THE TEST OF TIME
EXPLORING STATIONARY PLANETS

MICHELE FINEY

First published by Busybird Publishing 2022

Copyright © 2022 Michele Finey
All Rights Reserved

ISBN

978-1-922691-31-6 (paperback)

978-1-922691-32-3 (ebook)

This work is copyright. Apart from any use permitted under the *Copyright Act 1968*, no part of this publication may be reproduced, stored in a retrieval system or transmitted in any form or by any means, electronic, mechanical, photocopying, recording or otherwise, without the prior written permission of Michele Finey.

Cover Design: Busybird Publishing

Design and typesetting: Busybird Publishing

Busybird Publishing
2/118 Para Road
Montmorency, Victoria
Australia 3094
www.busybird.com.au

For Pop

Other Books by Michele Finey

Secrets of the Zodiac (Allen and Unwin) 2009

The Sacred Dance of Venus and Mars (The Wessex Astrologer) 2012

ACKNOWLEDGEMENTS

I want to express my gratitude and thanks to my partner Neil Dennis for his enduring love, as well as his invaluable assistance and making time to provide feedback. I also want to thank my clever friend Blaise van Hecke at Busybird Publishing for her guidance, skill and expertise. My sincere thanks also go to archivist Philip Graves for digging through his extensive library to locate Helen Keller's birth data source. I especially wish to acknowledge Associate Professor John O'Byrne at Sydney University for taking the time to answer my astronomical and statistical questions.

ABOUT MICHELE

Michele's interest in astrology was seeded at an early age by her artist grandfather George Finey and other family influences. Michele left school at the age of 16, but went on to complete diplomas in Astrology, Clinical Hypnotherapy and, Professional Writing and Editing. Since her first astrology article was published in 1985, her work has appeared in a wide range of publications including; *The Mountain Astrologer*, *The NCGR Journal*, *Wellbeing Astrology* and at *Astro.com*. Her two previous books are; *Secrets of the Zodiac* (Allen and Unwin 2009) and *The Sacred Dance of Venus and Mars* (The Wessex Astrologer 2012). Michele is now enjoying semi-retirement; playing golf several times a week and publishing her annual astrology calendar. She is also busy planning her next book. www.celestialinsight.com.au

CONTENTS

My Journey	1

SECTION ONE

Timewise	9
Interpreting Stationary Planets	15
The Astronomy of Stations	23

SECTION TWO

Personal Development	35
Mercury	55
Venus	67
Mars	77
Ceres	85
Juno	93
Pallas Athena	101
Vesta	109
Hygiea	117
Jupiter	123
Saturn	131
Chiron	141
Uranus	149
Neptune	157
Pluto	165
Eris	171

SECTION THREE

Disasters and Accidents	179
Lunar Phase Returns	191
Final Words	211
Appendix One	215
Appendix Two	229
Appendix Three	243
Endnotes	247

MY JOURNEY

I grew up in a somewhat eccentric household. My grandfather George Finey was a talented artist who painted, sculpted and wrote poetry. A caricaturist and political cartoonist too, he often said that we are born with a blueprint and go through life filling it in. He wasn't an astrologer, but as a wise Pisces fish, he was a bit of a philosopher and knew something about people and life. He was born exactly one week before astrologer Dane Rudhyar.

We lived in a basic rented house in the Blue Mountains west of Sydney, where I was raised by my mother and my grandparents. Pop used to complain about that 'other fish' which would interfere with his decisions just when he had made a plan. Later on, when I calculated his chart, I saw that not only did he have the Sun in Pisces, but he had the Moon and Ascendant in Sagittarius and four planets in Gemini. It was all this mutable energy in his chart that made him such a versatile artist and no doubt contributed to his restlessness.

As an only child of his youngest daughter, I recall Christmases when my two Taurean aunts would visit. I observed the adults around me and joined in with their conversations. I learned that my aunts had never got along. Each had their particular set of values. They were born one year apart. The younger of the two was a bit of a snob and only bought the most expensive items, while her elder sister was always looking for the best bargain. Their feud started when they were children during the Great Depression and they were each given the same birthday gifts. When her toy broke, the younger child who wanted nice things, stole her sister's toy and claimed it as her own.

My favourite aunt, the elder of the two, was born on the same day and year as Audrey Hepburn. She had her Moon in Pisces and enjoyed sailing. She and her husband, a Cancerian, named their yacht the *Cantaurus*. When my mother and I moved to Sydney in 1968 we would sometimes be invited to join them for a sail on the harbour and a barbeque at the yacht club.

In 1969, when I was about ten, my intuitive Cancerian mother, for reasons she was never able to adequately explain, bought a copy of Ronald Davison's book, *Astrology*. When I asked her many years later why she bought this book, she said she just felt that I might need it one day. It wasn't the only useful book she would buy me through the years.

When *Linda Goodman's Sun Signs* was published it became a sensation. I devoured it. There is a lot of truth in that well-written volume.

I was 21 when I calculated my first astrology chart. Transiting Uranus was in Scorpio and moving over my natal Jupiter and Ceres. Back then there were no computers to do the maths, so I had to learn how to calculate charts manually. Mathematics was my worst subject at school, so I taught myself to do logarithms. Suddenly they made sense. I did a short astrology correspondence course and bought lots of books to learn more.

As an only child born with most planets below the horizon, it's not surprising I'm an introvert. I've always enjoyed my own company, so I was content to study astrology privately on my own. Mostly I am self-taught, but after I moved to Melbourne in 1983, I took classes with Sean McNamara and went on to do my FAA exams in the mid-1980s. Though I had a regular job, I started seeing clients in the 80s

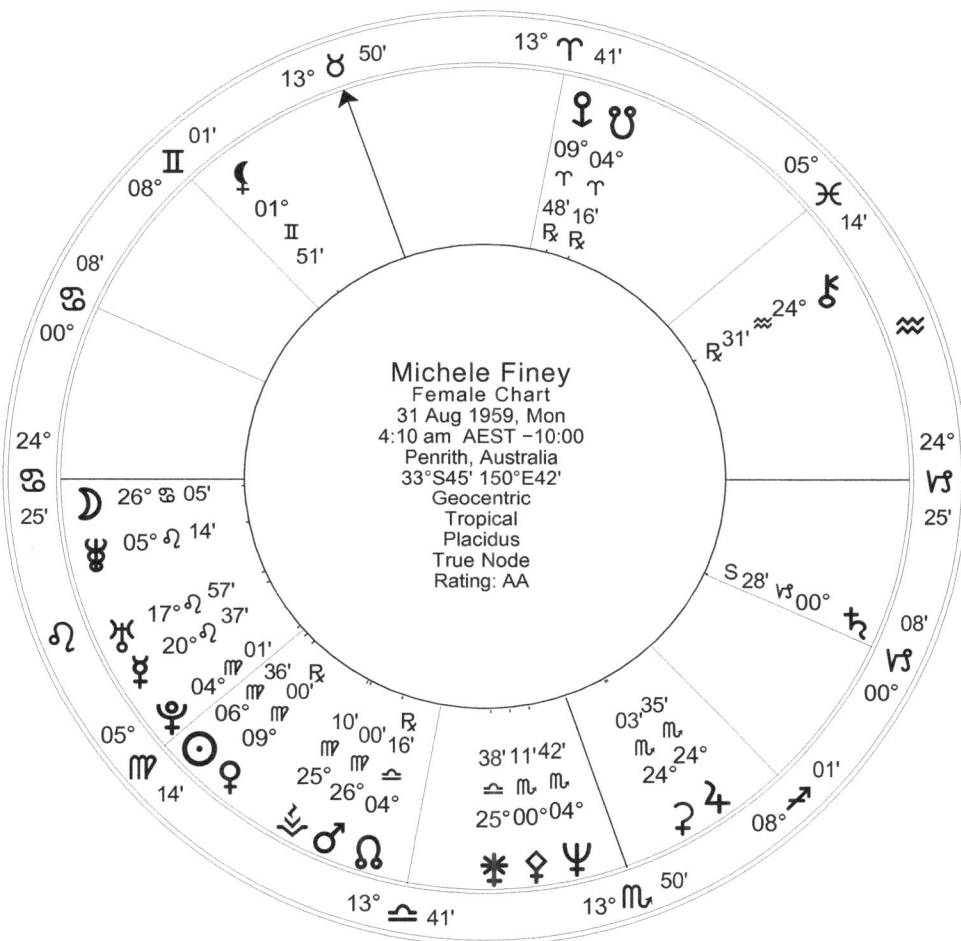

and wrote my first astrology article in 1985 which was published in the *Astrological Monthly Review*.

In the early 1990s I studied hypnotherapy and began seeing clients in that field too. In my client work my focus was on healing and counselling, but it was difficult to make a living that way. I saw more people for hypnotherapy than for astrology consultations, but truth be told I was always more interested in research and writing than consulting work or teaching. I have four planets in Virgo and a good smattering of Scorpio in my chart, so I guess that makes sense.

Over the years I developed my own style of astrology that is archetypal, psychological and symbolic, but also grounded in the actual movement of the planets. Planetary cycles, aspects, angular planets, transits and stations are my astrological bread and butter. I don't really consider the houses very much and I'm not convinced about some traditional techniques. I've always felt that essential dignities are a manufactured system imposed upon the planets, rather than an organic representation of the nature of the solar system.

Traditional astrology has never interested me. It's too fatalistic and predictive for my world view. People grow and evolve. As a hypnotherapist I've seen the dramatic changes that take place when a person is ready to step away from their pain, their past, or their bad habits. Once you know how, it's a relatively simple process to find a place of agreement between the conscious and unconscious mind.

Over the years I've dabbled in a range of associated fields including numerology, tarot and graphology, and picked up other pieces of esoteric knowledge along the way.

Stationary planets are one of my enduring passions. This book had its genesis some years ago when I wrote an article for *The Mountain Astrologer*. That material formed the basis of further research and sections of that article are included in this volume.

For simplicity, throughout this book I refer to all the planets, as well as the asteroids and dwarf planets as 'planets'. A number of abbreviations are used as follows;

SR	Stationary Retrograde
SD	Stationary Direct
AR	Aries
TA	Taurus
GE	Gemini
CN	Cancer
LE	Leo
VI	Virgo
LI	Libra
SC	Scorpio
SG	Sagittarius
CP	Capricorn
AQ	Aquarius
PI	Pisces

SECTION ONE

TIMEWISE

'Matter and light can, and do, turn into one another.'[1]

When big stars die, they eject masses of energy and material into space. These supernovae seed life elsewhere in the universe and create the many elements that make up the Earth and the planets, and even our bodies. We are made of stardust.

Science tells us that energy cannot be created or destroyed, only transformed. This principle is called the conservation of energy. It's one of the laws of nature. We also know that nothing can travel faster than the speed of light.[2] In fact, the only way to travel at the speed of light is to have no mass.

Whether we call it the soul, the spirit, the life force, or whatever it is that animates life, it has no mass. It's my hope that when we die and disconnect from our physical bodies, we become beings of light. While we may reincarnate into matter at some future time, being free to travel at the speed of light could account for all those near-death experiences and reports of tunnels of light. Yes, we are made of stardust, and who knows, maybe the stars are made from us.

'At the speed of light, time freezes.'[3]

Einstein discovered that time is only relative. Time measurements depend on one's location and perspective in the universal scheme of things. However, time is also our reality and the dimension we are bound by here on Earth, at least while we are alive. Our perspective and location in time may account for why it seems to move faster as we get older, but in reality we can't speed up time, nor slow it down.

Science tells us that everywhere we look in space, we are looking back in time. This even applies to our nearest stellar neighbours, so it's apparent that we can learn from the planets and their cycles, just as we can learn from history.

From the earliest times we have created calendars that chart the movement of the Sun, Moon and planets to measure time and guide human affairs. Day and night, the waxing and waning Moon and the rhythm of the seasons regulate life on Earth. When astrologers look to the heavens, we see a snapshot of time. Our task is to try to interpret the symbols and patterns in this sky map. We examine the prevailing stellar conditions so we can harmonise with these natural rhythms. Because cycles repeat over time, astrology helps us learn from the past and plan for the future.

Meanwhile, physicists are struggling to come up with a unified theory to explain everything from the very big, to the very small, but astrologers already have a theory. It's called, 'As above, so below'. This ancient tenet is a simple phrase that acknowledges that everything is interconnected. You cannot separate the macrocosm and the microcosm.

Many scientists continue to raise objections to astrology, but those who do have painted themselves into a very small corner of the universe. Scientists now know, as astrologers have always known, that there is something mysterious and unifying within all creation.

> *'For orthodox science, [too], the universe is becoming a seamless whole, with a dawning recognition that somehow what is taking place in one part of the universe is inseparable from what is happening elsewhere at the same instant.'*[4]

In the quantum world of the very small, it has been confirmed many times over that our actions influence the outcome of experiments at a distance. There is no causal mechanism to account for this. Simply by observing or witnessing an event we influence what's happening. It's our perceptions and our actions that make all the difference.

This confirms that the present moment, and our perspective, how we view the world, what we do, and even what we don't do, is the determining factor. Now is where we create the future. Our decisions and choices and events in every moment of time is where creative power resides. We are at the forefront of time. Astrologically, this suggests that we may have far more creative power than we assume.

The moment of our birth, our experiences and our environment all play an important role in development. Each moment can create an infinite number of possible scenarios.

For example, research into the background of serial killers has consistently shown that they often experience abuse and neglect in childhood. Serial killers are not born serial killers, but develop this way because of the abuse they have experienced as children. Head injuries can also play a role. But equally, there are children who experience abuse and neglect who do not become serial killers.[5] No two people are the same, nor will they have the same experiences, or reactions to them. Even identical twins will have differences.

Today, around 270 children are born every single minute on planet Earth. That's over 16,000 per hour, or about 380,000 each day.[6] They will be born into different cultures, to parents with a variety of parenting skills and a multitude of personal circumstances. Some will be boys, some will be girls, and some will be intersex. Some might be born with a physical or intellectual disability, and some may inherit a special talent. While thousands of people have similar birth charts and share many of the same aspects, their experiences and development will vary widely. Above all, astrology is a symbolic language. Each person is unique. Birth charts should always be interpreted with this in mind.

Many years ago, a friend introduced me to one of my astrological twins. She was born about 40 minutes after me and in a different location in Australia. When you look at the two charts there isn't much real time between them. Our Ascendants are around two degrees apart, which is around eight minutes time wise. My Moon is below the horizon, hers is above. The charts are virtually identical. I was fascinated to learn that like me, she had studied astrology and hypnotherapy, but there were many differences between us too. She didn't work in these fields as I had, she was a teacher. She has travelled extensively, but I have not. Throughout life we have had many different experiences. The mutual friend who introduced us said that she felt we had quite different personalities.

Similarly, my grandfather was born a few hours before another Australian artist, Lloyd Rees. Both men lived to the age of 92 and were interviewed together on the same television program later in life. My grandfather served in WWI as an underage private, but Lloyd Rees did not. My grandfather was a very animated and talkative character, Lloyd Rees was quieter and more reserved. Their artistic styles were very different.

An astrology chart can say a lot, but there are some things it cannot tell us. Like our death for example. As a hypnotherapist, I have worked with hundreds of people who made the conscious decision to quit smoking and live longer. Life is full of choices and events and all of them influence our development and path in life.

When you calculate an astrological chart it's a map for a moment in time. This chart of the solar system could be for the birth of a person, a cat, a bat or a fish. It may be a chart for an event, and idea, an eclipse, or some other astronomical alignment. Countless things take place at every moment across the world. The chart is a symbolic representation of time, nothing more. We need to have context to begin to interpret it.

When examining charts for individuals, or events for any common themes they may share, it's important to understand that there are billions of people in the world who have never had their charts calculated and so we may never know the real significance, or extent of a particular configuration. History too, is largely written by those who make it, and there are billions of people in the world whose stories have never been told. As astrologers we can only glimpse a tiny slither of the complexity of the world and its people. We only know what we know, and we don't know what we don't know.

As we grow, we learn, develop knowledge, form opinions and form relationships. Our values, preferences and skills develop throughout life as consciousness grows. Astrologically, the Sun represents consciousness, and this consciousness is something that evolves and develops over time. Consciousness is built by our experiences. The Sun is the centre of our solar system, our local source of light. All the planets revolve around this source of light and life. Stationary planets are defined by their relationship to the Sun as seen from our perspective on Earth. This means that planets that appear to stand still for a period of time provide significant opportunities for conscious development. They give us the time we need to absorb and process what we need to learn, thereby expanding consciousness. Indeed, when planets appear to stop moving, these may be the most significant moments we will ever experience.

INTERPRETING STATIONARY PLANETS

We measure time according to the movement of the Sun, Moon and planets as they travel along the zodiac. Each day, the Sun moves a degree or so, the Moon about 13 degrees and all the planets travel along the same band of sky at their various speeds. They move along the zodiac in direct motion, but now and then they appear to stop and back track before they are stationary again and resume forward motion. All the planets and asteroids (except the Sun and Moon) will be retrograde at one time or another.

Whether stationing retrograde, or direct, planets that have no (or very little) apparent motion hover at the same zodiacal position for days, sometimes weeks. If we think of the zodiac as being a journey through time, when planets are moving retrograde, they are, in a sense, venturing back into the past before resuming forward motion once more. When they are stationary, the present moment is symbolically magnified and highlighted. Time seemingly stands still.

For a given time the stationary planet becomes a key focus. For better or worse, it cannot be avoided. Stationary planets are not diluted by the passage of time, but are concentrated.

Whether in our birth chart, or when experienced as a transit, stationary retrograde (SR) planets are like huge STOP signs in our lives. Sometimes they ask us to alter course and retrace our steps. Have we forgotten something? Is there something we need to recapture, recall, remember, or take time to learn? Motionless planets present us with challenges that involve patience. Often, we have to dig deep to find the intestinal fortitude required to manage the tasks they represent. Progress can be halted altogether and a different approach or direction may be needed.

Retrograde motion is only apparent from our perspective on Earth; planets only APPEAR to slow, station, turn retrograde, station direct and move forward once more. This apparent retrograde motion therefore depends on one's point of view or perspective. Psychologically speaking, what we perceive to be our truth, IS our truth, but it's not necessarily the whole truth. Time will tell.

DIFFERING VIEWS

In traditional astrology, slow and stationary planets are generally perceived as debilitated, afflicted, or malefic. For the most part, they are considered to be weak. Yet, many astrologers, both ancient and modern, interpret stationary planets in quite a different way.

In Ptolemy's *Tetrabiblos,* we read that stationary planets are akin to rising planets in terms of their potency. Far from being weak or afflicted, Ptolemy stated that they are arguably the most powerful planets in a chart.

> '... the effect will be strengthened and augmented by their matutine or stationary position; but weakened and diminished by their being vespertine, or situated under the sunbeams, or by their midnight culmination.'[7]

How we interpret stationary planets may vary according to the type of chart we are examining. For example, in a horary chart, the stationary planet is thought to impede. Its lack of apparent motion is said to prevent further developments. This makes logical sense, because in horary work we are mostly concerned with that exact moment. As a rule, we don't examine transits or progressions to the horary chart. It's a chart that stands alone. It's constructed to answer a specific question. So if a key planet in the horary chart is stationary, then the matter concerned is most likely at a standstill, at least for the time being. As Deborah Houlding points out:

> *'Speedy motion symbolises strong impulse, so when a significator is direct in motion and moving swiftly, we judge whatever it signifies as moving directly towards its objectives and having a strong impetus to make something happen. This is a signature of someone with a strong will and a clear sense of purpose (however misguided that purpose may be). By contrast, a significator that moves slowly is regarded as hindered or impeded, suggesting hesitancy or protracted labouring over something difficult to accomplish.'*[8]

In the June/July 2014 issue of *The Mountain Astrologer*, Kenneth Johnson's article, 'The Many Faces of Mercury Retrograde,' discusses some of the ways that astrologers through the ages have interpreted stationary (and retrograde) planets. Vettius Valens, for example, was of the view that such planets were debilitated and weak, but Johnson points out that, in Indian tradition, retrograde and stationary planets were considered to be *stronger* than when moving direct.

So, where does that leave us? Just how should we interpret these seemingly motionless planets that appear to be changing direction?

Perhaps how we express and respond to stations may depend on other astrological factors, such as sign placement, or aspects to the stationary planet that can aid our interpretation. My interpretation of stationary planets is similar to the view Erin Sullivan outlines in her book, *Retrograde Planets*. Of the stationary retrograde (SR) planet she writes:

> *'One often finds it difficult if not impossible to express oneself to one's satisfaction. This can result in obsessive or compulsive types of behaviour or dedication to rigorous detailed work which through its thoroughness satisfies one's sense of completion and success.'*[9]

SR planets can present us with some big challenges. We have to dig deep to find the fortitude required to harness them. These planets therefore foster endurance, staying power, focus, and dedication. The frustration that can accompany the SR planet is often a catalyst, but for some individuals, the challenge may be too much. This could be why stationary planets are said to block or impede. There is a powerful urge to express the stationary planet, but its lack of motion means that it takes a great deal of stamina and effort to get results. Of the SD planet, Sullivan says:

> '[It] has already constellated a great amount of power and is virtually trembling for an avenue for expression. Unless there are other aspects to the planet that promote a channel for the energy, then it is likely to have little grounding in the early years of one's life.' [10]

So, when resuming forward momentum, the stationary direct planet urges us to get moving, but at the same time this planet is not easy to master, especially early in life. It's raw and fresh and has to move into uncharted territory. Over time we have an opportunity to develop this natal planet, to express it outwardly as it gains speed, but at first it can be a real monkey on our back.

STATIONARY RETROGRADE

The SR planet stops and then travels back over territory it previously traversed while in direct motion. This suggests that SR planets are thwarted as they attempt to continue as they have been up to that point. This is likely to engender a sense of **frustration**. A fresh original plan, a different approach, or new direction has to be worked out. In applying oneself to these problems we can eventually master them and achieve success.

STATIONARY DIRECT

The SD planet has been retrograde already. When the planet resumes forward motion, it goes back over territory already traversed too, but that history was made when the planet was retrograde. In resuming its forward momentum there is a powerful urge to get moving but at the same time it can be hindered by past experiences. This lends itself to a sense of **caution**, or **fear**, that we are going to experience the setbacks already encountered, but over time we can learn how to master them and achieve success.

It's also worth noting that if we have a stationary planet in our birth chart, the time before that took place in-utero, and those experiences are deeply embedded in our unconscious. If our natal planet is SR, it was direct before we were born. If our natal planet is SD, then it was retrograde before our birth.

With the passage of time, SD planets may have more opportunities to overcome fears and limiting early circumstances, but both SR and SD planets foster endurance and staying power and can propel us forward to great achievements and success. Perhaps it all comes down to how we manage our frustration (SR planets) and our fears (SD planets).

The way we interpret the inferior planets, Mercury and Venus, may differ to the rest of the planets that lie beyond Earth's orbit. This is due to the position where stations take place in relation to the Sun. All planets (except the Moon) are waxing (gaining light) when they rise before the Sun (visible in the morning sky) and are waning (losing light) when they rise after the Sun (visible in the evening sky). But the inner planets, Mercury and Venus, station direct in the morning sky, while all other planets station retrograde in the morning sky. Inner planets station retrograde in the evening sky, but all the others station direct in the evening sky.

This is important because we need to consider the location of stationary planets in relation to the Sun (consciousness). Retrograde motion and stations are a function of a planet's synodic cycle which is the time between two conjunctions with the Sun (or in the case of Mercury and Venus, two inferior conjunctions).

Station Positions Relative to the Sun	
Mercury and Venus	**All Other Planets & Asteroids**
Are Waxing when they Station Direct	Are Waxing when they Station Retrograde
Are Waning when they Station Retrograde	Are Waning when they Station Direct

On the face of it, this suggests that the planets beyond Earth's orbit are potentially more difficult to harness, and since they are less accessible anyway because their orbits are longer, this makes sense. It takes longer for us to develop the attributes associated with the planets that are further away from the Sun. The passage of time is always a determining factor in our development.

Superior planets when waxing are increasing in light as they head towards opposition (fullness) but it's during this waxing process that outer planets station retrograde. In the case of Mars, which is a personal planet, this creates a powerful contradiction.

Inner planets Mercury and Venus are waxing after inferior conjunction and will station direct in the morning sky. Reaching fullness at superior conjunction before waning again. Thus, when they turn direct, they are waxing. They are awakening, growing and exploring. They are guiding us to be open to new experiences, perhaps with a sense of caution or even fear, but nevertheless being engaged to explore and develop. When they are stationing retrograde in the evening sky, Mercury and Venus are waning and therefore, retreating. Although this may create a sense of frustration, there is probably more contentment with this frustration. As they are waning, they are more likely to be internalised, fostering a sense of introspection.

Planets that station retrograde, or station direct by progression can mark major turning points in life. Since stationary planets are in the process of changing direction, this implies they can herald reversals of fortune. A stationary direct (SD) planet in a natal chart will progress over the years and will pick up speed. Conversely, a planet that is slowing down will turn retrograde by progression at some future time.

In youth, before we develop a level of conscious awareness, a stationary planet can represent a blind spot. This blind spot may continue to be unconscious throughout life and may be projected onto others who are seen to represent the negative qualities of the planetary theme. While this is true for all disowned planetary archetypes to some extent, the stationary planet is both more accessible, and more challenging.

As we encounter challenges associated with the planet in question, it can lead to personal growth and mastery of the stationary planet within us. Alternatively, if we fail to learn its lessons, do not adapt and grow, then we will continue to disown the planet concerned and run into the same issues again and again. While this can be said for any challenging planetary aspect, our stationary planets may reveal the path we need to take to master these challenges. When we gain insight into these potential roadblocks we expand our self-knowledge which gives us a new way to approach them.

While a stationary planet can turn into a great asset once mastered, there is no guarantee that we will develop our stationary planet in a positive way. It could also develop into an overblown or exaggerated version of the archetype in question.

> *'The past can't be changed, but the future is ours to shape, if we make the effort.'*
>
> **His Holiness, the 14th Dalai Lama**
> *(Jupiter SD 13SC28)*

As planets move through the zodiac, they take us on a journey through time. Past, present and future are examined through the lens of a chart of the heavens calculated for a specific moment. Planets that appear to be stationary represent key moments in that journey when, in a sense, time appears to stand still. The stationary retrograde planet might be more challenging than the stationary direct one, but they are both capable of empowering us.

The different ways that astrologers interpret stationary planets may come down to the fact that, for some of us, challenges can push us to strive for bigger and better things, but for others, these challenges can become insurmountable obstacles. Either way, stationary planets are incredibly powerful.

THE ASTRONOMY OF STATIONS

HOW TO IDENTIFY STATIONARY PLANETS IN A CHART

As seen from the Earth, the inner planets, Mercury and Venus, station retrograde when they are evening stars, and station direct after their inferior conjunction with the Sun, when they are morning stars once more.

The planets beyond the orbit of the Earth, including Mars and the asteroids, station retrograde when approaching solar opposition, and turn direct again as they head back towards the Sun.

From a chart perspective, a good way to remember where planets will station is to look at the position of the Sun. Think of the chart as a clock face and the Sun as being at the 12 o'clock position. The inner planets, Mercury and Venus, station retrograde when located at about the 11 o'clock position relative to the Sun and turn direct at about the 1 o'clock position. All the other planets and asteroids station retrograde around the 4 o'clock position relative to the Sun and station direct around the 8 o'clock mark. Using the Sun as a guide, when looking at a chart with planets flagged S, you will know right away whether they are SR or SD.

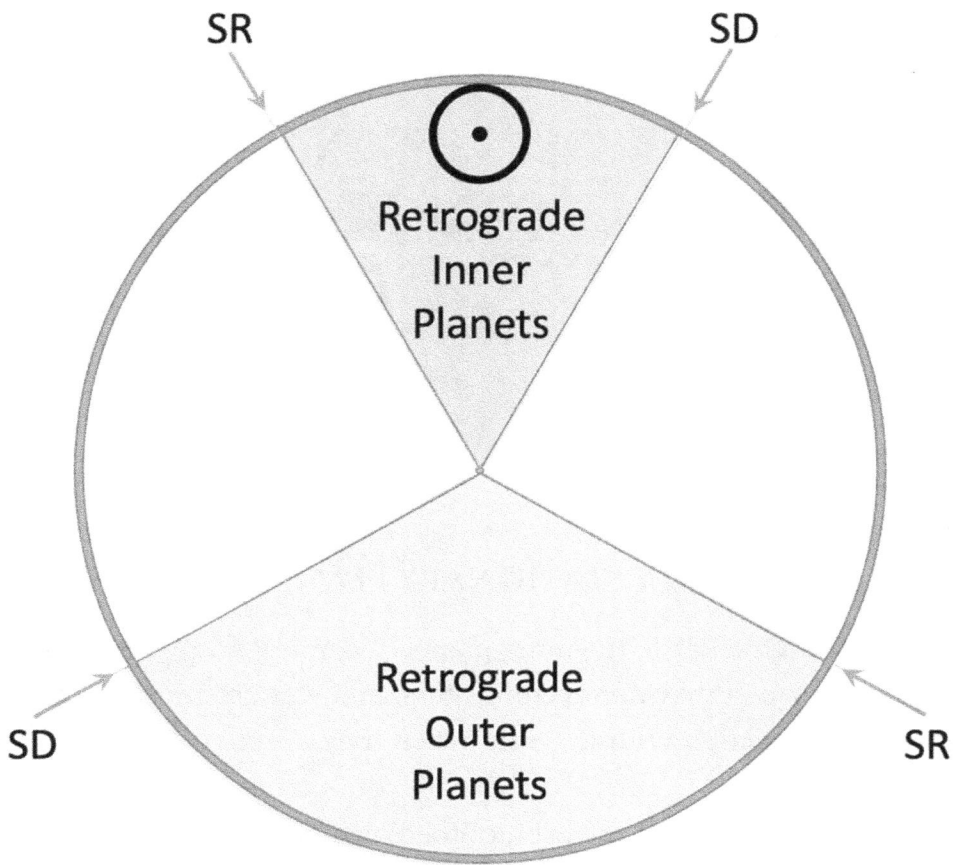

Diagram 1. Using the Sun as a guide to find stations. If it's easier to visualise, try rotating charts so that the Sun is at the top.

SYNODIC CYCLES

Apparent retrograde motion occurs as part of a planet's synodic cycle which is the number of days between one conjunction with the Sun and the next. In the case of Mercury and Venus, each of which makes two solar conjunctions per cycle, this is the number of days between two inferior conjunctions.

Most astrology software programs allow a few days orb for stations and stationary planets are flagged S accordingly. But if you consider that the speed and orbital length of each planet differs, these differences should be taken into account.

Using a percentage of a planet's average daily motion is one way to do this. But it turns out that a planet's average speed is not an easy thing to calculate. It depends on a range of factors, such as the time period over which its motion is averaged and other factors that can yield quite different results. This is particularly relevant for Mercury and Venus whose daily motion is at times faster than the Sun.[11] However, Mercury and Venus move in tandem with the Sun and are therefore commonly set to the same average daily travel, 59'08" per day. This is the basis upon which charts are calculated.

PLANET	SYNODIC PERIOD
Mars	780 days
Venus	584 days
Vesta	504 days
Juno	473 days
Ceres	467 days
Pallas Athena	466 days
Hygiea	445 days
Jupiter	399 days
Saturn	378 days
Chiron	373 days
Uranus	369 days
Neptune	367 days
Pluto	367 days
Eris	366 days
Mercury	116 days

Table 1. The number of days of each planet's Solar synodic cycle.[12]

In Solar Fire, the default setting flags stationary planets with an S for two days before and two days after each exact station. This gives four days at station retrograde and four days at station direct. Any planet falling within this time range will be flagged with an S to indicate that it's barely moving. You will notice that the colour of the S in a chart will change at the exact moment of the station. But there are other options for calculating stations and one of them is based on the different speeds of the planets.

THE 30 PERCENT RULE

For a long time, I used the default setting for stations until it occurred to me that choosing a variable orb would take into account the different synodic periods and the various speeds of the planets and would therefore be more accurate and meaningful. In Solar Fire, preference four lets you choose a percentage of a planet's average speed so that any planet moving slower than this will be flagged S.

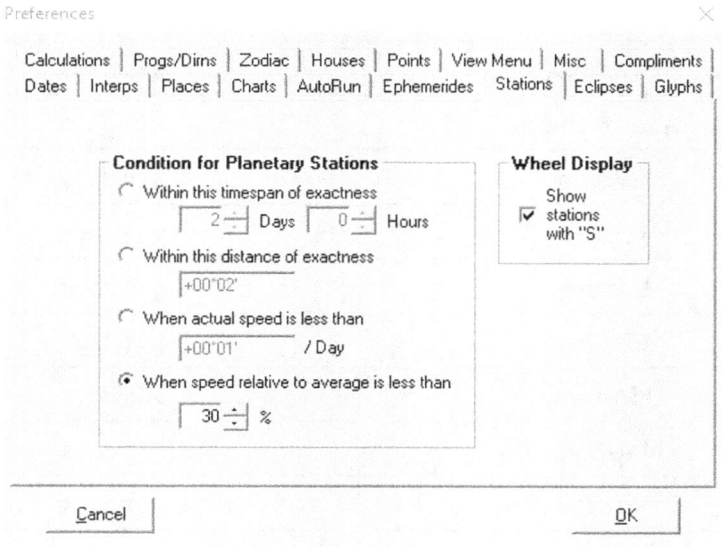

Diagram 2. Solar Fire's preference settings for stationary planets. The default setting is option 1 which is set to two days. Option four, as a percentage of average speed gives you a variable orb which is relative to the speed of each planet. I settled on 30 percent as a good benchmark.

So, what kind of orb should we allow for a stationary planet? In other words, how slowly does a planet have to be moving to have some kind of added intensity, or other effect? After choosing this setting, I set to work examining every chart in my database, in total, thousands of charts. I tweaked the percentage up and down, looking at natal and event charts to determine an orb that I was happy with. I wanted to be sure that the symbolism of the stationary planet in question was apparent.

After spending weeks looking through my database and trying different percentages, I decided to use 30%. This means that whenever a planet is moving slower than 30% of its average daily motion, it will be flagged with an S.

Because some planets have a more elliptical orbit than others, some station orbs will differ slightly from one chart to another. This is especially true for Mercury, Mars, Chiron and Pluto which have quite elliptical orbits.

While 30% might seem high, keep in mind that this is a percentage of *average speed,* and average speeds are much slower than a planet's fastest motion. Though the way in which average daily motion is calculated can vary, this setting seems to work well — that is, the themes of the stationary planet in question appear to be quite obvious in the chart being examined. It's also astronomically more valid than having a blanket four-day orb per station for every planet.

PLANET	AVERAGE MOTION	HIGHEST	LOWEST
Sun	00°59'08"	01°03'00"	00°57'10"
Moon	13°10'35"	16°30'00"	11°45'36"
Mercury*	01°23'00" or 59'08"	02°25'00"	−01°30'00"
Venus*	01°12'00" or 59'08"	01°22'00"	−00°41'12"
Mars	00°31'27"	00°52'00"	−00°26'12"
Ceres	00°12'40"	00°30'00"	−00°16'00"
Jupiter	00°04'59"	00°15'40"	−00°08'50"
Saturn	00°02'01"	00°08'48"	−00°05'30"
Uranus	00°00'42"	00°04'00"	−00°02'40"
Neptune	00°00'24"	00°02'25"	−00°01'45"
Pluto	00°00'15"	00°02'30"	−00°01'48"
Pallas	00°12'20"	00°40'30"	−00°22'30"
Juno	00°14'15"	00°39'00"	−00°18'00"
Vesta	00°16'15"	00°36'00"	−00°17'32"
Chiron	00°02'00"	00°10'00"	−00°06'00"

Table 2. Average daily movement of the planets. For more information about Mercury and Venus refer to this useful blog by Anthony Louis.[13]

Since Mars has the longest synodic cycle, it also has the longest orb duration for its stations. Using the 30% rule, Mars will be flagged S for about three to four weeks at each station.

PLANET	SYNODIC PERIOD	APPROXIMATE TIME PER STATION USING THE 30 PERCENT RULE
Mars	780 days	21–28 days
Venus	584 days	15 days
Ceres*	467 days	18–20 days
Jupiter	399 days	15 days
Saturn	378 days	12 days
Chiron	373 days	8–14 days
Uranus	369 days	8 days
Neptune	367 days	7 days
Pluto	367 days	4–7 days
Mercury	116 days	4–8 days
Eris	366 days	2 days

*Table 3. Planetary synods and their station orbs using the 30% rule. *The asteroids not listed in this table spend a similar amount of time stationary to Ceres.*

SHADOWS AND ORBS

Over the years there has been a lot of discussion about so called 'shadow periods'. These are times when a planet is moving in direct motion, before and after its retrograde period and passing over the same degrees it travels when retrograde. It has been said that these 'shadows' have some of the elements of retrograde periods, only to a lesser extent.

Personally, I am not convinced that shadow periods have any merit. If you factor in these shadow degree areas and plot them over time, you will see why.

In the case of Mercury, there are three retrograde passages every year, each of which span three weeks. If we add in the shadow periods, we have an extra six weeks of shadow time per retrograde. Taken together, this equates to around six months every year when Mercury will be either retrograde, or in shadow. Although Mercury is well known for its capacity as a trickster, 50% of the time is rather excessive. Using the 30% rule instead, gives you an orb window of between four and eight days per station.

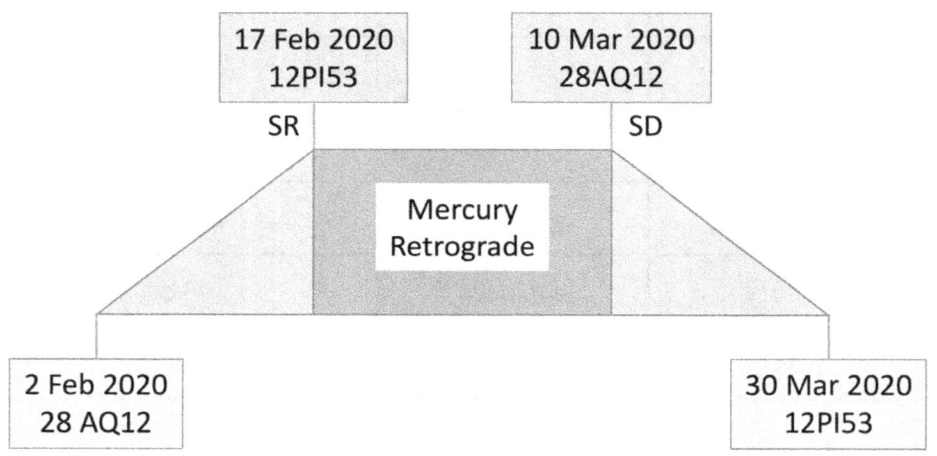

Diagram 3. One Mercury Retrograde period plus its shadow period covers two months. As Mercury retrogrades three times annually, this means that Mercury will be retrograde or in shadow for six months every year.

Mars will be in shadow or retrograde for about six months every two years, or roughly 25% of its synodic period. With the slower-moving planets, you end up with overlapping or double shadows. Uranus is always in shadow or retrograde and in the case of Neptune and Pluto, one shadow period is still in effect when the next shadow period commences.

I have not personally investigated these 'double shadows' to see if they have any particular astrological significance, but on the face of it, overlapping shadows call into question the whole concept of shadow periods. If you go along with the idea of shadow periods, then you also have to accept that Neptune and Pluto have overlapping shadows and that Mercury will be in shadow, or retrograde six months every year.

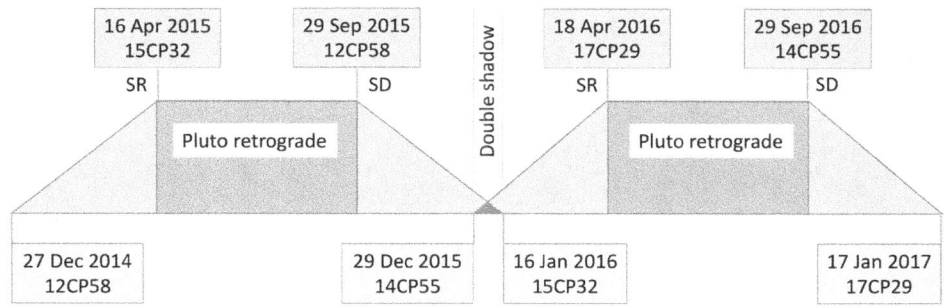

Diagram 4. Pluto's shadow. Two successive retrograde periods of Pluto are shown with their shadow periods. Note that the first shadow period ends after the second one commences, creating a double or overlapping shadow.

NOTE: The 30 percent rule has been used as the basis for all charts, people and events listed in this book.

SECTION TWO

PERSONAL DEVELOPMENT

The planets in our birth charts and their cycles symbolise our potential and how that potential develops over time. When planets station and move retrograde it's an opportunity to reflect on our past, our present and where we are headed. At the station retrograde we can take a step back from the external world to some extent and spend more time reflecting on our experiences. These musings may or may not lead to important decisions. But when we reflect on our life, we have the opportunity to call a halt to situations that are not working and make a fresh start when the planet resumes forward motion.

If our upbringing was painful or dysfunctional, or if our present situation is not working out, when we are ready to step away from these experiences we can. Sometimes this means we must alter our values, our behaviour, or make other changes. Because stationary planets are a reflection of their relationship to the Sun, they are directed by the light of consciousness.

Some personal issues may be blind spots, but even blind spots can become visible when we focus on them. Whether in the natal chart, when transiting or progressing, stationary planets provide an opportunity to focus on their theme and message for long periods which can assist personal development. Working through personal issues can take time and stationary planets give us that time.

In this section I have listed some of the symbols and functions of each planet, including some of the ways they can operate when dysfunctional and when acting at their best. These scenarios could also be applied to other features in the natal chart, such as difficult aspects, or when we are faced with challenging transits. Like hard aspects, stationary planets can test our resolve. It takes time and patience to master them.

Upon reflecting on our life path and present circumstances, we have the opportunity to call a halt to any situation that is not working out and make a fresh start when the planet in question turns direct.

Personal Development

MERCURY

Our capacity to learn and communicate

DIFFICULTIES ASSOCIATED WITH MERCURY CAN INCLUDE;

- **Mental arrogance**
- **Using ignorance as an excuse**
- **Confused thinking or communication – mixed messages**
- **Learning difficulties**
- **Mental illness**
- **Fear of speaking up – stammer/stutter**
- **Frustration at not being able to communicate effectively**
- **Too much, or not enough focus on detail**

OVERCOMING ISSUES ASSOCIATED WITH MERCURY CAN LEAD TO;

- **Communicating an important message**
- **Prolific communication**
- **Original ideas and inventions**
- **Negotiation and diplomatic skills**

THINGS TO CONSIDER WHEN MERCURY IS STATIONARY

This is an opportunity to rethink activities and projects and take time out from busy schedules. Take a step back from doing too much. Consider whether to learn a new skill. Recalculate, reanalyse, reschedule, review and rest.

VENUS

Our capacity to formulate personal preferences,
core values and relationships

DIFFICULTIES ASSOCIATED WITH VENUS CAN INCLUDE;

- ∞ **Putting up with dysfunctional or abusive relationships**
- ∞ **Fear of being alone**
- ∞ **Over valuing others and undervaluing ourselves**
- ∞ **Over valuing or undervaluing money and material resources**
- ∞ **Low self-esteem**
- ∞ **Fear of relationships**
- ∞ **Withdrawal from social contact**
- ∞ **Celibacy, or sexual addiction**

OVERCOMING ISSUES ASSOCIATED WITH VENUS CAN LEAD TO;

- ∞ **Love and respect**
- ∞ **Long lasting and worthwhile relationships**
- ∞ **Financial and material wealth**
- ∞ **Negotiation and diplomatic skills**

THINGS TO CONSIDER WHEN VENUS IS STATIONARY

This is an opportunity to re-evaluate and reassess our relationships, our personal standards, values and financial situation. A time to let go of any situation, relationship or commitment that is not worth our while. A time to reaffirm those commitments that sustain us. When Venus turns direct it's time to decide about making new commitments and starting new relationships.

MARS

Developing willpower so we can take action and be assertive

DIFFICULTIES ASSOCIATED WITH MARS CAN INCLUDE;

- ∞ **Allowing others to abuse us**
- ∞ **Bullying others**
- ∞ **Feeling powerless and frustrated**
- ∞ **Angry outbursts when we don't get our own way**
- ∞ **Childish behaviour in adults**
- ∞ **A sense of entitlement**
- ∞ **Impatience or recklessness**
- ∞ **Passive-aggressive behaviour**
- ∞ **Sexual or physical abuse**

OVERCOMING ISSUES ASSOCIATED WITH MARS CAN LEAD TO;

- ∞ **Tremendous staying power and endurance**
- ∞ **Knowing when to stop and when to keep going**
- ∞ **Leadership or pioneering achievements in any field**
- ∞ **Heroic acts**

THINGS TO CONSIDER WHEN MARS IS STATIONARY

This is an opportunity to reassert our efforts and decide how much we are willing to apply towards our desires. Are the challenges we are facing too much to handle? Do we have the energy for the long haul? How much endurance do we have? What sacrifices do we have to make? Are we willing to ask for help and if so, who can provide assistance?

CERES

The capacity to care for others and respect the natural environment

DIFFICULTIES ASSOCIATED WITH CERES CAN INCLUDE;

- ∞ **Mother-daughter issues**
- ∞ **Mother-son issues**
- ∞ **Neglect**
- ∞ **Trauma associated with mother**
- ∞ **Dependency on mother, or on children**
- ∞ **Deep insecurity**
- ∞ **Desperation or obsession around mothering**

OVERCOMING ISSUES ASSOCIATED WITH CERES CAN LEAD TO;

- ∞ **Good parenting skills**
- ∞ **Capacity to nurture and care for children beyond the family**
- ∞ **Nurturing and caring for the wider community, animals and the environment**

THINGS TO CONSIDER WHEN CERES IS STATIONARY

This is an opportunity to reflect on the give and take in our family relationships and make adjustments to reach a better power balance. Reflecting on our role in the family. Setting boundaries within the family structure. Letting go of family attachments if necessary.

JUNO

Developing the capacity for tolerance, respect
for others and forgiveness

DIFFICULTIES ASSOCIATED WITH JUNO CAN INCLUDE;

- ∞ **Jealousy**
- ∞ **Retribution**
- ∞ **Passive-aggressive behaviour**
- ∞ **Sibling issues**
- ∞ **Relationship issues**
- ∞ **Power struggles**
- ∞ **Dependency on one's spouse**

OVERCOMING ISSUES ASSOCIATED WITH JUNO CAN LEAD TO;

- ∞ **Long lasting relationships**
- ∞ **Rising to positions of power and influence**
- ∞ **Respect from one's colleagues and the public**
- ∞ **The capacity to share**

THINGS TO CONSIDER WHEN JUNO IS STATIONARY

This is an opportunity to reconsider the power balance we have with our partners and siblings. How far do our loyalties stretch? How do we make adjustments so that we can be loyal to ourselves as well? Where do we draw the line?

PALLAS ATHENA

Developing an understanding of fair play and justice

DIFFICULTIES ASSOCIATED WITH PALLAS ATHENA CAN INCLUDE;

- ∞ **Father-daughter issues**
- ∞ **Father-son issues**
- ∞ **Nepotism**
- ∞ **Thinking we are above the law**
- ∞ **Taking the law into our own hands**
- ∞ **Fear of one's own power**
- ∞ **Inequality and dysfunction related to gender bias**

OVERCOMING ISSUES ASSOCIATED WITH PALLAS ATHENA CAN LEAD TO;

- ∞ **Diplomatic skills**
- ∞ **Calling out unjust laws and actions**
- ∞ **Stepping into positions of power, especially in law or politics**
- ∞ **Powerful social influence**
- ∞ **Becoming a positive role-model for gender equality and social justice**

THINGS TO CONSIDER WHEN PALLAS ATHENA IS STATIONARY

This is an opportunity to reflect on our understanding of social justice and fairness. Do we support equal opportunities for all, no matter their gender, race, or sexual preference? What are we personally willing to do to call out injustice when we encounter it?

VESTA

Developing self-awareness

DIFFICULTIES ASSOCIATED WITH VESTA CAN INCLUDE;

- ∞ **Inability to consider other viewpoints – tunnel vision**
- ∞ **Social isolation**
- ∞ **Skewed beliefs**
- ∞ **Pig-headed insistence that our views are correct**
- ∞ **Inability to cope with change**
- ∞ **Perfectionist standards that are impossible to meet, or maintain**

OVERCOMING ISSUES ASSOCIATED WITH VESTA CAN LEAD TO;

- ∞ **Tremendous inner focus**
- ∞ **Self-sufficiency and selflessness**
- ∞ **The capacity to take on big responsibilities without being asked**
- ∞ **Being respected as a guide who assists the self-development of others**

THINGS TO CONSIDER WHEN VESTA IS STATIONARY

This is an opportunity to reflect on our capacity for inner focus and self-sufficiency. How well do we manage when alone? Do we spend too much time alone? An opportunity to refocus on our main priorities.

HYGIEA

Establishing the criteria that we consider pure and healthy

DIFFICULTIES ASSOCIATED WITH HYGIEA CAN INCLUDE;

- ∞ **Lack of self-care**
- ∞ **Skewed ideas of what is pure, clean and healthy**
- ∞ **Self-harm and eating disorders**
- ∞ **Obsessive-compulsive behaviours – cleaning and checking**
- ∞ **Constant health issues – psychosomatic disorders**
- ∞ **Hypochondria**

OVERCOMING ISSUES ASSOCIATED WITH HYGIEA CAN LEAD TO;

- ∞ **The ability to manage one's health effectively**
- ∞ **The capacity to heal others**
- ∞ **Healthy habits**
- ∞ **The ability to change unhealthy habits**

THINGS TO CONSIDER WHEN HYGIEA IS STATIONARY

This is an opportunity to reassess our health and have a check-up. A time to re-establish healthy habits and let go of bad habits that are impacting our wellbeing. Revitalising, rejuvenating and refreshing.

JUPITER

The capacity for personal growth

DIFFICULTIES ASSOCIATED WITH JUPITER CAN INCLUDE;

- ∞ **Hubris, superiority complex, messiah complex, racism, narcissism**
- ∞ **Lack of confidence - inferiority complex**
- ∞ **Feeling invincible and bullet proof - recklessness**
- ∞ **Glass half-empty attitude - poor me**
- ∞ **Reckless indulgence in drugs or alcohol**
- ∞ **Handballing responsibility to, or blaming 'god'**
- ∞ **Sense of entitlement**
- ∞ **Social inadequacy**

OVERCOMING ISSUES ASSOCIATED WITH JUPITER CAN LEAD TO;

- ∞ **A sense of joy in living**
- ∞ **Confidence and a positive outlook**
- ∞ **Accepting that we must try new things in order to grow and learn**
- ∞ **The capacity to correctly evaluate risks**
- ∞ **Developing a worldview that sustains us**
- ∞ **Having a sense of meaning and purpose in life**

THINGS TO CONSIDER WHEN JUPITER IS STATIONARY

This is an opportunity to reflect on our general outlook on life. What risks are we willing to take in order to grow? What is our attitude to the society we inhabit? Are we willing to continue to learn?

SATURN

Developing to maturity and taking on adult responsibilities

DIFFICULTIES ASSOCIATED WITH SATURN CAN INCLUDE;

- ∞ **Excessive fear or worry**
- ∞ **Overly serious, harsh or critical attitudes**
- ∞ **Avoidance of responsibility**
- ∞ **Clashes with authority figures, government, or employers**
- ∞ **Making up our own rules – run-ins with the law**
- ∞ **Denial of reality because it's too hard, too scary, or too depressing**
- ∞ **Lack of self-discipline**
- ∞ **Depression**
- ∞ **Excessive focus on materialism**
- ∞ **Inability to say no**
- ∞ **Inability to organise anything**

OVERCOMING ISSUES ASSOCIATED WITH SATURN CAN LEAD TO;

- ∞ **Consciously deciding on, and committing to one's goals, vocation or profession**
- ∞ **Rising to a position of authority and respect in one's profession**
- ∞ **Rising to a position of authority and respect in public life**
- ∞ **Setting up one's own business and making a success of it**
- ∞ **Capacity to take on, manage and organise adult responsibilities**
- ∞ **Recognition from our peers**

THINGS TO CONSIDER WHEN SATURN IS STATIONARY

This is an opportunity to reassess our long-term goals, vocation and professional standing. Are we on the right path? Are we behaving responsibly? Do we have too many responsibilities? What is our plan for retirement and old age?

CHIRON

Understanding and accepting that our wounds have value

DIFFICULTIES ASSOCIATED WITH CHIRON CAN INCLUDE;

- ∞ **Allowing our wounds to paralyse us**
- ∞ **Keeping ourselves locked away because we feel too damaged to participate in life**
- ∞ **Thinking that we are in a worse situation than everyone else**
- ∞ **Thinking that no-one else can understand what we have experienced, or endured**
- ∞ **Poor me**
- ∞ **Self-harm**
- ∞ **Chronic health issues**

OVERCOMING ISSUES ASSOCIATED WITH CHIRON CAN LEAD TO;

- ∞ **Capacity to reach out to others to offer help – healing and mentoring**
- ∞ **Understanding that our wounds have unique value**
- ∞ **Ability to accept help and guidance from others**
- ∞ **A positive attitude to ageing**
- ∞ **Participating in life regardless of our pain and suffering**

THINGS TO CONSIDER WHEN CHIRON IS STATIONARY

This is an opportunity to reflect on our attitude towards ageing and to our personal pain and wounds. What have our experiences taught us? What are the positives we have learned from our wounds and suffering? Coming to terms with our wounds. Psychological healing. Mentoring others.

URANUS

The freedom to create

DIFFICULTIES ASSOCIATED WITH URANUS CAN INCLUDE;

- ∞ **Rebellion because we feel powerless**
- ∞ **Inflexibility**
- ∞ **Hiding our creativity behind Saturn's regulations and obligations**
- ∞ **Throwing away everything we have achieved in order to be free**
- ∞ **Stress and anxiety from constantly fighting against social rules**
- ∞ **Inability to cope with change**
- ∞ **Fear of the future**

OVERCOMING ISSUES ASSOCIATED WITH URANUS CAN LEAD TO;

- ∞ **Conscious awakening of creativity and originality**
- ∞ **Knowing we are free and creative**
- ∞ **Taking responsibility for everything we create**
- ∞ **Inventiveness and social reforming**
- ∞ **Utilising our unique talents**
- ∞ **Progressive attitudes to future possibilities**
- ∞ **Being free to create while also accepting our responsibilities**
- ∞ **Knowing that Saturn and Uranus are not mutually exclusive**

THINGS TO CONSIDER WHEN URANUS IS STATIONARY

Finding new ways to manage stress and change. How do we see the future? This is an opportunity to break free from the past and make long overdue changes that have prevented us from expressing our individuality and creativity.

NEPTUNE

The universal desire to belong and believe

DIFFICULTIES ASSOCIATED WITH NEPTUNE CAN INCLUDE;

- ∞ **Worshipping spurious concepts and beliefs**
- ∞ **Worshipping messiahs and gurus who we believe have all the answers**
- ∞ **Playing the victim**
- ∞ **Disillusionment and depression**
- ∞ **Avoiding reality**
- ∞ **Mental illness**
- ∞ **Lack of empathy and compassion**
- ∞ **Avoiding personal responsibility by blaming 'god'**
- ∞ **Drug and alcohol abuse**

OVERCOMING ISSUES ASSOCIATED WITH NEPTUNE CAN LEAD TO;

- ∞ **Meaningful experiences**
- ∞ **Developing a personal belief system that guides our behaviour, morals and ethics**
- ∞ **Compassion, understanding and empathy**
- ∞ **Deep love and appreciation of music, art and the natural world**
- ∞ **A sense of meaning and purpose**

THINGS TO CONSIDER WHEN NEPTUNE IS STATIONARY

This is an opportunity to reflect on our dreams. Do we feel we belong? Do we feel we are connected to our spiritual self? What do we believe? A time to re-engage with nature, music, meditation, art or whatever provides nourishment to our soul.

PLUTO

The need to survive

DIFFICULTIES ASSOCIATED WITH PLUTO CAN INCLUDE;

- ∞ Blaming others for our misfortune, choices or actions
- ∞ Allowing others to manipulate or control us
- ∞ Manipulating others to feel a sense of control
- ∞ Deep-seated fear – especially fear of death
- ∞ Overly concerned with money and material survival – never having enough
- ∞ Hoarding
- ∞ Constant power struggles
- ∞ Paranoia
- ∞ Inability to let go
- ∞ Cruelty, abuse, greed and violence

OVERCOMING ISSUES ASSOCIATED WITH PLUTO CAN LEAD TO;

- ∞ Capacity to let go and to grieve
- ∞ Accepting that death is part of life and should not be feared
- ∞ The capacity to reinvent ourselves
- ∞ The ability to rise above destructive behaviour and situations
- ∞ Accepting the mysteries of life and death
- ∞ Knowing the difference between things we can control and those we can't
- ∞ Rising to positions of power and influence without exploiting others

THINGS TO CONSIDER WHEN PLUTO IS STATIONARY

This is an opportunity for releasing, resurrecting, regenerating or reinventing ourselves. How much control do we feel we have? How much control do we need to have? What is our attitude to death? Being willing to let go and to grieve when necessary.

ERIS

How we cope with events that make us feel invisible

DIFFICULTIES ASSOCIATED WITH ERIS CAN INCLUDE;

- ∞ **Stirring up trouble just for fun**
- ∞ **Stirring up trouble to retaliate, get even, or feel superior**
- ∞ **Jealousy**
- ∞ **Resentment**
- ∞ **Feeling like the world is against us**
- ∞ **Feeling guilty and deserving of punishment**

OVERCOMING ISSUES ASSOCIATED WITH ERIS CAN LEAD TO;

- ∞ **Accepting that what goes around comes around, but sometimes not in our lifetime**
- ∞ **Accepting that we are beautiful, no matter our situation, or circumstances**
- ∞ **Effective management of conflict, whether personal or global**

THINGS TO CONSIDER WHEN ERIS IS STATIONARY

This is an opportunity to know we are loved and beautiful even when we feel invisible and are caught up in conflicts beyond our control.

MERCURY

Mercury is the fastest of all the planets (except the Moon) and governs all aspects of travel and communication. As the first planet from the Sun, Mercury represents the first stages of development.[14] Children learn quickly. Communication involves not just speaking, writing and reading, but also observing and listening.

Mercury is retrograde three times each year for a period of three weeks each time. These retrograde periods recur in the same element several times before moving backwards into the previous element; against the normal order of elements. So, Mercury will retrograde in Water several times, then several times in Air, then Earth, then Fire.

Known as the archetypal trickster, Mercury is well known for his antics when retrograde. Mercury's retrograde periods offer us an opportunity to 'rethink'. But sometimes rethinking can complicate matters when we start second guessing ourselves. As we start fiddling and tweaking trying to fix issues, we can make problems worse.

Computer glitches, transport breakdowns and other random annoyances often crop up at these retrograde intervals. As I write this, Mercury is retrograde in Gemini. Since Mercury stationed retrograde two weeks ago, Apple has been rolling out a software update that has affected thousands of people who subsequently lost access to a program containing all their passwords!

Mercury operates differently in the morning sky (Promethean) to when it's in the evening sky (Epimethean). Promethean types (meaning forethought) tend to think more independently, while Epimethean types (meaning afterthought) prefer to take into account other views and try to arrive at a consensus.

We see these different communication styles in the example of musicians Paul Simon and Art Garfunkel who were born three weeks apart. Paul's Mercury is SR (evening sky) and Art's is SD (morning sky). The duo originally met at school. Throughout their critically acclaimed musical collaboration, they were always at odds with one another. Communication between them was always fraught and they have never been able to reconcile their differences. Interestingly, Paul Simon's SR Mercury (11SC52) is exactly quincunx Art Garfunkel's SD Mars (11AR11) which is an awkward aspect in itself, adding to the tension in their relationship.

It's worth noting that a number of incredibly prolific writers were born with stationary Mercury, including Agatha Christie (15LI13 SR), Georges Simenon (03AQ40 SD), Linda Goodman (02TA36 SR) and J.K. Rowling (00VI02 SR). Other influential writers and orators with stationary Mercury include Charles Baudelaire, Noel Coward, F. Scott Fitzgerald, Dylan Thomas and Stephen Fry.

One of the most prolific writers of the 20th Century was Winston Churchill. He doesn't have Mercury stationary within the 30 percent rule, but Mercury did station direct five days before his birth, so it was slow and just outside the orb. In the chart for prolific screenwriter Dalton Trumbo (*Spartacus* et al,), Mercury is retrograde, but it stationed retrograde three or four days before his birth. These two examples could be an argument for widening the orb for stations, but of course there are many writers who don't have stationary Mercury. Mercury aspects also play a key role and it's important to consider the Moon in the charts of writers. As the groundbreaking research of Michel Gauquelin revealed, the Moon is often rising, or culminating in these charts. In every chart there are always many factors to consider.

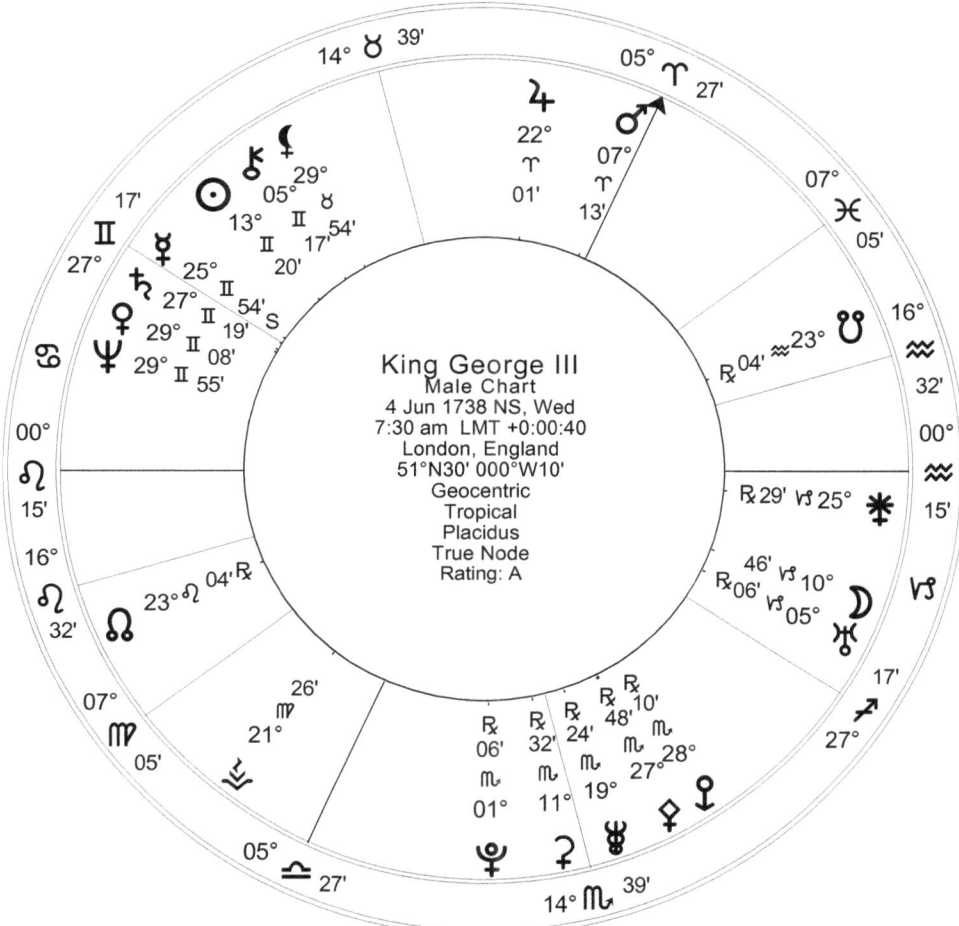

In the chart for King George III, we see SR Mercury in its own sign Gemini and involved in a stellium with Venus, Saturn and Neptune. The actual station of Mercury took place three and a half days before his birth.

King George III, known as 'Mad King George,' developed a peculiar condition that was never fully understood. Some sources have suggested that it was a genetic blood disorder called porphyria. Recent research seems to have virtually ruled out this theory, and it is now thought that he suffered from a type of mania, or other psychiatric condition.[15] Perhaps it was a combination of the two.

One of the key symptoms of his illness was a tendency to talk incessantly. His speech became manic, and he would rave on incoherently, unable to stop himself. His written correspondence showed this same tendency; sentences would run on and on as his train of thought became increasingly confused. Towards the close of his life, he talked nonstop for days, not pausing to eat or sleep.

When his illness first surfaced, George himself was of the view that the condition was triggered by his intense grief over the loss of his youngest and beloved daughter, Princess Amelia, who died at the age of 27 on 2 November, 1810.

Whatever the cause, natal SR Mercury located in its own sign Gemini accurately describes his inability to stop talking. In his chart the Sun and Chiron are also positioned in Gemini, making a total of six planets in the sign of communication. The sextile between Mercury in Gemini and Jupiter in Aries would have served to exacerbate this condition. Sextile aspects naturally evoke the energy of air signs Gemini and Aquarius which are 60 degrees from 0 Aries.

King George III simply had no way out of this compulsion. He was destined to endlessly repeat himself, literally stuck in time. Whether or not it was grief that triggered his condition, by the end of his life he was completely insane — also blind and deaf, suffering from dementia and unable to walk. George III died in January 1820.

Mercury plays a key role in travel as well as in communication. If you calculate the chart for Christopher Reeve's 1995 accident using the four day default setting for stations, Mercury appears retrograde and asteroid Hygiea (health and healing) is direct. But if you calculate this event chart using the 30 percent rule, both Mercury and Hygiea are flagged S, which highlights the fact that both planets were about to station and were therefore significant factors at that time. Similarly, in Reeve's natal chart, using the standard four-day orb, Hygiea would be flagged R, but using the 30 percent rule, it's flagged S.

At the time of his accident, the transiting Mercury station (17GE55) was in tight opposition to Reeve's natal 5th house Mars (18SG15).

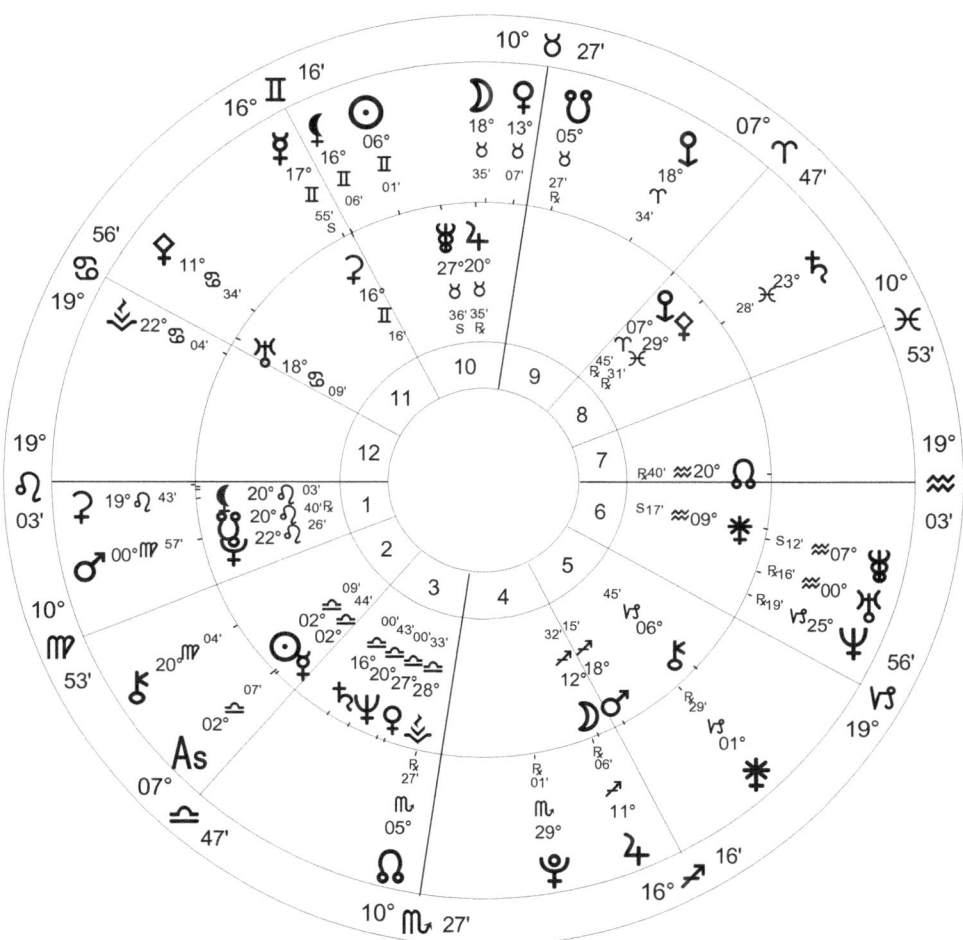

Inner Wheel: Christopher Reeve. 25 September 1952. 3.12am, New York, New York. (A)
Outer Wheel: His accident. 27 May 1995. 3.03pm, Culpeper, Virginia. (A)

According to Reeve himself, it was a sudden decision to enter the equestrian competition in Culpeper, Virginia. The family had originally planned to go sailing that weekend, but a last minute invitation from a friend had changed his mind. Reeve states in his book *Still Me*, that after the accident he learned that this kind of impulsive decision is typical of many accidents.

'I've often thought that if I'd stuck to the original plan nothing bad would have happened. But Dana pointed out that if we'd gone sailing that weekend instead, I could just as easily have been hit in the head by the boom, knocked overboard, and drowned.'[16]

Reeve has a very tight quincunx between Mars and Uranus in his natal chart, an aspect symbolically associated with the potential for accidents. This aspect was repeated in the heavens on the day he fell from his horse, breaking his top two vertebrae and leaving him a quadriplegic. With the transiting Mercury station powerfully positioned in its own sign of Gemini, opposing Reeve's natal Mars, we have an extra factor that suggests the potential for an accident.

The transiting Hygiea station (07AQ12) was within two degrees of Reeve's only other stationary planet, namely Juno, (09AQ17).

Some moments in time are indeed more significant than others. While Mercury stations imply that we might change our mind and alter course, this story also tells us that sometimes a 'rethink' is not the best idea.

TRAVELLING WHEN MERCURY IS STATIONARY - A TRUE STORY

In May 2010 my partner and I drove from Melbourne to Sydney to visit my aunt who had recently broken her hip. We decided to extend our trip and spend a few days away.

On 13 May 2010 around 24 hours after Mercury stationed direct, but was still slower than 30 percent of its average speed, we were scheduled to fly to Lord Howe Island for a five day break. I have travelled before on a Mercury station without incident, but this was to be an eventful journey in more ways than one.

We arrived at the airport early, which turned out to be a good thing because Neil realised he had left his camera in the car and went back to retrieve it. The flight was delayed owing to bad weather in the Lord Howe region. We boarded about an hour late and took off for paradise.

Unfortunately, I had a come down with a heavy head cold the previous day and was chock full of drugs, lozenges and nasal spray so my eardrums would survive the journey. I was feeling pretty miserable, but nonetheless looking forward to a wonderful few days holiday.

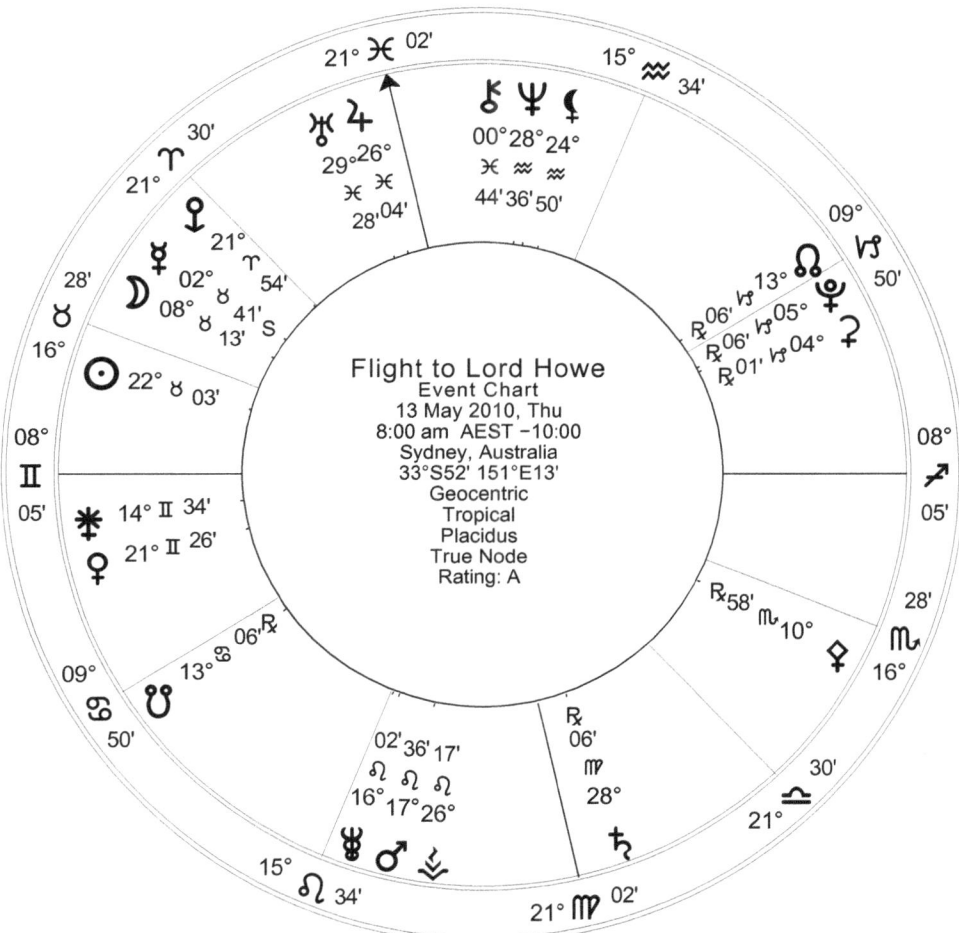

The flight from Sydney to Lord Howe takes around two hours. As we began our descent, we caught a glimpse of the beautiful island below us.

The plane circled and circled, and then started to gain altitude.

Just then the pilot announced, 'We've been waiting for some weather to clear over the island, but now it's developed into an electrical storm. Unfortunately, we don't have enough fuel to wait any longer, and we don't have enough to get back to Sydney, (Gasp!) so we will be flying to Port Macquarie. Sorry for the inconvenience.'

After we breathed a sigh of relief that we were not about to ditch into the Pacific Ocean, the plane turned around and headed for Port Macquarie. We had assumed that we would be staying in Port Macquarie for the night, but no. We sat on the plane and after refuelling we flew back to Sydney. So here we were, Mercury was stationary and we had been travelling all day to arrive back exactly where we started.

Arrangements were made for us to stay at a hotel for the night. We had to wait a while for the shuttle bus. By this time it was getting dark. Feeling cold and tired, we loaded our luggage into the trailer behind the bus and found seats with our fellow passengers. It had been a full flight, so a second bus was needed to ferry us all to the hotel. We were on the first bus and duly disembarked at the hotel. Luggage was unloaded from the trailer, but to our horror, Neil's case was not there!

I stood there cursing to myself, with a runny nose, sore throat and blocked ears, feeling miserable, knowing full well that I should have known better than to travel on a Mercury station. We stood waiting in the cold evening air, hungry, tired and frustrated, not knowing what to do. After a few minutes which seemed like an eternity, the second shuttle bus arrived. Fortunately, a fellow passenger had noticed Neil's bag was left sitting on the curb and had made sure it was loaded on the second shuttle bus. Thank the heavens.

We checked into the hotel then headed down to the restaurant for dinner, discussing the day's Mercury station events. It was then, looking at the menu, that I realised we were staying at the MERCURE Hotel!

The next day we headed back to the airport for an early flight which fortunately arrived at Lord Howe without a problem.

Lord Howe is a stunningly beautiful island, but while we were there the weather was a bit variable to say the least. The first day it was incredibly windy. Every day we had intermittent showers, wind, then sun, then showers again. It changed every half hour. Over the four days we were there, several other flights were not able to land. The island seemed to create its own weather.

Lord Howe was uninhabited (by humans at least) until it was unexpectedly discovered in 1788. I noted the date and the time of its discovery which we found in an original document housed in Lord Howe's small museum. How appropriate that the island was discovered unexpectedly when the Sun was in Aquarius and Uranus was exactly on the Ascendant!

It's a truly unique place. World Heritage listed because of its vast range of rare and unique flora and fauna; many species are found nowhere else on Earth.

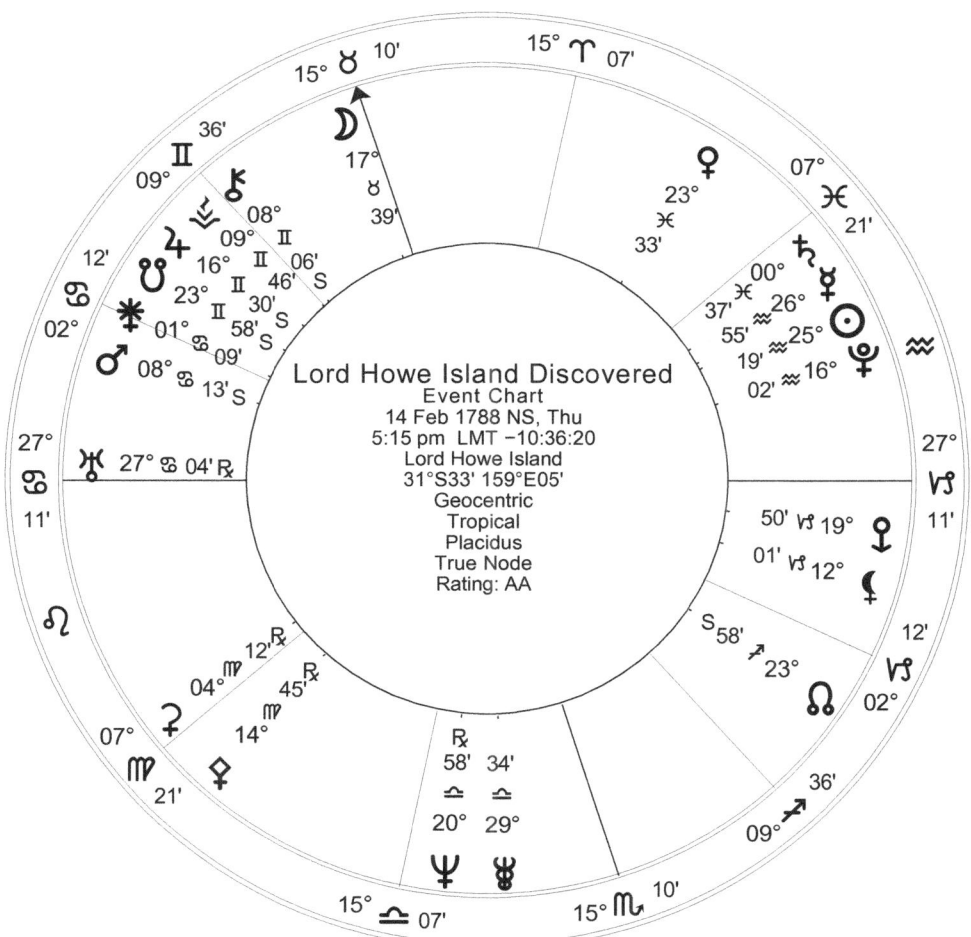

On the day we were due to fly back to Sydney, the morning was still and calm; not a breath of wind, but there were clouds gathering. After a morning spent kayaking on the lagoon, we had lunch, then headed for the airport.

The clouds were getting thicker. The wind picked up and rain started to fall. We waited for the incoming flight to land which would take us back to Sydney.

We watched the plane break through the clouds and approach the runway, but it just flew past, fifteen metres or so over the tarmac. A fly-by.

The airstrip at Lord Howe is short with the Pacific Ocean at both ends. Plus, it's sandwiched between two mountains on one side and a flat plain on the other, which makes it prone to windshear, so we learned. It's a difficult place to land at the best of times, but especially in bad weather.

As the plane headed back to the skies, we knew, based on our first aborted trip, they only had about 20 minutes to land safely, or they would have to fly back to Port Macquarie.

We waited and watched as the rain started to really pelt down. The wind had dropped, but the windsock was moving in all directions. After fifteen minutes the plane had not reappeared. We were beginning to think that we would be staying for five nights after all.

A few minutes later the plane appeared through the clouds for a second time. It was still bucketing down. Thankfully, the plane landed safely to a chorus of applause from the waiting passengers and from the ground staff in the control booth behind us. Mercury was now fully direct.

Mercury SR[17]

Ruth Bader Ginsburg	07AR12
John Belushi	20AQ10 - (conjunct Mars)
Jeanne Calment[18]	16PI38 - see also Ceres & Jupiter
Agatha Christie	15LI13
Hillary Clinton	21SC243 - see also Pallas Athena & Hygiea
Nicholas Copernicus	26PI30
Michael Faraday	20LI08 - see also Venus & Pallas Athena
F. Scott Fitzgerald	24LI48 - (conjunct Venus) see also Neptune
Jane Fonda	15CP33 - see also Neptune & Eris
Benjamin Franklin	12AQ19 - see also Saturn
Stephen Fry	24VI48 - see also Vesta
King George III	25GE54 - (conjunct Saturn)
Linda Goodman	02TA36 - see also Juno
Patty Hearst	16PI04 - see also Saturn
John Howard	24LE02 - see also Jupiter
Jeff Kennett	21AQ39 - see also Vesta & Uranus
Dr Phil McGraw	02LI14 - (conjunct South Node)
Spike Milligan	10TA23 - see also Mars, Pallas Athena & Neptune
John Nash[19]	12CN07 - (conjunct Pluto)
Pablo Picasso	24SC14 - (opposite Jupiter)
J.K. Rowling	00VI02 - see also Ceres & Neptune
Paul Simon	11SC52 - see also Jupiter
Ringo Starr	05LE12 - (conjunct Moon, Mars & Pluto)
Dylan Thomas	22SC587 - (conjunct Mars) see also Vesta
Greta Thunberg	28CP26 - see also Hygiea
John Travolta	15PI56 - see also Saturn
Harry S. Truman	01GE16 - (conjunct Pluto, Pallas Athena & Chiron)
Vincent Van Gogh	25AR36

Events

1947 Roswell Alien Crash	27CN04 - see also Pallas Athena & Chiron
1955 James Dean's fatal accident	28LI37 - (conjunct Neptune)
1994 Nicole Simpson's murder	08CN24 - see also Juno
1995 Christopher Reeve's accident	17GE55 - see also Hygiea
2010 Deepwater Horizon Explosion	12TA12 - see also Ceres

Mercury SD[20]

Marshall Applewhite	04TA07 - see also Vesta, Ceres & Neptune
Charles Baudelaire	27PI23 - (conjunct Pluto) see also Uranus & Ceres
Bjorn Borg	00GE14 - see also Venus, Hygiea & Vesta
Lindy Chamberlain	21AQ33 - (opposite Mars) see also Uranus & Vesta
Glenn Close	09PI31 - see also Jupiter
Noel Coward	05SG49 - (conjunct Uranus)
Bob Crane	03CN32 - see also Ceres & Uranus
Clint Eastwood	23TA48 - see also Juno
Lady Gaga	18PI04 - see also Juno & Uranus
Art Garfunkel	26LI27 - see also Mars & Pluto
John Glenn	11CN09 - (conjunct Pluto) see also Chiron
Philip Seymour Hoffman[21]	12CN39 - see also Saturn
Steve Jobs	14AQ21 - see also Saturn, Juno and Hygiea
James Earl Jones	06CP03 - see also Pallas Athena
Jim Jones	03TA35 - see also Ceres & Neptune
Paul Keating	08CP54 - see also Mars & Vesta
Christine Keeler	11AQ36 - see also Venus
John F. Kennedy	20TA36 - see also Uranus, Juno & Hygiea
David Koresh[22]	07LE51 - see also Venus
14th Dalai Lama	25GE35 - see also Jupiter
K.D. Lang	22LI33 - see also Pallas Athena & Juno
Heath Ledger	26PI09 - (conjunct Mars & Vesta)
Charles Manson	02SC59 - (conjunct Jupiter & Descendant)
Oscar Pistorius	13SC05 - see also Venus & Vesta
Georges Simenon	03AQ40 - see also Mars & Pallas Athena
Wallis Simpson	16GE04 - see also Pallas Athena & Chiron

Events

1977 Granville Train Disaster	07CP07 - see also Jupiter, Pluto & Hygiea
2021 Florida Building Collapse	16GE11 - see also Jupiter and Neptune

VENUS

After the Moon, Venus is our closest celestial neighbour. Her proximity to Earth places Venus at the heart of our core values and self-esteem which determine our personal preferences and how we relate to others. Venus symbolises our likes and dislikes that start to develop in childhood. Do we like the taste of carrots? What is our favourite colour? Do we like our sister, our aunt, our appearance?

Named for the goddess of love and beauty, the morning and evening 'star' symbolises our standards and values, and by extension, how we engage with others who may, or may not share them. Hence, Venus symbolises our relationships, both social and intimate.

Venus is semi-sextile the Sun when stationary.[23] The semi-sextile aspect of 30 degrees speaks to the natural arrangement between two adjacent signs. Adjacent signs have different polarities, and neither element, nor quality in common, yet they share a cusp. They are neighbours and because of their proximity, they have to learn to get along.[24] The fact that Venus stations when 30 degrees from the Sun, just after emerging as the morning star, and again just before vanishing when the evening star, evokes the intrinsic need within us to engage with others. To do that we have to figure out the similarities and differences that exist between our values and those of others, and if we are able to reach a position of compromise.

The synodic cycle of Venus is intrinsically beautiful, tracing a perfect flower shape in the heavens. The Fibonacci series of numbers, where two numbers in the sequence added together produce the next number: 1, 1, 2, 3, 5, 8, 13, 21, 34, 55 and so on, when expressed geometrically, produces a unique spiral pattern. This is the same natural pattern of growth that we see in flowers, ferns, antlers, shells and other spiralling life forms. Known as the Golden Mean, or Golden Ratio, this innately beautiful pattern is embedded in the Venus-Earth relationship.

Morning and evening placements of Venus differ somewhat in their expression. Morning star types born with Venus waxing tend to be more vulnerable and active in seeking relationships, whereas waning evening star types are more self-contained and less engaged with others. However, in both cases, those born with stationary Venus often experience intense and highly passionate encounters.

The Venus evening star station is a time for retreat and withdrawal. It signals a time to *re-evaluate* our connections and commitments. What is most important to us? Do we feel valued? What is worth our while? With whom do we wish to associate? Which people, groups, relationships and financial commitments are in our best interests? Do we feel appreciated? When the Venus cycle is about to end and a new one is about to recommence at inferior conjunction,[25] it doesn't mean that our relationships are doomed, rather it means it's time to consider if there is an imbalance between our inner standards and outer circumstances. The station retrograde tells us it's time for this re-evaluation.

During the evening star phase, Venus is waning. As her crescent shape diminishes, she also gets closer to us. This tells us that during this period we focus more of our attention on less. We scrutinise details and become more choosey and particular.

As the next planet inward from the Earth, Venus represents our inner feelings from which outer expression unfurls. Venus's preferences lie at the heart of our decisions and choices. It's when Venus is in the middle of her retrograde cycle, at inferior conjunction, that she is at her closest to the Earth. Her proximity to us gives us an opportunity to re-engage with our core values and discover what and who we hold most dear.

Sometimes we put energy into relationships that may not be viable. Sometimes relationships, whether personal or professional, simply outlive their time. When Venus stations retrograde, we are given an opportunity to re-assess the merit of these ties and whether we should continue to invest our time, money and resources. The key question is; is it worth it? If the answer is no, choices can be made. If the answer is yes, but … then a heart-to-heart conversation can help to clear the air. Changes might be needed and these may, or may not be workable. Either way, Venus is guiding us to honour our inner goddess and needs.

Do we need to alter our opinions and the values that underpin them, or do outer circumstances need to change? Retrograde Venus focuses our attention on these important questions, which makes this a significant time for personal reflection and decision making.

Her station direct is the perfect time to re-engage with others and the outside world, or embark on a new relationship, whether business, or personal. However, the success of these new ventures often depends on how well we evaluate their suitability during the retrograde period. Once direct, Venus is slow at first and we should try to follow her pace and take the initial stages of any new relationship slowly.

On Valentine's Day 2013 at around 3am in Pretoria, South Africa, Oscar Pistorius shot and killed his girlfriend, Reeva Steenkamp. Transiting Saturn was located at 11SC30 and it was stationing retrograde.

In Oscar's natal chart Mercury is SD (13SC05) around half an hour from its exact station and Venus is also SD (08SC10). At the time of the shooting Oscar's progressed Venus had reached 13SC27 the same degree as his natal SD Mercury.

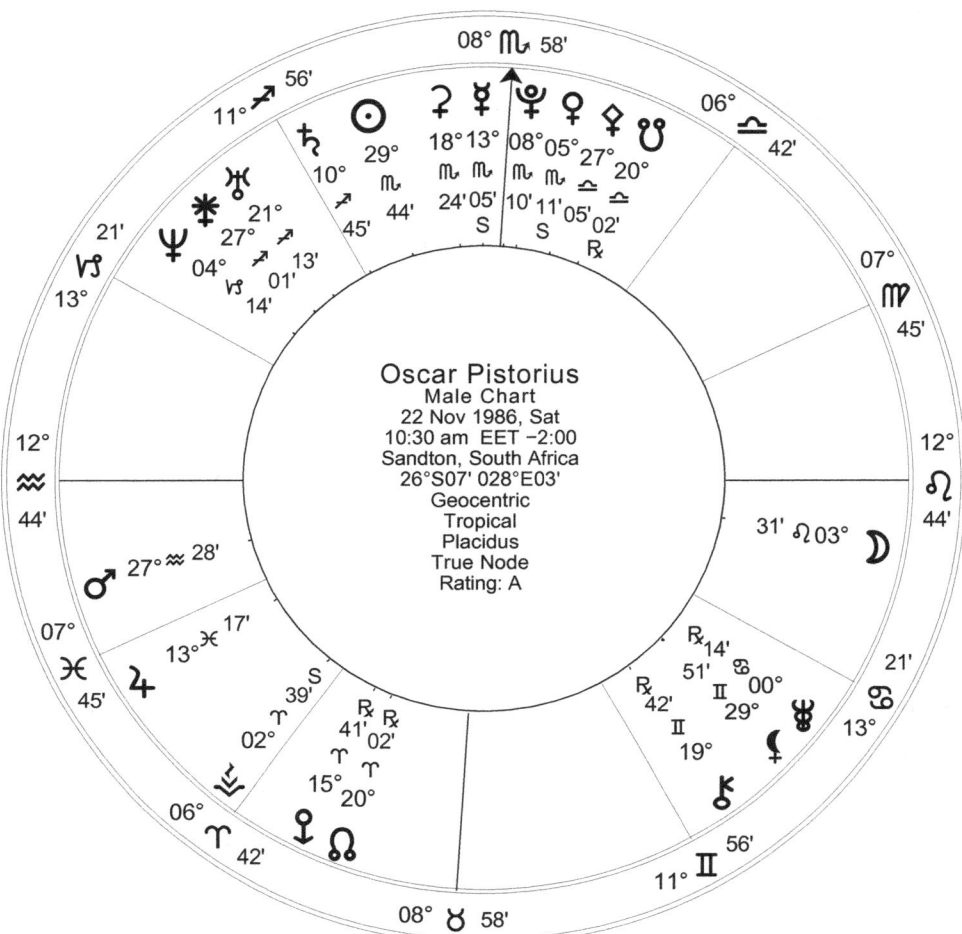

Assuming his time of birth is 100% accurate, Pluto is right on his Midheaven, which suggests a fervent desire to command his destiny as well as possible control issues. A powerful Pluto is often seen in the charts of those who undergo major reversals of fortune, for better or worse.

Living in a gated community and in a country where fear of home invasion is a real concern, Oscar's defence was that he thought there was an intruder. He said that he was in fear of his life and feeling vulnerable. This is consistent with the Scorpio propensity for paranoia and with his vulnerable SD Venus. Scorpio is also known for its deep and intense emotions including jealousy and possessiveness. Mars,

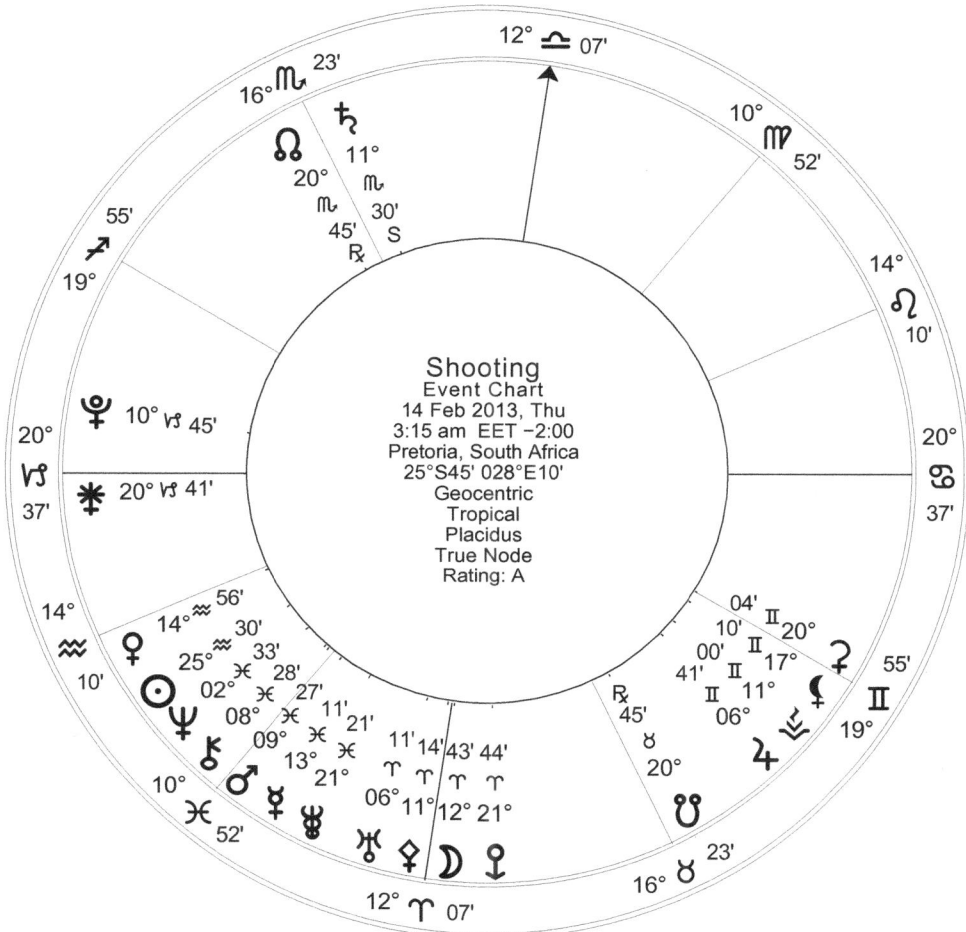

the co-ruler of his Scorpio planets, squares his Scorpio Sun, adding heat to his passionate nature.

Oscar Pistorius was born without any bones in his lower legs. At 11 months of age, his legs were amputated and he was fitted with prosthetics. Pistorius learned to walk and run with these prosthetics and was nicknamed 'the blade runner'. Achieving amazing success as an athlete, he was given permission to run against able bodied athletes in the 2012 Olympic Games in London. But everything changed in the early hours of 14 February 2013.

Reeva Steenkamp was born on 19 August 1983 in Cape Town, South Africa. There is no known birth time for Reeva, but we know she was born with Venus retrograde (04VI52). She died at the age of 29, having just been through her Saturn Return. At the time of her death, Venus was stationing direct by progression (23LE17) and was in a tight conjunction with progressed Mars (22LE26). In this progressed chart, Juno, goddess of marriage, is also stationary retrograde (05TA31).

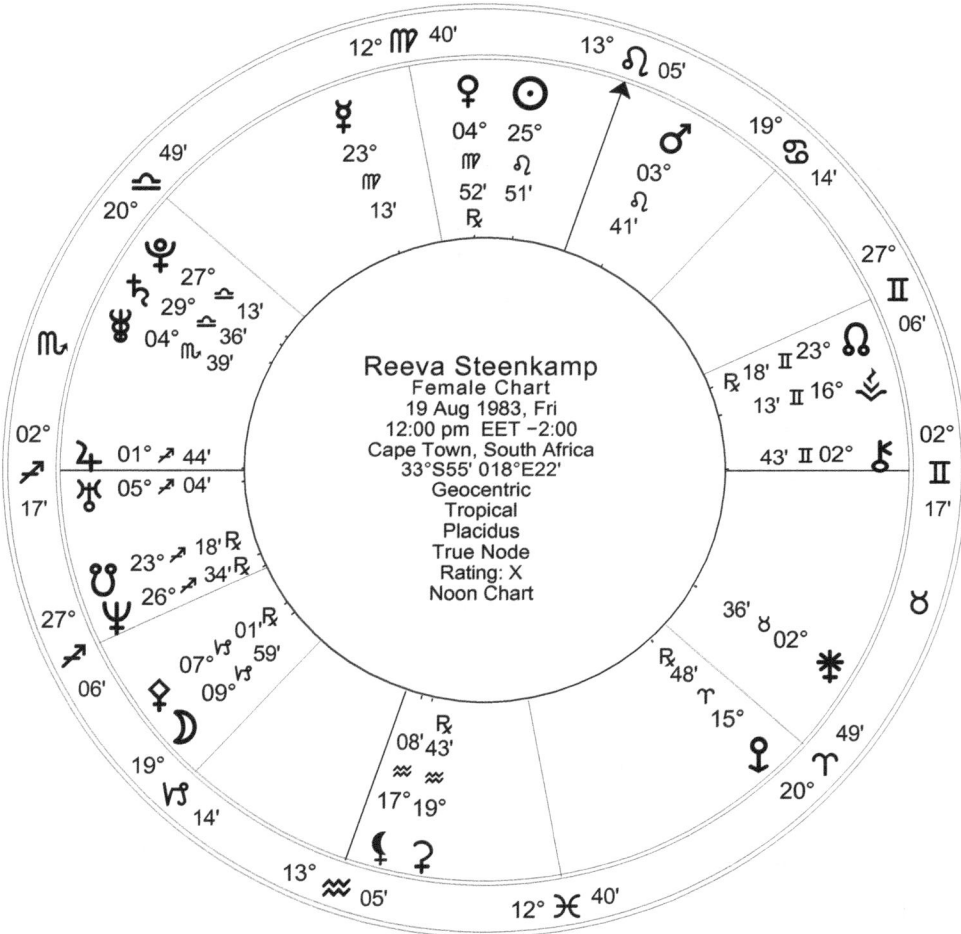

We often see Venus-Mars cross aspects in the charts of lovers. Hard aspects are not always experienced as difficulties in relationships. They can be highly creative and loving too. In this case we have Reeva's Venus (04VI52) in wide opposition to Oscar's Mars (27AQ28), an aspect of powerful sexual chemistry. In addition, Oscar's Venus (05SC11) squares Reeva's Mars (03LE41) which was probably more problematic, as fixed squares tend to be. Their two Venus's are in a very close sextile.

At the time of the shooting, transiting Saturn was stationary retrograde (11SC30). This places it at the midpoint of Oscar's Mercury-Pluto conjunction and not far from his stationary Venus.

Of course, not all stations of Venus have such a horrific tale to tell. Stationary Venus can impart a tremendous sense of artistry as seen in the charts of Michelangelo and Beethoven among others. That being said, many of those with stationary Venus, at least in this list of well-known individuals, have had relationship issues. Warren Beatty, Charles Chaplin, Tom Jones, Heidi Fleiss, Courtney Love, Patricia Neal, Mata Hari and Christine Keeler have all been in the news, at one time or another, concerning their personal relationships.

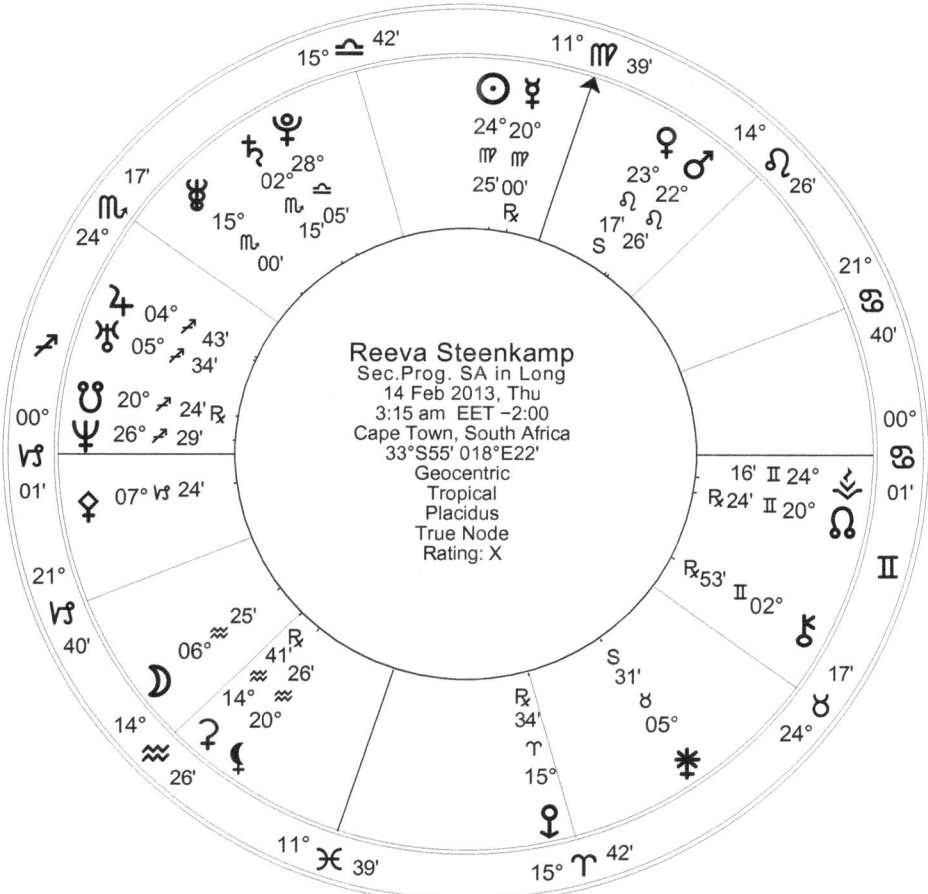

Venus SR

Muhammad Ali	20AQ40 - (conjunct Desc) see also Saturn & Hygiea
Warren Beatty	05TA37 - (conjunct Uranus)
Beethoven	26CP46 - see also Neptune
Bjorn Borg	08CN15 - see also Mercury, Hygiea & Vesta
Fidel Castro	24VI02 - see also Chiron
Charles Chaplin	18TA06 - see also Saturn
Michael Faraday	03SC20 - see also Mercury & Pallas Athena
Heidi Fleiss	13AQ07 - (conjunct Asc & Mars)
Stephen Hawking	20AQ46
Tom Jones	13CN15 - (conjunct Mars)
David Koresh	15VI14 - (conj Mars & Vesta) see also Mercury
Michelangelo	24AR41 - see also Saturn
Patricia Neal	25AQ56 - see also Pallas Athena
Nostradamus	02AQ23 - (opposite Chiron)

Events

1865 Lincoln Assassination	25TA39 - see also Jupiter
1962 Cuban Missile Crisis	29SC09 - see also Jupiter
1970 West Gate Bridge Collapse	24SC37 - (opposing Juno) see also Juno

Venus SD

Jason Alexander	29LE53
Daniel Andrews	18GE24 - (conjunct Saturn)
Julie Andrews	06VI38
Tony Blair	15AR01
Rubin Carter	19AR34 - see also Juno
King Charles II	05TA10
George Clooney	13AR04 - see also Saturn
Peter Gabriel	04AQ07 - see also Mars
Tom Hanks	22GE50 - see also Neptune
Mata Hari	14CN02 - see also Chiron & Neptune
Harold Holt	06CN32 - (conjunct North Node)
Buster Keaton	18VI43 - see also Hygiea and Vesta
Christine Keeler	05AQ31 - see also Mercury
Alan Leo	18CN20 - (opposite Mars) see also Mars & Pluto
Courtney Love	20GE24 - see also Vesta, Juno, & Pallas Athena
Erik Menendez	09SC56
Oscar Pistorius	05SC11 - (conjunct Pluto) see Mercury & Vesta
Cybill Shepherd	03AQ09 - see also Mars
Cat Stevens	25GE08 - see also Chiron
Kenneth Williams	10AQ58 - see also Hygiea
Amy Winehouse	23LE12 - see also Juno

Events

1804 Juno discovered	04LE10 - (conjunct South Node) see also Vesta
1937 Hindenburg disaster	19AR33 - see also Juno

MARS

We now venture beyond the inner solar system. Our first stop is Mars. This is where we develop willpower and a spirit of enterprise and drive. Named for the God of War, the red planet shares the same symbolic meaning as this dynamic primary colour. Mars is active, passionate and energetic. He has fighting spirit and can be angry and aggressive. He's courageous, thrives on competition and he likes to win. Just as red is the first colour of the spectrum, Mars puts himself first. Mars rules Aries, the first sign of the zodiac.

In many ways, Mars is in a category all his own. Given his independent and forthright nature, he's probably quite comfortable with this classification. Planet Mars is a solid world located in the inner solar system before we reach the asteroid belt, which is the natural division between the inner planets and the more distant and massive gas and ice worlds. Yet Mars lies beyond Earth's orbit and follows the same retrograde pattern as his more distant neighbours.

It's a relatively common mistake to think that the outer planets such as Pluto, or Eris have the longest synodic cycles, when it's actually Mars. From one year to the next, Pluto does not move very far, so its conjunctions with the Sun happen at 367 day intervals. Mars, however, is situated in a similar part of the solar system to the Earth.

So, when viewed from Earth, Mars and the Sun unite in a conjunction every 780 days, making Mars the longest planetary synod.

Mars is associated with forward momentum, action, vitality and activity. Being stationary and potentially frustrated and impeded is contrary to the very nature of the red planet. Consequently, it's fair to say that Mars retrograde, and its stations, are probably the most challenging.

Mars is not known for his patience. When progress comes to a halt Mars can have a temper tantrum. Although stationary Mars can impede one's energy and drive, it can also produce incredible stamina and staying power. The challenges symbolised by a slow Mars provide opportunities to rise to great achievements that inspire others.

Mars begins to slow in pace around the time of its waxing square to the Sun and stations occur between 130-145 degrees from the Sun, around the four o'clock mark. Retrograde periods last between 60-82 days. This variation is due to the fact that Mars has a highly elliptical orbit.

The painstaking research undertaken by Michel Gauquelin (who was born with SR Mars) revealed that Mars rising, or culminating is associated with sports champions.[26] It's a proven signature of athletic prowess. A strong Mars provides the competitive spirit that athletes need. Yet there are many outstanding athletes who have stationary Mars including tennis champions Martina Navratilova (SD), Rafael Nadal (SR) and Samantha Stosur (SR).

Far from being weak, or impeding one's energy and drive, this reinforces Ptolemy's observation that stationary planets can be just as powerful as those near the Ascendant or Midheaven.

Sprinter Usain Bolt has Mars SD (12CP01) which is the apex of a cardinal T-square involving Venus (14LI17) and SR Vesta (17AR24) with Eris (16AR30).

Drug cheat Lance Armstrong is another athlete with stationary Mars (SD) and Moto GP champion Marc Marquez (SD) is another.

Swimming champion Mark Spitz also has Mars stationary (SR). He won a total of nine gold medals, seven of them at the 1972 Munich Olympics, all in world record time. Having an 'immobile' Mars has not impeded the competitive spirit, energy or drive of these athletes, but has intensified it.

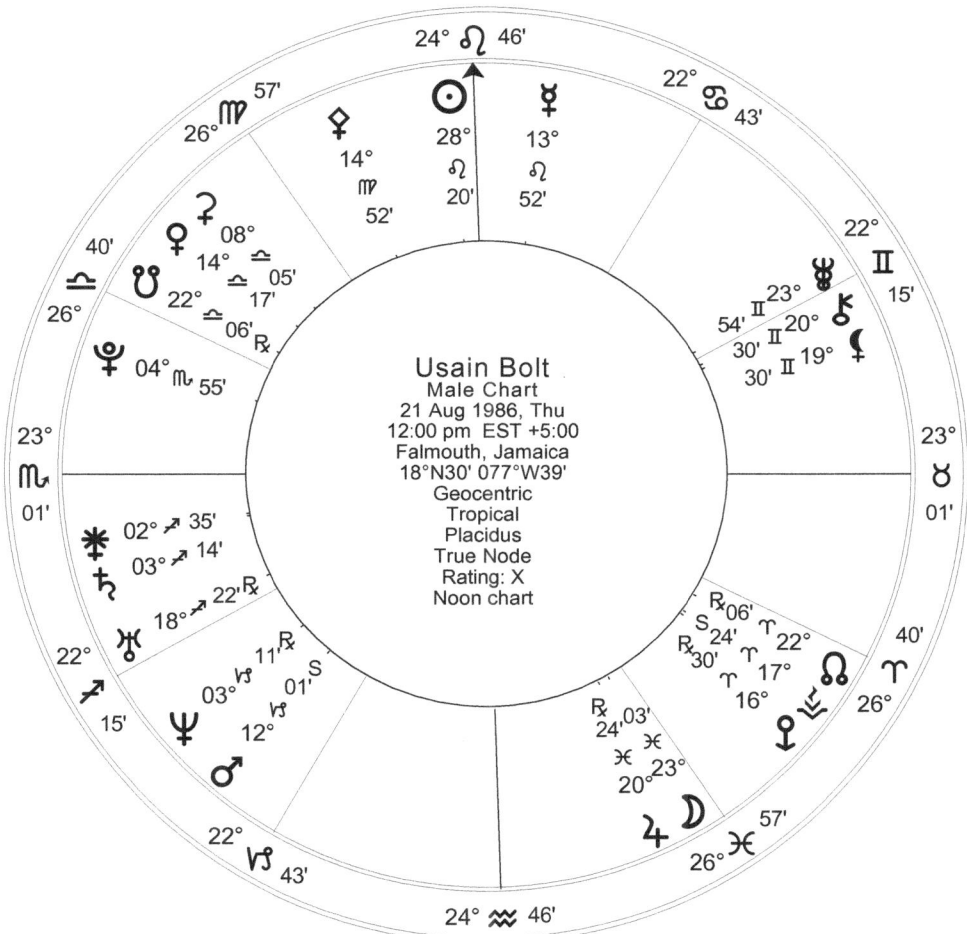

It seems that stationary Mars urges us to persist and strive to overcome obstacles. Of course, there is no guarantee that we will succeed in our quest. Heroes can stumble and fall. The challenge of a stationary Mars may be too great.

It could be a different kind of challenge that heroes face, totally unrelated to physical stamina and endurance, as in the case of Julian Assange.[27] Few people will have experienced the level of frustration and stress that he has faced over many years. He has SR Mars (21AQ32) near his North Node. Mars stationed retrograde eight days after his birth. He has a close Chiron-Eris conjunction in his chart. Both Chiron and Eris stationed retrograde a week or two after his birth. So, during his formative years, Mars, Chiron and Eris all stationed retrograde by progression.

Assange had a nomadic childhood attending over 30 different schools. His mother and father separated before he was born. His

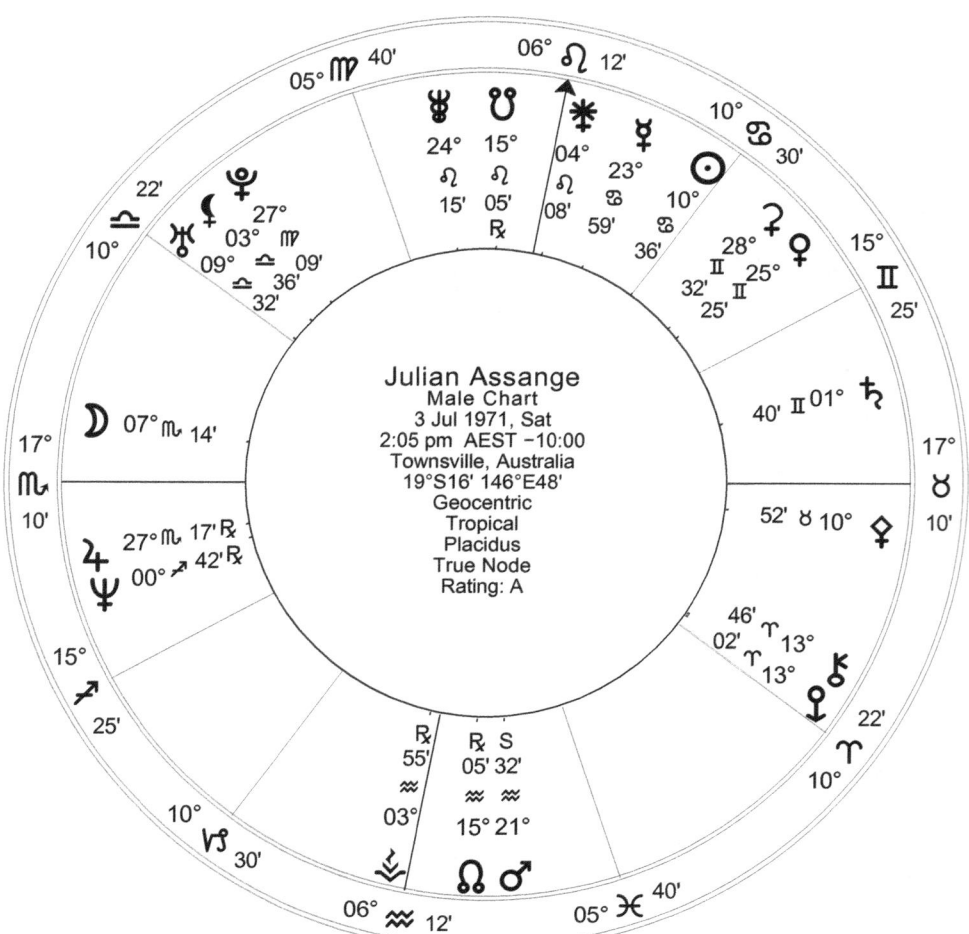

mother remarried when Julian was one year old and he took the surname of his stepfather, Brett Assange. Brett and his mother Christine divorced in 1979 when Julian was eight and his progressed Mars stationed retrograde.

It was at this time that his mother became involved with Leif Hamilton, who was a member of the Australian cult known as 'The Family'. It was in trying to get away from Leif Hamilton (aka Leif Meynell) that Julian and his mother had to keep moving.[28] We can only speculate how this unstable upbringing impacted his subsequent development and worldview, but clearly it had a major influence.

While each of us will respond differently to the hurdles we encounter in our journey through time on planet Earth, those born with stationary planets may have higher hurdles to jump than the rest of us, especially in the case of Mars. If they manage to get over these hurdles, they have an opportunity to really stand out from the crowd.

Mars SR

Julian Assange	21AQ32 - (conjunct North Node)
Sonny Bono	23LI58
Paul Cezanne	29VI16 - (conjunct South Node)
Peter Gabriel	11LI01 - (conjunct South Node) see also Venus
Michel Gauquelin	09CN16
Pauline Hanson	08CP26
John F. Kennedy Jnr.	18CN30 - (opposite Saturn)
Dr William Masters	29LE43 - see also Ceres
Bette Midler	03LE10
Ennio Morricone	09CN16
Elon Musk	20AQ56 - (conjunct North Node)
Rafael Nadal	22CP56
Jack Nicholson	05SG07
Dennis Nilsen	02LE20
Edith Piaf	28LE50
Tim Robbins	02GE15 - see also Hygiea
Rosalind Russell	18CP53
Cybill Shepherd	10LI44 - see also Venus
George Simenon	16LI05 - see also Mercury & Pallas Athena
Mark Spitz	11LI01 - (conjunct South Node)
Samantha Stosur	28SC05 - (opposite Chiron)
Harvey Weinstein	18SC18 - see also Uranus

Events

1933 The Third Reich	19VI42 - (conjunct Jupiter) see also Chiron
1975 Whitlam Dismissal	02CN30 - see also Vesta, Pallas Athena & Saturn
2014 MH370	27LI18 - see also Vesta, Ceres, Jupiter, Saturn

Mars SD

Lance Armstrong	12AQ26 - (conjunct North Node) see also Saturn
Lauren Bacall	25AQ35 - see also Hygiea & Ceres
Usain Bolt	11CP59 - see also Vesta
Truman Capote	25AQ48 - (conjunct North Node) see also Vesta
Jimmy Carter	25AQ53 - (conjunct North Node) see also Vesta
Blake Edwards	11SG44 - see also Hygiea & Chiron
Carrie Fisher	14PI00 - see also Pallas Athena
Joe Frazier	05GE11 - (conjunct Uranus) see also Vesta
Sigmund Freud	03LI22 - see also Chiron
Art Garfunkel	11AR11 - see also Mercury & Pluto
Mikhail Gorbachev	27CN38 - see also Jupiter
Carl G. Jung	21SG22 - see also Chiron
Paul Keating	05GE14 - see also Mercury & Vesta
Martin Luther King Jr	21GE53 - see also Chiron
Jay Leno	22VI11 - see also Juno, Hygiea & Pluto
Alan Leo	20CP10 - see also Venus and Pluto
Jayne Mansfield	01VI11 - (conjunct South Node)
Marc Marquez	08CN42
Spike Milligan	14VI27 - see also Mercury, P Athena & Neptune
Mozart	00CN19 - see also Jupiter & Ceres
Rupert Murdoch	27CN29 - see also Jupiter
Martina Navratilova	13PI35 - see also Chiron & Pallas Athena
Matthew Newton	14GE44 - see also Ceres
Jimmy Page	04GE51 - (conjunct Uranus) see also Neptune
Franklin D. Roosevelt	27GE00 - see also Chiron
Karen Silkwood	14CN07 - see also Uranus & Juno
Lily Tomlin	24CP23 - see also Uranus & Vesta

Events

1788 Lord Howe Island discovered	08CN14 - see also Jupiter & Chiron
1939 WWII first shot	24CP22 - see also Uranus & Vesta

CERES

The asteroid belt is a natural division in the solar system where we find thousands of minor planets, remnants of its early formation. There are multitudes of asteroids so there is no practical purpose in charting them all. However, it's worth examining the main ones which symbolise key aspects of the feminine and provide gender balance to the chiefly masculine hierarchy of the solar system.

Most asteroids orbit the Sun in around three to six years. As well as representing female archetypes, they symbolise qualities that we develop around the period of childhood when we transition from infancy, expand our social circle and start school.

With Ceres, the largest body in this group, now classified as a dwarf planet, we learn more about nurturing and care. At this time, we begin to separate from mother with the hope she provided us with a feeling of security and safety that we can carry with us.

Ceres personifies the mother archetype and as the goddess of grain and crops, she also has a strong connection to the natural environment. As Mother Earth, Ceres governs the bounty of the Earth, representing the capacity to nurture and care for both children and the natural world, and by extension the animal kingdom.

Stationary Ceres can manifest as trauma associated with one's mother. Prince William and Prince Harry both have stationary Ceres, highlighting the pain they experienced with the death of their mother, Princess Diana. Prince William has Ceres SD (12SC56) in his 10th house and his brother Prince Harry has Ceres SR (25TA16) conjunct his Moon and the North Node in the 4th house. Both the 10th and the 4th houses are associated with parental influences. Chiron and Hygiea are also at a standstill in Harry's chart.

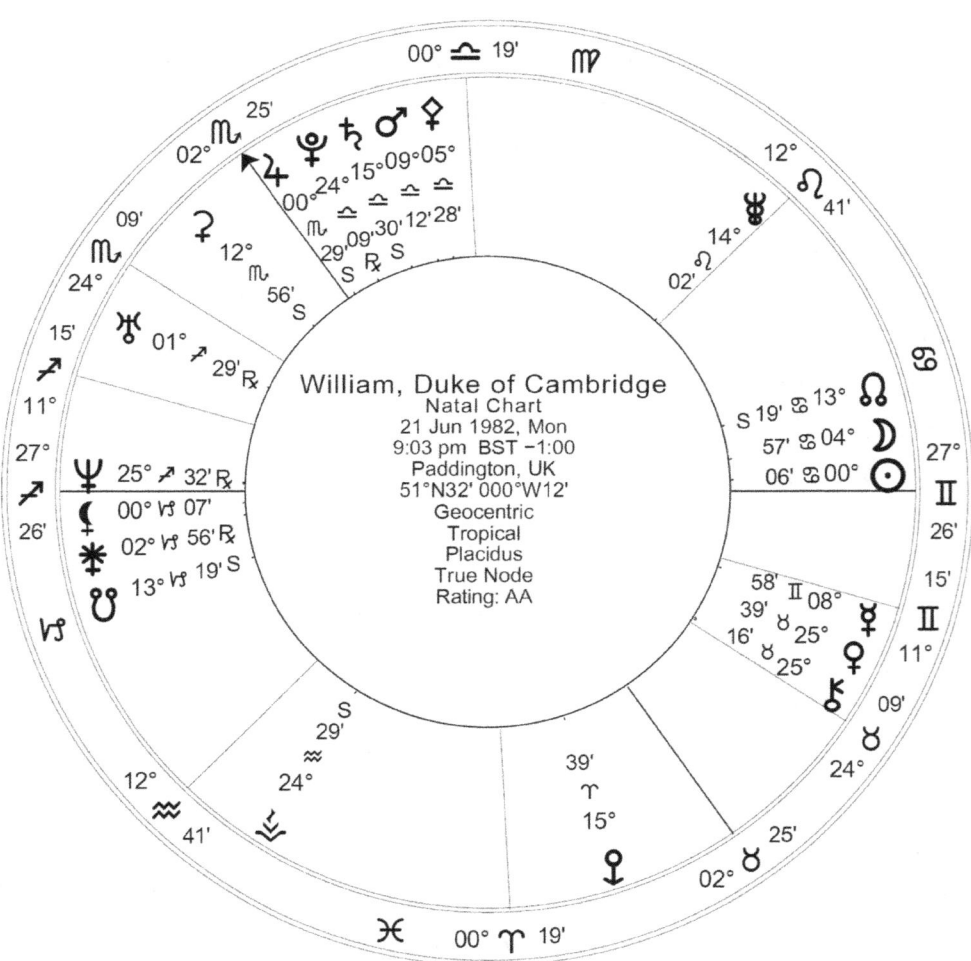

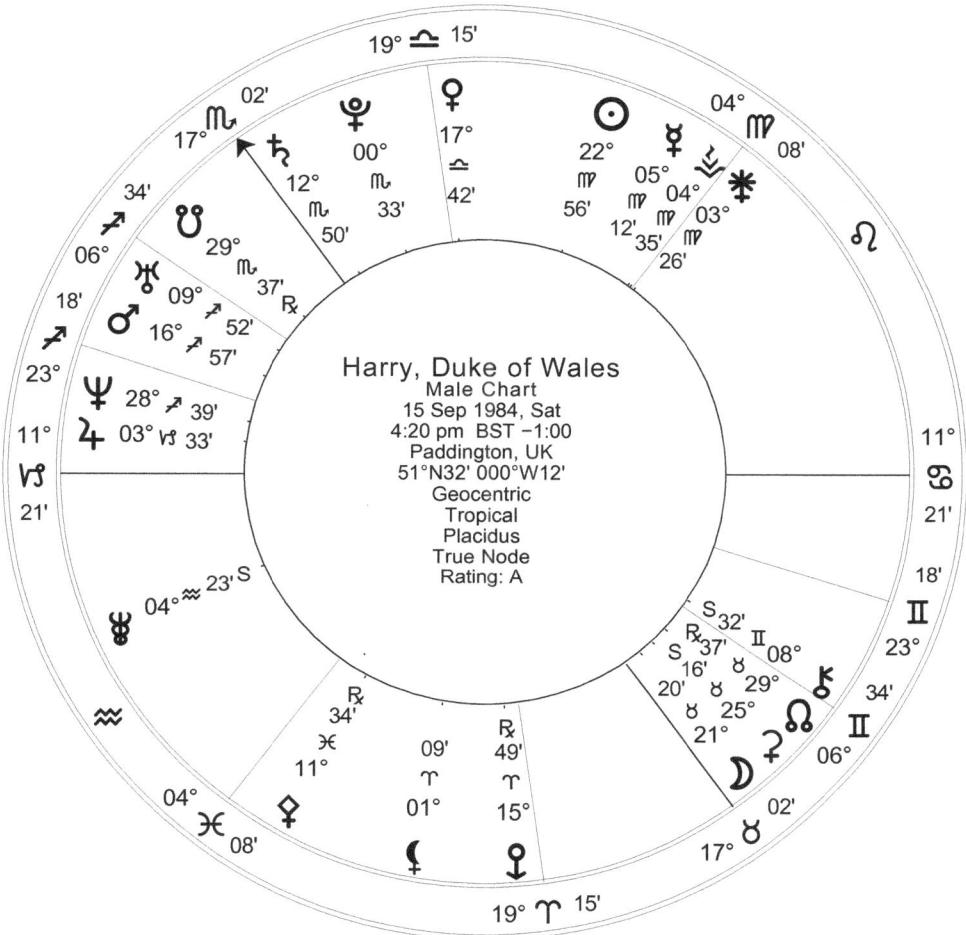

Mothering can turn to smothering, or to neglect with Ceres stationary. At its worst, dysfunctional Ceres may lead to child sexual abuse as we see in the examples of Jeffrey Epstein and allegedly Roman Polanski, who was first arrested in 1977, but managed to avoid several convictions.

Donald Trump has five stationary planets, the most I have seen in any natal chart. This may account for his range of psychological issues. Jupiter, Neptune, Chiron, Ceres and Juno are all stationary. All except Ceres, are located in Libra in his 2nd house. His stationary Ceres opposes his 12th house Pluto, suggesting control and power issues connected with his mother. This opposition speaks to the myth of Pluto's abduction of Ceres' daughter, Proserpina. It suggests an inability to reconcile this conflict and power imbalance, unlike the myth where a compromise was eventually worked out. It speaks to Trump's scant regard for women, animals and the environment.

Trump has rarely spoken of his mother. In her tell-all book, *Too Much and Never Enough*, Mary Trump, Donald's niece, a clinical psychologist, describes her grandmother as incapable of providing comfort or nurturing. 'She attended to them when it was convenient to her.' She describes her as, 'often unstable and needy' and says she used her children to comfort her, rather than nurturing them.[29]

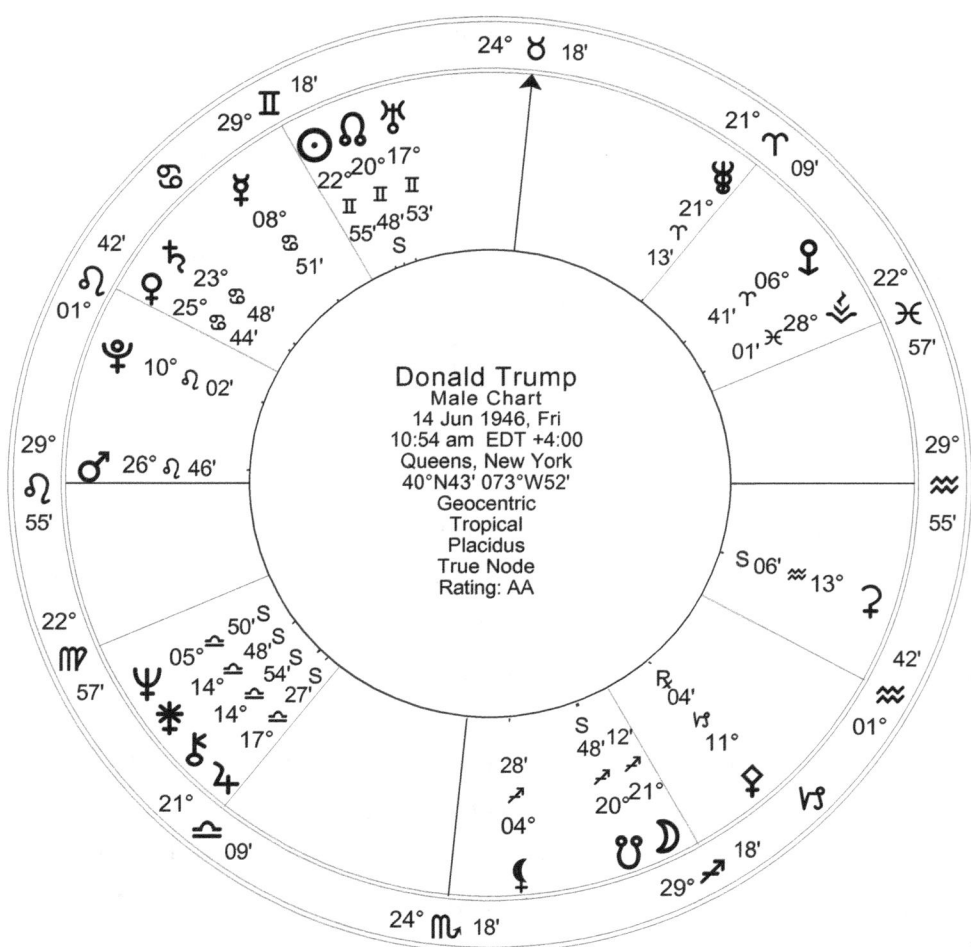

With four planets stationary in Trump's 2nd house of money, *Too Much and Never Enough,* is an apt title. Planets without much movement can be over emphasised, or under-developed and both extremes can be seen in one individual at different times, or even at the same time in different circumstances.

It's worth noting that in the US Sibly chart we find Ceres stationary retrograde (08PI41). The US has four planets in Cancer, the sign most associated with motherhood, and the addition of SR Ceres amplifies the desire for security. National security is a chief concern of the US and all manner of actions and political decisions have been made in its name.

The United States is in a way the archetypal 'mother' not just for the many immigrants who have made their home there, but also having adopted a maternal role on the world stage. In the US Sibly chart Ceres makes a tight square to Uranus (08GE55), planet of individuality and freedom. Both security and freedom are paramount values in the US and are enshrined in their constitution. The square aspect between these bodies suggests a delicate balance and tension between these two disparate themes.

It's interesting that Trump's successor, Joe Biden, was also born with stationary Ceres. Clearly his Ceres is in better shape than Trump's. Ceres has a lot to say about the environment, and Biden has the future of the planet in mind. One of his first acts after his inauguration was to set targets to tackle the effects of climate change.

Environmentalist, James Lovelock (aged 102 at the time of writing) who is best known for proposing the Gaia hypothesis, was born with SR Ceres (05AR14) in a close conjunction with Chiron. He clearly understands the wounds (Chiron) that the human animal has inflicted on the environment (Ceres). He was the first to detect the presence of CFCs in the atmosphere and their role in depleting the ozone layer. By way of comparison, naturalist David Attenborough does not have Ceres stationary, but it is powerfully aspected. In his chart Ceres is conjunct Neptune and part of a Fixed Grand Cross involving the Sun, Saturn and Jupiter.[30]

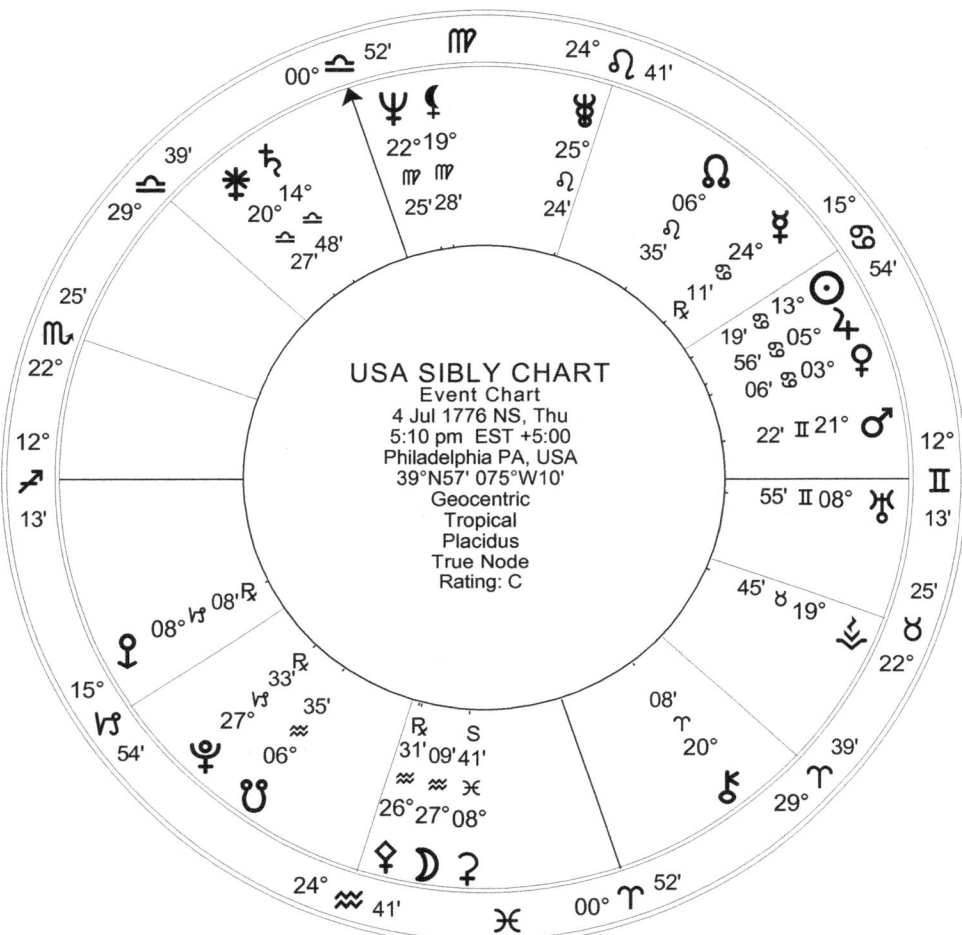

Ceres SR

Lauren Bacall	08TA10 - see also Mars & Hygiea
Charles Baudelaire	08SG02 - see also Mercury & Uranus
Erin Brockovich	29AQ10 - (conjunct Chiron)
Mark David Chapman	25CP04 - see also Chiron
Bob Crane	17PI58 - see also Mercury & Uranus
Nicholas Culpeper	20GE22 - see also Chiron & Uranus
James Dean	15LI24
Cadel Evans	10LI27 - see also Uranus
Mohandas Gandhi	03GE12
Julia Gillard	26TA46 - see also Vesta, Jupiter & Saturn
Prince Harry	25TA16 - see also Chiron & Hygiea
Brian Houston	13LI03 - see also Jupiter & Saturn
James Lovelock	05AR14 - (conjunct Chiron)
Mozart	05LI54 - see also Mars & Jupiter
Roman Polanski	22AR13 - opposite Mars, square Moon & Pluto
Vladimir Putin	17GE17 - see also Juno
Gina Rinehart	13LI14 - see also Jupiter
J.K. Rowling	02AR46 - see also Mercury & Neptune
Peter Sutcliffe	13AQ11 - see also Juno
Donald Trump	13AQ07 - see also Juno, Chiron, Jupiter & Neptune
Robin Williams	16PI35 - see also Juno

Events

1612 Galileo first sees Neptune	29LE42 - see also Neptune
1776 USA Independence (Sibly)	08PI41 - (square Uranus)
1846 Neptune discovered	04GE15
1914 Arch Duke Ferdinand Killed	01PI25 - see also Chiron
1989 Berlin Wall comes down	05CN04 - (conjunct Jupiter)
2010 Deepwater Horizon Explosion	04CP26 - (conjunct Pluto) see also Mercury
2014 MH370	01SC38 - see also Mars, Vesta, Jupiter, Saturn

Ceres SD

Peter Allen	24GE25 - see also Uranus
Marshall Applewhite	02LI13 - see also Mercury, Vesta and Neptune
Jeffrey Archer	06VI31 - see also Pluto
Joe Biden	20PI05
Richard Branson	06SG01 - see also Hygiea
Eileen Brennan	12CP28 - see also Chiron
Jeanne Calment	00CN23 - see also Mercury & Jupiter
Patsy Cline	12CP37 - see also Chiron
Jeffrey Epstein	03GE23
Alexander Fleming	10SG06 - (conjunct North Node)
Judy Garland	26LI02 - see also Jupiter
Shane Gould	06AR50
Jim Jones	02LI14 - see also Mercury & Neptune
Monica Lewinsky	03SG58 - see also Chiron & Juno
Queen Mary I	07CN34 - see also Jupiter
Mary Queen of Scots	01TA32 - see also Pallas Athena
Dr William Masters	15TA30 - see also Mars
Henri Matisse	19TA09 - see also Jupiter
Kylie Minogue	23LI02 - (opposite Saturn)
Matthew Newton	01GE19 - see also Mars
Geoffrey Robertson	29CP24 - see also Uranus
Robert Louis Stevenson	24PI48 - see also Neptune
Henri Toulouse-Lautrec	11AR42 - see also Hygiea, Chiron & Eris
Prince William	12SC56 - see also Vesta, Jupiter & Saturn

Events

1801 Ceres Discovery	23TA23

JUNO

All the bodies located in the asteroid belt spend a lot of time stationary. This is due to their close proximity to the Earth. Although Juno is the smallest of the main asteroids, smaller even than Hygiea, Juno packs a punch. Despite having similar orbits, there are more people and events with stationary Juno than the other asteroids I have examined.

Juno was the mythic wife of Jupiter and was known for her loyalty to her husband. Although they stayed together, Juno and her husband had a marriage full of tension. Juno is known for her vengeance against those who Jupiter seduced, as well as his illegitimate offspring.

She was not only the wife of Jupiter, but also his sister, so sibling rivalry could be a factor in how Juno behaves. The month of June is named for Juno. Because of her loyalty to her husband/brother, June is traditionally considered the best time of year to marry. Given the volatile nature of their relationship, I'm not sure I would agree.

When the asteroid Juno was discovered on 1 September 1804, it was involved in a powerful Cardinal Grand Cross. Juno was located in forthright Aries (02AR20) opposing Mercury (03LI59) and Saturn (03LI16), and was squaring Mars (04CN23) and Chiron (05CP49). Juno was also in a tight quincunx with her mythic spouse Jupiter (02SC31). Perhaps these tense aspects at the time of her discovery have contributed to Juno's capacity for acting out.

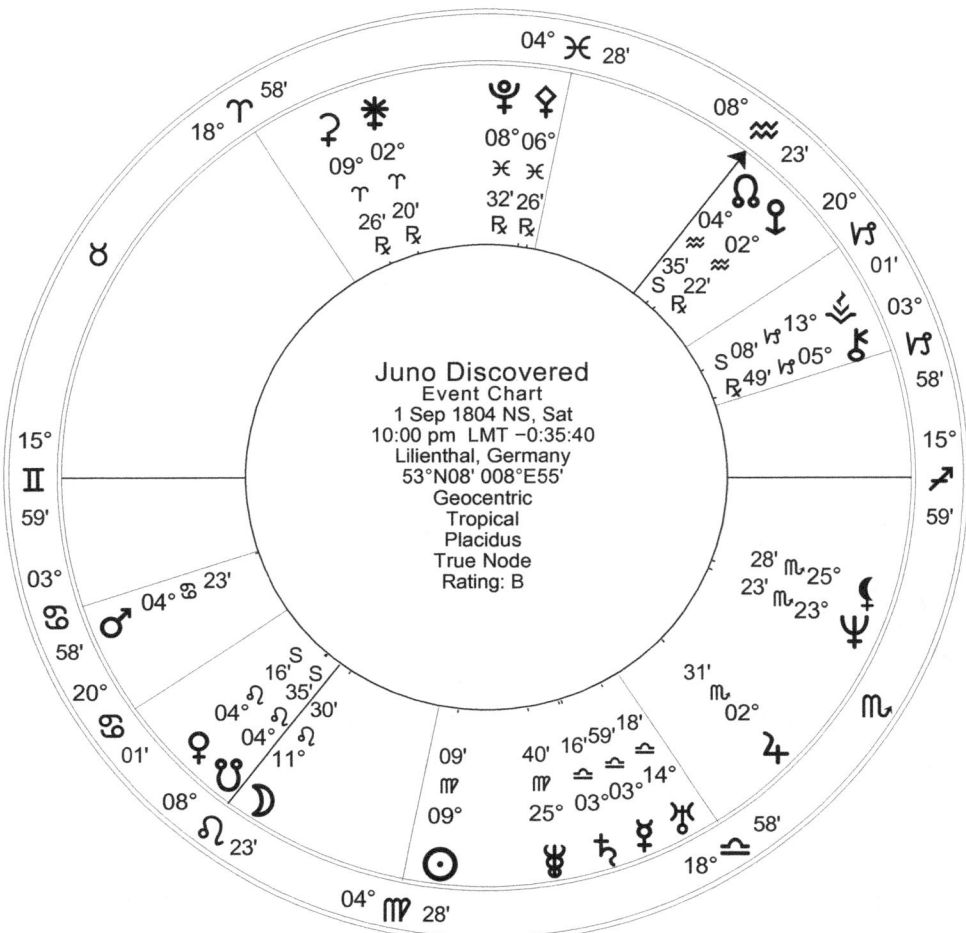

Don't cross swords with Juno, for she will often retaliate. Juno is a figure who can manipulate and work behind the scenes to exert control and wield power.

Those with stationary Juno can express total devotion to their spouse, as we see in the example of Edward VIII who abdicated the English throne to marry his lover Wallis Simpson. Interestingly, in the synastry between Edward VIII and Wallis we see Edward's SD Juno (05SC24) opposite Wallis's Juno (08TA52). Wallis remained loyal to her husband through the years, though some historians have suggested she felt trapped in the marriage and obliged to remain with him.

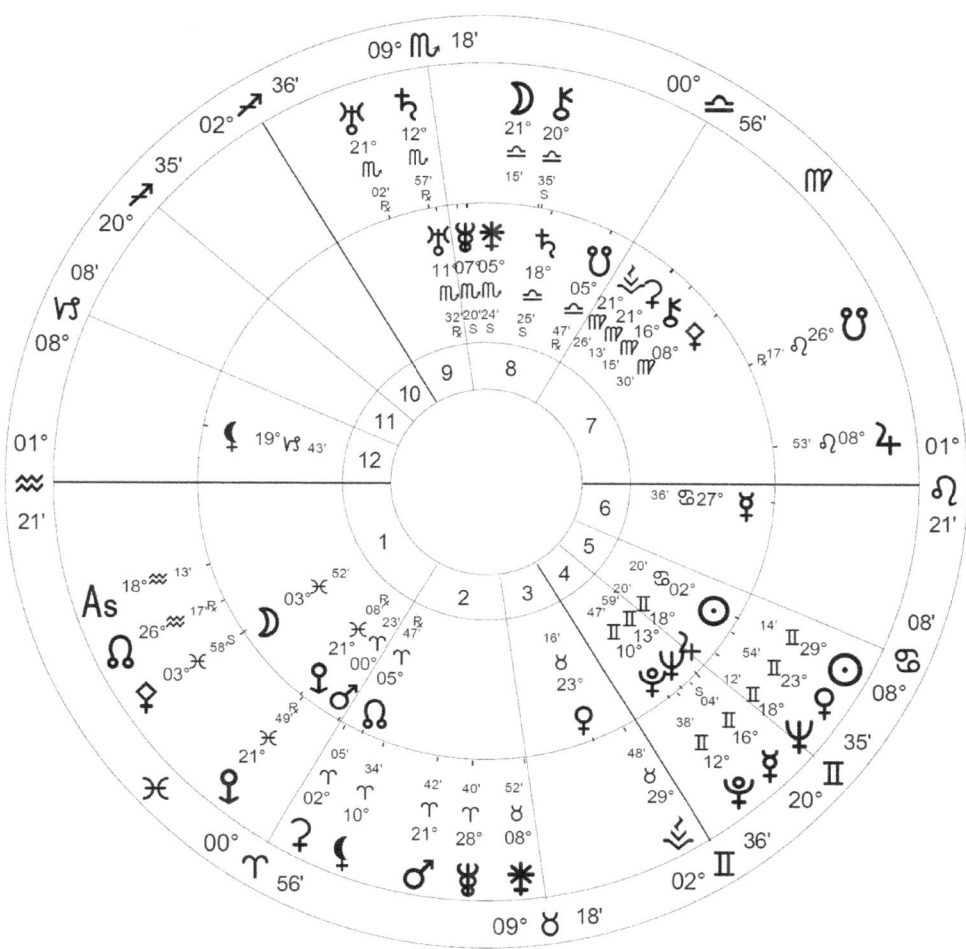

Inner Wheel: Edward VIII. 23 June 1894. 9.55pm, London, England. (AA)

Outer Wheel: Wallis Simpson. 19 June 1896. 10.30pm, Blue Ridge Summit, Pennsylvania. (DD)

Another interesting example of stationary Juno is Frida Kahlo. Her Juno is SD in passionate Scorpio (00SC41). Her volatile relationship with husband Diego Rivera was depicted in the movie *Frida*. Like Jupiter himself, Diego was frequently unfaithful and the couple often argued. While there is some uncertainty as to his exact date of birth,[31] whatever that date is, his Jupiter is no more than two degrees away from Frida's SD Juno.

What's more, the most likely location of his Juno (18CP03) places it in an extremely tight conjunction with his Mars (18CP05) and both planets are opposing his Saturn (21CN24) and Frida's Jupiter (20CN26). These powerful aspects no doubt contributed to the combustible nature of their relationship, also fuelled by her passionate Venus-Pluto conjunction.

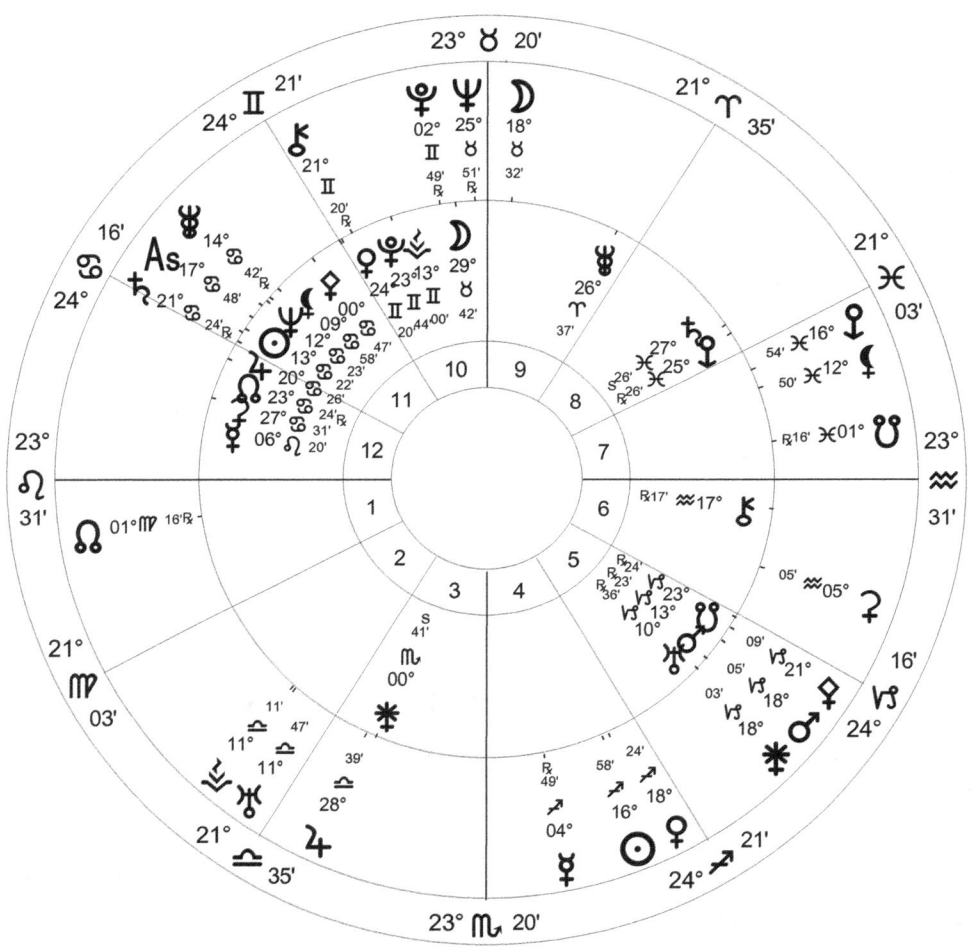

Inner Wheel: Frida Kahlo. 6 July 1907. 8.30am, Coyoacan, Mexico. (AA)
Outer Wheel: Diego Rivera. 8 December 1886. 7.30pm, Guanajuato, Mexico. (DD)

In keeping with Juno's diverse mythic roles and many epithets,[32] it seems that the loyalty of a stationary Juno can express itself in a devotion to a range of values, principles and causes that she will fight to uphold.

Juno can represent political power, and the power behind the throne. Stationary Juno is often seen in those who have entered into relationships with prominent figures including Princess Mary Donaldson, Yoko Ono and Monica Lewinsky. It's also seen in the charts of people who have themselves risen to a position of power and influence, such as John F. Kennedy, Lyndon B. Johnson, Ronald Reagan, Vladimir Putin, Gough Whitlam, Tony Abbott, Barack Obama, Donald Trump and Catherine the Great.

Catherine the Great was implicated in the murder of her husband. She seized control of Russia and ruled as Empress for 34 years until her death in 1796. With her Juno in Capricorn (05CP04), Catherine oversaw the expansion and development of Russia. Clearly, she was more loyal to Russia and its people, than to her unpopular husband. Peter III only ruled for a few months before Catherine decided she could do a better job of leading the country, which she did.

Juno SR

Tony Abbott	18GE15
Kathleen Battle	13AR33 - see also Jupiter
Justin Bieber	02SC31 - see also Jupiter & Pluto
Robert Browning	15CP42 - see also Eris
Rubin Carter	25VI28 - see also Venus
Catherine the Great	05CP04
Princess Mary Donaldson	19LI45 - (conjunct Moon) see also Saturn
Clint Eastwood	06AQ19 - see also Mercury
Lady Gaga	16SG28 - see also Mercury and Uranus
Linda Goodman	20SG14 - see also Mercury
Steve Jobs	18SC07 - see also Mercury, Saturn and Hygiea
John F. Kennedy	13AQ06 - see also Mercury, Hygiea & Chiron
Nick Kyrgios	04CP28 - see also Neptune
Shirley MacLaine	07CP56 - see also Vesta
Harvey Milk	06AQ01
Barack Obama	00AR39
Yoko Ono	05SC50
Robert Plant	13AR48 - see also Jupiter
Charlotte Rampling	00SC04 - see also Jupiter & Chiron
Ronald Reagan	23LI14
Vanessa Redgrave	11LI03
Karen Silkwood	00SC26 - see also Mars & Uranus
Nina Simone	05SC52
Amy Winehouse	05TA31 - see also Venus

Events

1977 KLM Pan Am Disaster	29SC47 - see also Pallas Athena
1912 Titanic hits iceberg	24SG59 - (conjunct Asc)
1970 West Gate Bridge Collapse	26TA11 - opposite Venus

Juno SD

Woody Allen	20AR29
Chuck Berry	01PI38 - see also Jupiter & Pluto
Lucrezia Borgia[33]	18VI03 - see also Pallas Athena (conjunct Saturn)
Prince Charles	01AR29
Schapelle Corby	14SC20 - see also Eris
Margaret Court	07SC42
Olivia De Havilland	17SC35 - see also Chiron
King Edward VIII	05SC24 - see also Saturn & Hygiea
Adolph Eichmann	09LE27 - see also Neptune
Harrison Ford	07SC34
Alfred Hitchcock	14SG22 - see also Uranus
Lyndon B. Johnson	04CP27 - (conjunct South Node)
Frida Kahlo	00SC41 - see also Saturn
Ethel Kennedy	01VI14 - (opposite Mars, conjunct Neptune)
Ted Kennedy	12CN13 - (conjunct Desc)
K.D. Lang	17PI24 - see also Mercury & Pallas Athena
Jay Leno	18VI52 - see also Mars, Hygiea & Pluto
Monica Lewinsky	06SG45 - see also Ceres & Chiron
Courtney Love	19SC26 - see also Venus, Pallas Athena & Vesta
Vladimir Putin	09AQ29 - see also Ceres
Christopher Reeve	09AQ17 - see also Hygiea
Joan Rivers	20LI09
Peter Sutcliffe	14LI44 - see also Ceres
Shirley Temple Black	01VI17 - (conjunct Neptune)
Pamela Travers	14SG20 - see also Chiron & Uranus
Donald Trump	14LI48 - also Ceres, Jupiter, Chiron & Neptune
Gough Whitlam	17SC13
Robin Williams	23SC54 - see also Ceres
Brian Wilson	07SC39 - see also Pallas Athena and Vesta

Events

1911 Titanic Launch   07LI26
1937 Hindenburg Disaster   25VI27 - (opposite Moon) see also Venus
1994 Nicole Simpson's murder   17LI04 - see also Mercury

PALLAS ATHENA

Athena is a goddess associated with intelligence, ideas and the mind. In myth, Pallas Athena was born out of the head of Zeus (Jupiter). She is a symbol of wisdom and justice. Athena is also known for her capacity to solve problems and as a strategic thinker. Associated with the archetypal daughter, she is independent and forward thinking. Politics, education, the arts and the law are some of her areas of interest. Those with Pallas Athena stationary are often found in these settings. They are highly engaged with justice and the law, in particular in advocating for change regarding unjust laws. Those with stationary Athena include suffragette leader Emmeline Pankhurst, former political prisoner and South African President Nelson Mandela, and in the 17th Century, Oliver Cromwell, who asserted the rights of the English Parliament against King Charles I and led their forces against the monarchists, becoming Lord Protector.

Another key theme that emerges for those in this group, is the powerful impact that their fathers had on their lives.

We can glimpse its meaning in the charts of women like Jacqueline Kennedy Onassis, whose chart has Pallas Athena conjunct Uranus. An icon of creativity and feminine strength, she came from a wealthy family. Her father, John Vernou Bouvier III, was a stockbroker, but he was an alcoholic and had many extramarital affairs. "Black Jack" as he was known, lavished praise on Jacqueline as a child and she looked up to her father. Jacqueline's parents separated in 1936 when she was aged seven and her mother remarried. Through the years Jacqueline stayed in touch with her father, but he was reportedly too drunk to escort her down the aisle when she married Jack Kennedy in 1953. Her father died of liver cancer in 1957. With her Pallas Athena conjunct unpredictable Uranus, no doubt she had a lot of difficulty with his erratic behaviour.

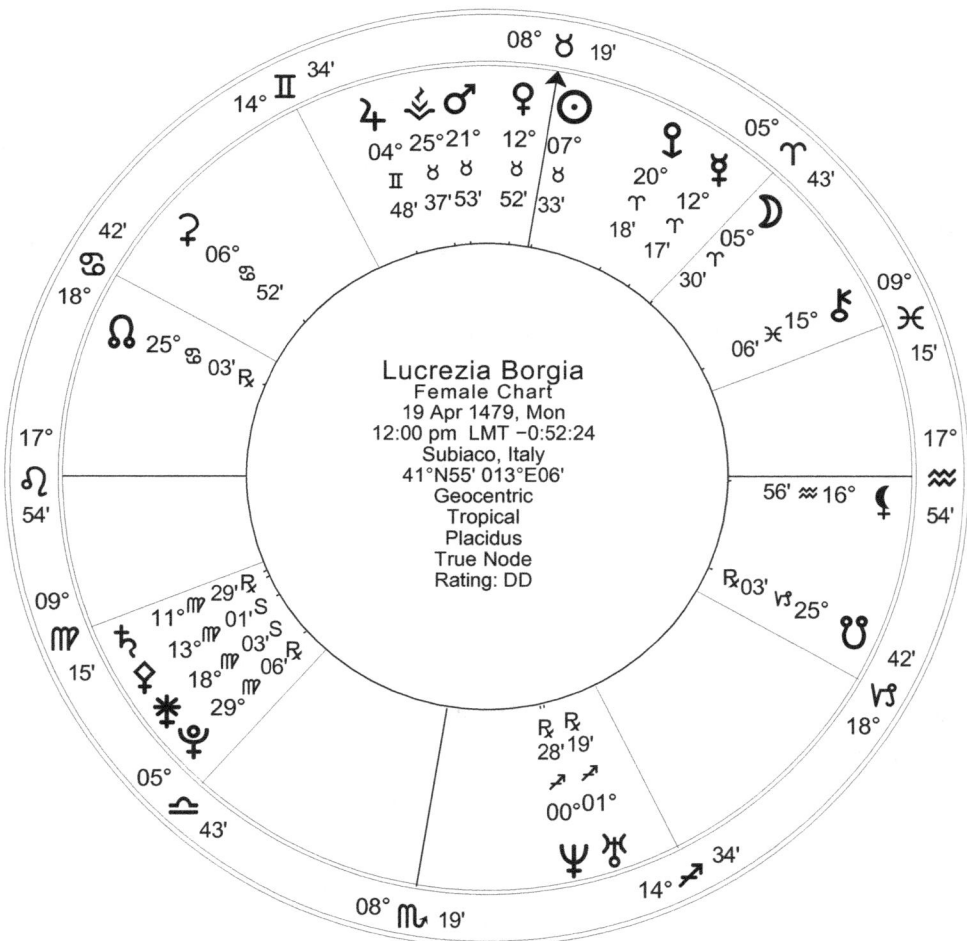

Lucrezia Borgia's 1479 noon chart. Note DD Rating. Pallas Athena is SD in this chart. In her 1480 chart Pallas Athena is SR at 08CP26.

Pallas Athena

Lucrezia Borgia was the daughter of the notorious Pope Alexander VI, Rodrigo de Borgia. Her mother was one of his mistresses. History has characterised Lucrezia as an evil woman, guilty of murder and incest, but it turns out there is little real evidence to support this view.

In order to further his political standing, Lucrezia's father arranged several marriages for her, the first when she was just 12 years of age. Lucrezia was well educated, but her father used her as a pawn to increase his influence and power. She rose to a position of authority and was often left in charge of the papal court when her father was away. She handled much of the correspondence and administration.

There is some uncertainty about her birth year. Astro-Databank makes a compelling argument for 1479,[34] but most other sources say 1480. Normally I would not include such doubtful data, but whether we use 1479 or 1480, Pallas Athena is stationary. In the 1479 chart Athena is SD (13VI01) and in the 1480 chart it's SR (08CP26). I've chosen the 1479 chart which also has goddess of marriage Juno SD in a conjunction with Pallas Athena which seems apt, given Lucrezia's many marriages to powerful figures. After her father died, Lucrezia established herself as a patron of the arts and became a key figure during the Renaissance.[35]

The challenge for many of those born with stationary Athena is to find a way to express themselves despite their father's psychological influence, whatever that may be. For better or worse, it seems that those with stationary Pallas Athena will experience their father as a larger than life, mythic figure who will have a significant impact on their identity and development.

Bindi-Sue Irwin embodies the symbol of the archetypal daughter, adopting the persona and role of her late father Steve Irwin. Bindi-Sue has SR Pallas Athena (02AR11) conjunct her Ascendant and SR Jupiter.

Other people with stationary Pallas Athena include actor James Earl Jones who was fatherless. The trauma of moving to live with his grandparents led him to develop a stutter that was so bad he did not speak for many years. Later, the actor developed a rich and distinctive voice. Sophia Loren's father abandoned her mother. Sophia only met him a few times. Brian Wilson, founder of the Beach Boys, suffered years of abuse from his father which had a dramatic impact on his life.

Politics is a key theme for those with stationary Pallas Athena. Both Bill and Hillary Clinton have Athena stationary direct. Bill Clinton's father died in a car accident before Bill was born. Hillary's father was a successful businessman, and a staunch Republican supporter. Hillary swapped to become a Democrat.

A particularly interesting example of stationary Athena is O.J. Simpson whose father was a drag queen. He announced he was gay late in life and died of AIDS in 1986.

O.J.'s parents separated in 1952 when he was five. His mother struggled to raise O.J and his siblings in a poor neighbourhood. O.J. looked outside the family for a father figure and became involved in gang violence.

For a sports champion like O.J. with a large supply of testosterone and masculine energy, one can imagine how having a gay drag queen for a father would have affected him. Indeed, it may have contributed to his passion for sport, his aggression and violent behaviour. He may have tried to repress any feelings he construed as feminine or sensitive, which he may have perceived as weak. As a child, O.J. was probably confused by his father's behaviour, especially as his father was in denial of his own sexuality. It's been stated that O.J. was highly antagonistic towards gay men.[36]

O.J. Simpson has the Sun in Cancer with stationary Pallas Athena in Pisces (16PI51). Jupiter is also stationary in Scorpio (17SC45) on the I.C. making a Grand Trine with the Sun (16CN35) and Pallas Athena. His Moon is in Pisces. Water signs are sensitive, caring and understanding, but in supressing his innate sensitivity, he became aggressive which led him to abuse and kill his former wife, Nicole Brown and her friend Ronald Goldman. Though acquitted in the murder trial, O.J. Simpson was found responsible for their deaths in a 1997 civil trial that was initiated by the parents of both victims. He was later convicted of 12 counts of armed robbery. He was released from prison in 2017.[37]

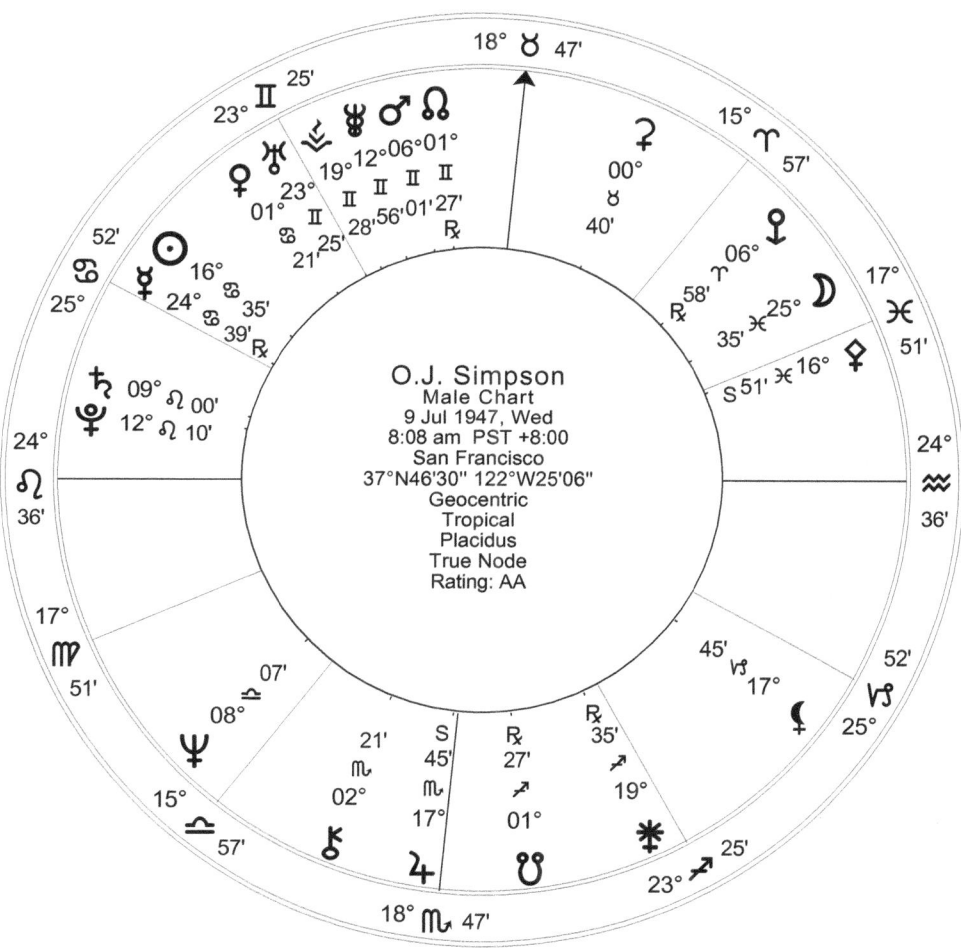

Pallas Athena SR

William Bligh	04TA24 - see also Saturn and Vesta
Joseph Campbell	04SG48
Coco Chanel	22AR04
Jeffrey L. Dahmer	29CP04 - see also Vesta
Princess Diana	25PI37 - (conjunct Juno) see also Hygiea
Michael Faraday	16TA09 - see also Mercury & Venus
Betty Ford	19SG13 - see also Saturn
Bindi-Sue Irwin	02AR11 - (conjunct Asc) see also Jupiter
James Earl Jones	18VI50 - see also Mercury
Jacqui Kennedy Onassis	12AR42 - (conjunct Uranus & Hygiea)
Sophia Loren	17TA17 - see also Chiron
King Louis XVI	04TA28 - see also Pluto
Paul McCartney	26AQ07 - see also Vesta
Spike Milligan	19SG05 - see also Mercury, Mars & Neptune
O.J. Simpson	16PI51 - see also Jupiter
Wallis Simpson	03PI58 - see also Mercury & Chiron
Brian Wilson	26AQ02 - see also Vesta & Juno

Events

Roswell Alien Crash	16PI58 - see also Mercury & Chiron

Pallas Athena SD

Lucrezia Borgia[38]	13VI01 - see also Juno (conjunct Saturn)
Bill Clinton	27SG57 - see also Hygiea
Hillary Clinton	28AQ28 - see also Mercury & Hygiea
Oliver Cromwell	17VI38 - see also Neptune
Carrie Fisher	17AQ10 - see also Mars
Robert Graves	07SG52 - see also Uranus
K.D. Lang	07PI22 - see also Mercury & Juno
Courtney Love	18SC25 - see also Venus, Vesta & Juno
Nelson Mandela	00SG32
Jim Morrison	05AR00 - see also Jupiter
Martina Navratilova	17AQ06 - see also Mars & Chiron
Patricia Neal	11GE09 - see also Venus
Emmeline Pankhurst	26SC23
George Simenon	01CN00 - see also Mercury & Mars

Events

1917 Czar Nicholas II Abdication	05LE12 - see also Pluto
1960 OPEC Formed	10CP41 - see also Saturn
1975 Whitlam Dismissal	17PI42 - see also Mars, Saturn & Vesta
1977 KLM-Pan Am disaster[39]	13LE19 - see also Juno
1986 Challenger Shuttle disaster	22GE41 - (opposite Uranus)

VESTA

Vesta is a female goddess associated with self-sufficiency. She's not interested in relationships or worldly success. She's content to focus on the hearth and the home, and is the keeper of the eternal flame. Vesta is a spiritual goddess, self-contained and attuned to her inner vision.

Despite the fact that the asteroids orbit in the same area of the solar system and spend a similar amount of time stationary, there are not as many well-known people in this group compared to the other main asteroids. This fits with Vesta's internal focus.

Those with stationary Vesta share this capacity for concentration. This is in keeping with the fact that the word 'focus' is Latin for the hearth or fireplace, representing the warmth at the centre of the home.[40]

The ability to commit to a task or objective and remain focused for the duration is a key attribute of Vesta. Taken to extremes, stationary Vesta can manifest as a tunnel vision mentality that, for better or worse, refuses to consider alternatives.

We see this attitude in Thomas Edison, who persisted with his direct current model even when confronted by the much better alternating current method developed by Nikola Tesla and George Westinghouse. Captain William Bligh is another example of the potential for pigheadedness that can accompany stationary Vesta. A positive example is seen with Galileo, who persisted with his scientific observations of the planets and supported the Copernican model of the solar system although it was considered heresy by the Church, which placed him under house arrest.

Spiritual matters may become overblown with stationary Vesta and there is the potential for involvement in cults. We see this dark manifestation of Vesta in the examples of Marshall Applewhite and Anne Hamilton Byrne, whose charts both have Vesta stationary. A number of other cult leaders have Vesta strongly aspected. Although not stationary in the chart of David Koresh, Vesta is conjunct his Mars and SR Venus in Virgo, and in the chart for Jim Jones, Vesta is 12 days away from its station, conjunct Saturn, and opposing Jupiter and Pluto.

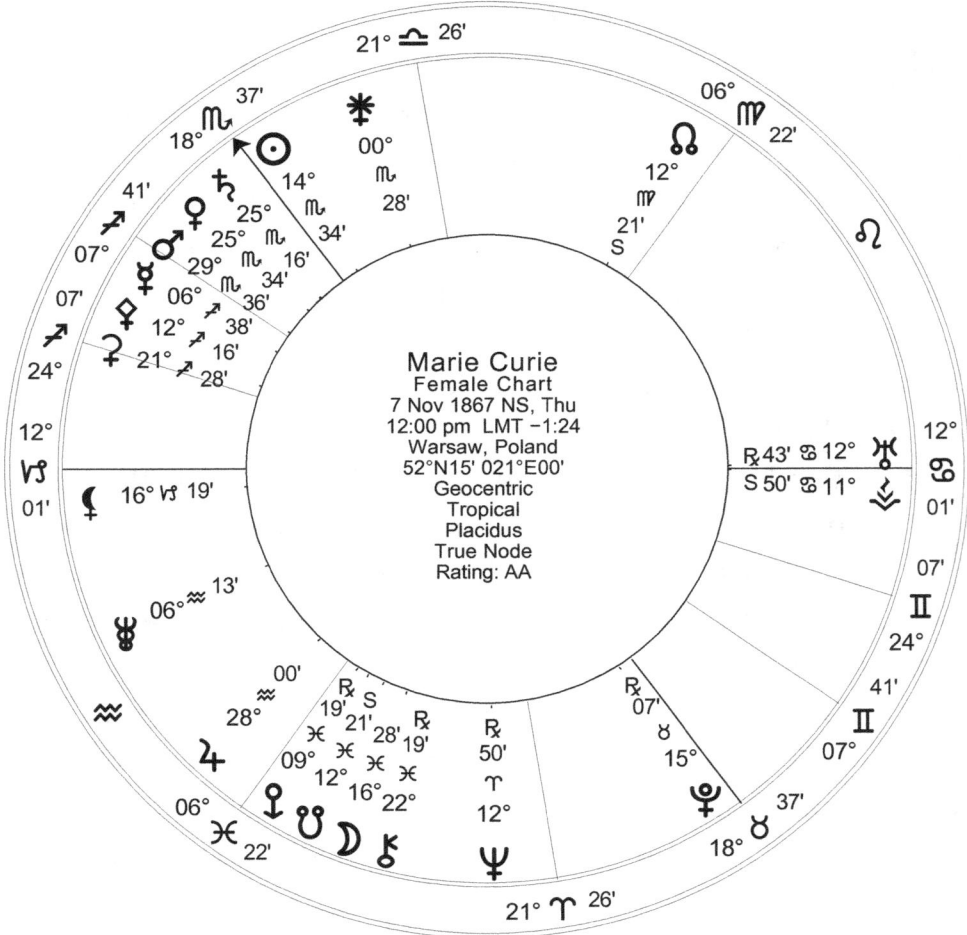

A perfect example of the passion, dedication and focus associated with stationary Vesta is seen in the life of physicist and chemist, Marie Curie. Her Scorpio Sun opposes Pluto which no doubt gave her tremendous staying power, but in addition she was born around nine hours before Vesta stationed retrograde (11CN50). Vesta is in a tight conjunction with Uranus, symbolising her intense passion for science. Along with her husband Pierre, she discovered radioactivity and two new elements, radium and polonium. Her painstaking research led to the development of x-rays and radiation treatment for cancer, and unfortunately also led to the nuclear bomb.

In 1903, along with her husband, she was awarded the Nobel Prize in Physics, becoming the first woman to ever receive a Nobel Prize. Pierre died in 1906 when he was run down by a horse drawn carriage. Marie continued with her work and in 1911 she was awarded a second Nobel Prize in Chemistry. During World War I she became a director of the Red Cross, set up mobile x-ray units and managed their installation in hundreds of field hospitals across war-torn Europe.

Like Vesta, Marie Curie disliked public attention and preferred to spend time alone researching. Despite becoming ill from radiation poisoning, she kept on working in her laboratory until her death in 1934.[41]

A different story emerges in the life of Frances Farmer, who was also born with stationary Vesta conjunct Uranus. In this case Vesta was SD and in Aquarius.

Like Marie Curie, this aspect contributed to her passionate individuality and insistence on expressing herself without interference from others. Vesta and Uranus are in her 5th house of creative expression. Unfortunately, Frances became emotionally unstable, possibly with bi-polar disorder, or perhaps, as she stated in an interview in 1958, she was suffering from acute stress that led to a nervous breakdown. Whatever the cause, it was her rebellion against the authorities that first led to her arrest. Events soon escalated. She was imprisoned and later committed to a mental institution for many years.

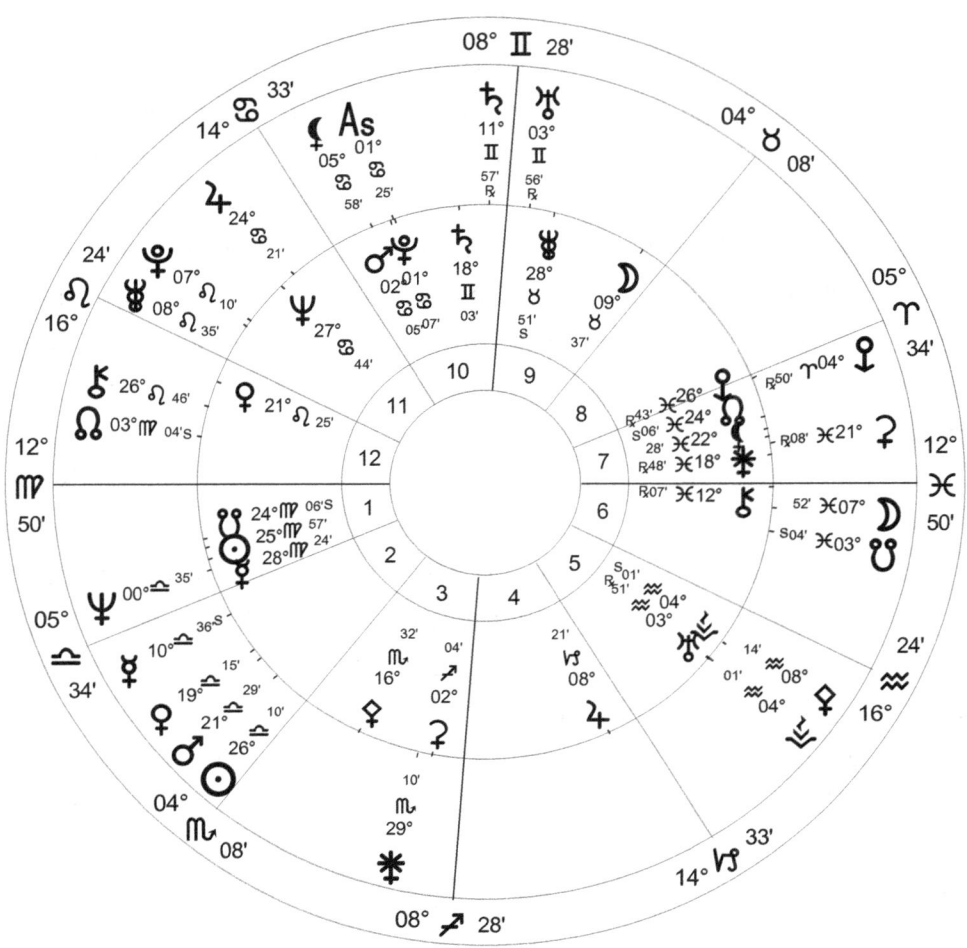

Inner Wheel: Frances Farmer. 19 September 1913. 4.45am, Seattle, Washington. (AA)

Outer Wheel: Traffic Violation. 19 October 1942. Santa Monica, California. Time estimate 10pm.

Her first run in with the law took place on the evening of 19 October 1942 in Santa Monica, California when she was pulled over for driving with her headlights on high beam when there was a wartime order in place to dim them.[42] Unbelievably, she was having an exact Vesta Return that day. Vesta was located at precisely 04AQ01 in her birth chart and at the time of this traffic infringement. She was 29 and in the midst of her Saturn Return.

Vesta

In her chart, the midpoint of her two stationary planets, SR Hygiea and SD Vesta is 01AR26 a point that squares her dynamic Mars-Pluto conjunction (midpoint 01CN36). This no doubt contributed to her rage and aggression towards those who were trying to control her erratic behaviour, including the police, studio officials, family members and the psychiatric fraternity.

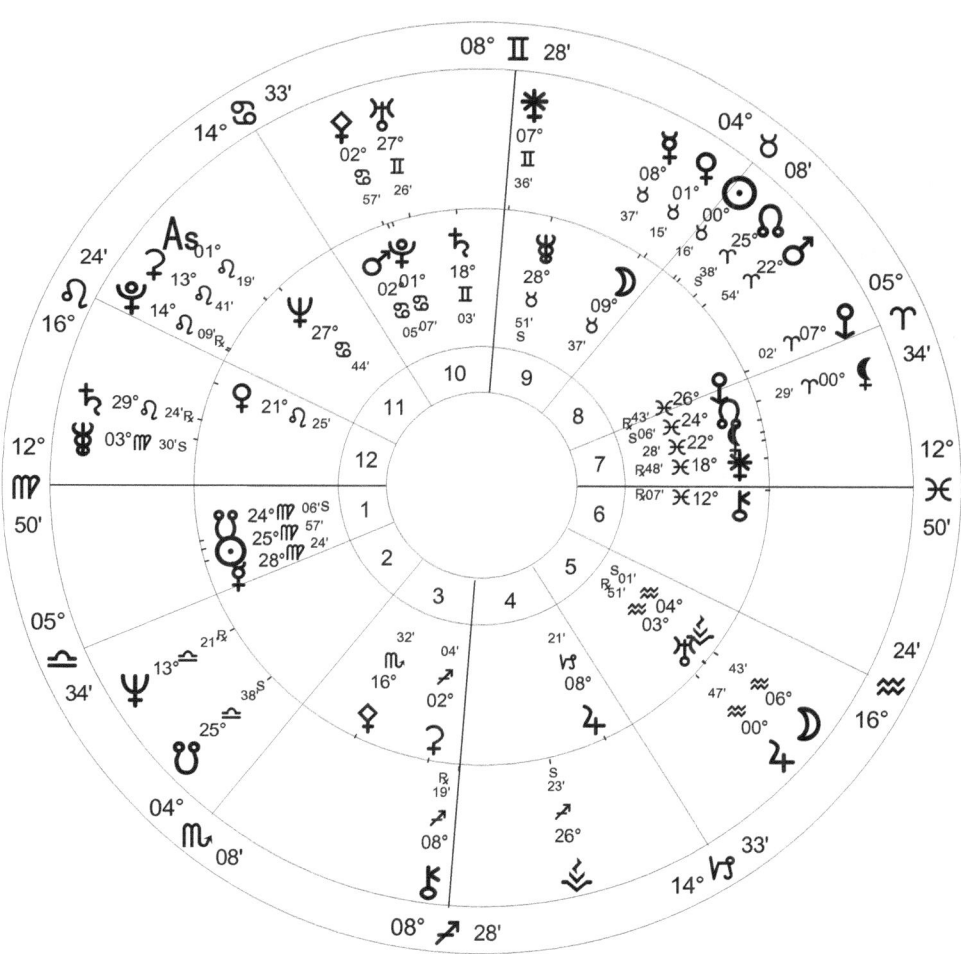

Inner Wheel: Frances Farmer. 19 September 1913. 4.45am, Seattle, Washington. (AA)

Outer Wheel: Jessica Lange. 20 April 1949. 11.00am, Cloquet, Minnesota. (AA)

One can barely imagine the trauma she must have endured through the years. She wrote in her autobiography, *Will There Really Be A Morning* that she was, 'raped by orderlies, gnawed on by rats and poisoned by tainted food…chained in padded cells, strapped into strait jackets and half drowned in ice baths.'[43] In the movie she undergoes a frontal lobotomy, however it's unlikely this ever took place.[44]

Stationary Vesta conjunct her Uranus in the 5th house in Aquarius, is a powerful signature for an independent and creative mind. Add to that her wilful Mars-Pluto conjunction, and you can see how this would have intensified her rebellion.

Her tragic story was dramatised in the movie *Frances*, starring Jessica Lange, who was born to play this role, for she too has both Vesta and Hygiea stationary. Jessica has SR Vesta (26SG23) and SD Hygiea (03VI30). Jessica Lange's Moon Jupiter conjunction is tightly aligned with Frances Farmer's Vesta-Uranus.

Vesta SR

Marshall Applewhite	21CP57 - see also Mercury, Ceres & Neptune
William Bligh	17TA05 - see also Saturn and Pallas Athena
Usain Bolt	17AR25 - see also Mars
Marie Curie	11CN50 - (conjunct Uranus)
Jeffrey L. Dahmer	17CP13 - (conjunct Saturn) see also Pallas Athena
Thomas Edison	19LI33 - (conjunct North Node)
Stephen Fry	21AR32 - see also Mercury
Galileo	02SC11 - (opposite Moon) see also Hygiea
Julia Gillard	04GE28 - see also Ceres, Jupiter & Saturn
Ulysses S. Grant	00CP50
Bob Hawke	16LE16 - see also Neptune
Jessica Lange	26SG23 - see also Hygiea
Courtney Love	16PI46 - see also Venus, Pallas Athena & Juno
Paul McCartney	11AQ40 - see also Pallas Athena
Dylan Thomas	22GE58 - see also Mercury
Lily Tomlin	08TA47 - see also Mars & Uranus
Prince William	24AQ29 - see also Ceres, Jupiter & Saturn
Brian Wilson	11AQ34 - see also Pallas Athena

Events

1939 WWII first shot	08TA47 - see also Mars & Uranus
1997 Death Princess Diana	01TA45
2014 MH370	29LI5 - see also Mars, Ceres, Jupiter, Saturn

Vesta SD

Bjorn Borg	28LI05 - see also Mercury & Venus & Hygiea
Lord Byron	08GE30 - (conjunct Chiron) see also Neptune
Truman Capote	20AQ56 - (conjunct South Node) see also Mars
Jimmy Carter	20AQ56 - (conjunct South Node) see also Mars
Lindy Chamberlain	14CN13 - see also Mercury & Uranus
Frances Farmer	04AQ01 - (conjunct Uranus) see also Hygiea
Joe Frazier	04GE16 - (conjunct Uranus) see also Mars
Indira Gandhi	26PI38 - (conjunct Chiron)
Anne Hamilton-Byrne	09TA49 - (square Neptune)
Paul Keating	04GE15 - see also Mercury & Mars
Buster Keaton	25AQ40 - see also Venus & Hygiea
Jeff Kennett	14CN12 - see also Mercury & Uranus
Nicole Kidman	17SC56 - (conjunct Neptune)
Shirley MacLaine	21VI06 - see also Juno
Luciano Pavarotti	07PI17 - (conjunct Saturn)
Oscar Pistorius	02AR39 - see also Mercury & Venus

Events

1804 Juno discovered	13CP06 - see also Venus
1975 Whitlam Dismissal	18PI09 - see also Mars, Saturn & Pallas Athena

HYGIEA

I decided to include one more important asteroid. Hygiea is the 4th largest body in the asteroid belt after Ceres, Pallas Athena and Vesta. Juno is smaller. Hygiea is associated with health and healing and is the origin or the word hygiene. One could say she's a female counterpart to Chiron. Significant matters associated with health are often seen in those with Chiron or Hygiea stationary.

I recall attending a presentation by the late Roderick Kidston, whose astrological passion was asteroids. Roderick spoke of the importance of purification with the influence of Hygiea, but he also pointed out that in order to 'heal' and 'cleanse' her function can sometimes become perverted or distorted. He described Hygiea as an agent for healing and cleansing on many levels, not just physically.

Dysfunctional Hygiea can manifest as an abuse of power that needs to be purged. He said that Hygiea can give rise to a type of 'fever', whose function is to cleanse, sometimes by extreme acts that can make matters worse before they get better.

Personal health issues have a way of affecting us mentally; equally, our emotional state can impact our physical and mental health. Hygiea represents how we react to stress, and she plays a key role in our general sense of wellbeing.

John F. Kennedy had SR Hygiea (09AQ51) and suffered from a number of serious health issues. In childhood he almost died from scarlet fever. He also had digestive issues, possibly colitis. His back problems required a number of surgical procedures that proved unsuccessful. He also had Addison's disease. He took massive amounts of steroids, pain killers and other drugs to manage his many illnesses. He downplayed and publicly denied many of these medical problems. It's worth mentioning that Kennedy also had Chiron in his 6th house of health. Ultimately his life was cut short on that fateful day in 1963.

Hygiea wants things to be pure and somehow perfect, and she is not at all comfortable when they don't measure up to her high standards. This concept of 'pure' can be applied to any number of settings and aspects of life, for example we may apply it to ourselves, to others, our living circumstances, job, political views, world view, or our beliefs.

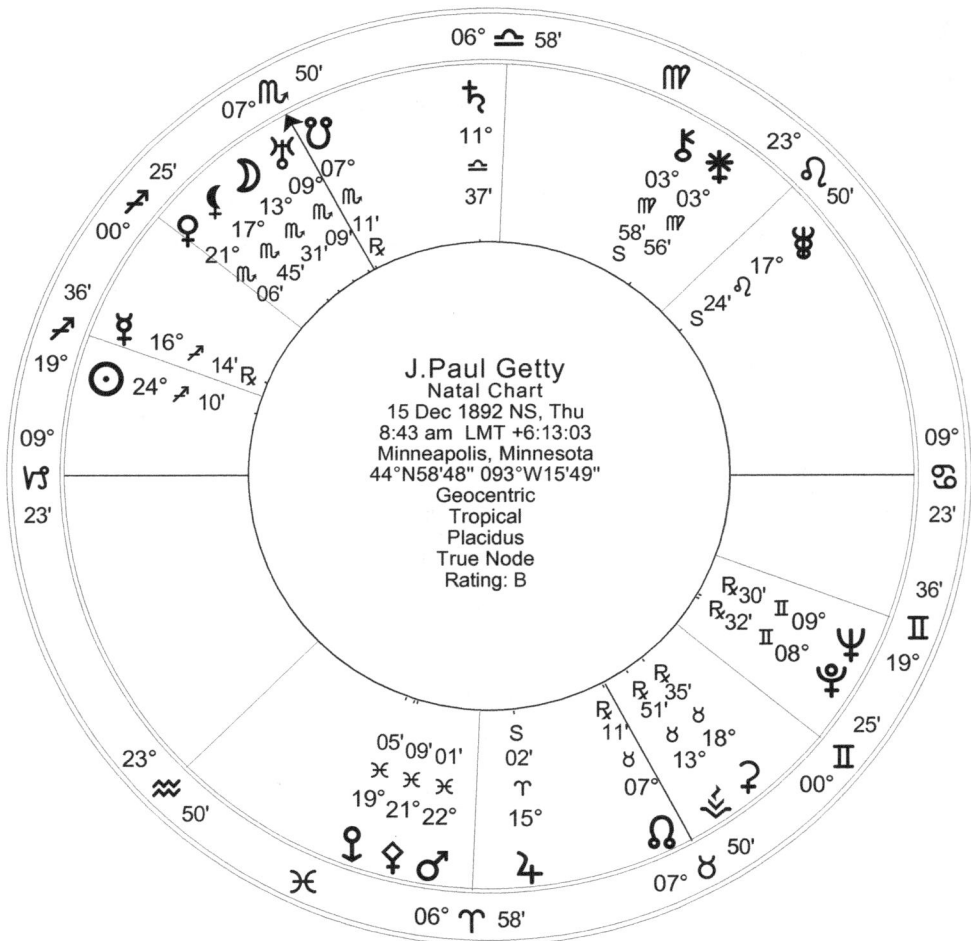

We see the twisted expression of stationary Hygiea in the example of John Paul Getty, once the richest man in the world. His chart has SR Hygiea (17LE24) in trine aspect to SD Jupiter (15AR02) plus SR Chiron is in a very tight conjunction with Juno. His refusal to pay ransom money when his grandson, J.P. Getty III was kidnapped, is the subject of the 2017 movie, *All the Money in the World*. Getty senior's SR Hygiea in Leo tightly squares his Black Moon in Scorpio, which is the midpoint of his Venus and Moon. Hygiea also squares Ceres in Taurus. Fixed squares are known to be determined and can be stubborn, and Taurus-Scorpio are the signs related to money. Getty was notorious for his frugal penny-pinching ways, and not just in refusing to pay the ransom. There are numerous tales of him trying to obtain the lowest possible price for even minor expenditures.[45]

His dysfunctional Hygiea had a devastating impact on his grandson, who was not only tortured and mutilated by his kidnappers, but who subsequently turned to drugs. Following a drug overdose in 1981 he suffered a stroke that left him a quadriplegic and almost blind. He died in 2011 at the age of 54.[46] It's worth noting that Getty senior's SR Hygiea (17LE24) and the other points in his Fixed T-square triggered his grandson's Pallas Athena (18AQ09).

In Steve Jobs, co-founder of Apple, we see a man driven by perfection.[47] His SR Hygiea (19LI51) is the focal point of a T-square involving Venus (21CP10) and Jupiter (20CN30). In 2003 he was diagnosed with pancreatic cancer, though he kept it quiet until 2004. It's been widely reported that he delayed treatment despite having a rare type of the disease that is slow to develop and can be easier to treat. He opted for alternative natural management, delaying surgery for nine months.[48] It was a decision he later regretted. He died in 2011 at the age of 56. While complementary medicine is often beneficial for a range of diseases, on its own it was of no use against this aggressive illness.

Above all, there seems to be powerful desire for idealised perfection in those with stationary Hygiea. Similar in some ways to

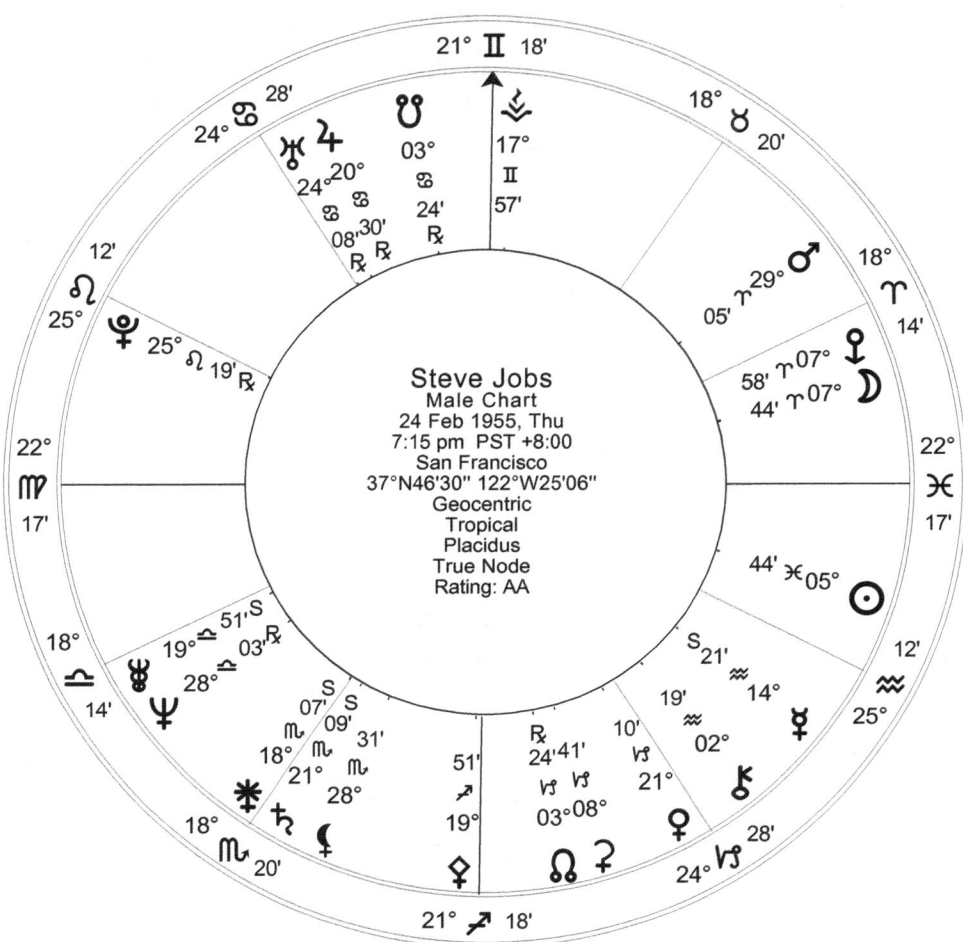

Vesta, those with stationary Hygiea can have a very single minded, tunnel vision mentality. For better or worse, the idea of perfection or purity can manifest in numerous ways according to the specific values and standards of the individual.

SR Hygiea

Lauren Bacall	21TA15 - see also Mars & Ceres
Bjorn Borg	00AQ03 - see also Mercury, Venus & Vesta
Martin Bryant	14CP23 - (opposite Ceres)
Bill Clinton	01TA43 - see also Pallas Athena
Hillary Clinton	04CN19 - see also Mercury & Pallas Athena
Tom Cruise	06PI57 - (conjunct Chiron) see also Jupiter
Frances Farmer	28TA51 - see also Vesta
John Paul Getty	17LE24 - see also Jupiter & Chiron
Steve Jobs	19LI51 - see also Mercury, Saturn & Juno
John F. Kennedy	09AQ51 - see also Mercury, Juno & Uranus
Robert Kennedy	23CN39 - (conjunct North Node)
Jay Leno	22SG28 - see also Mars, Juno & Pluto
Christopher Reeve	27TA36 - see also Juno
Tim Robbins	23GE11 - see also Mars
Henri Toulouse-Lautrec	08LE50 - see also Ceres, Chiron, & Eris

Events

1977 Granville Train Disaster	21VI00 - see also Mercury, Jupiter & Pluto
1995 Christopher Reeve's Accident	07AQ12 - see also Mercury

SD Hygiea

Muhammad Ali	25TA17 - (conjunct Uranus) see also Venus & Saturn
Roald Amundsen	03SG07 - see also Chiron
Richard Branson	10SG57 - see also Ceres
Sam Cooke	04GE19 - see also Chiron
Princess Diana	19SC05 - see also Pallas Athena
King Edward VIII	07SC20 - see also Juno & Saturn
Blake Edwards	03SG03 - see also Mars & Chiron
Galileo	15CN48 - see also Vesta
Prince Harry	04AQ23 - see also Ceres & Chiron
Buster Keaton	16AQ17 - see also Venus & Vesta
Jessica Lange	03VI30 - see also Vesta
Eleanor Roosevelt	24AQ50
Steven Spielberg	18AR39
Greta Thunberg	08TA38 - see also Mercury
Kenneth Williams	10CN25 - see also Venus

Events

2020 Saturn-Pluto	27TA18 - see also Uranus and Eris

JUPITER

Beyond the asteroids we arrive at the largest planet in our solar system. Named for the chief sky god, larger than life itself, with the most rapid rotation of any planet, Jupiter is clearly in charge.

Jupiter's orbit of around 12 years corresponds to the age when adolescence begins. This is when we enter high school and once again our social circle expands. We have a whole new learning curve ahead of us. Jupiter symbolises this rapid expansion as we learn about the world around us, including different cultures and beliefs. Jupiter is where we develop our world view.

Michel Gauquelin's research showed that just as Mars is connected with sport and medicine, Jupiter is associated with actors, top executives, military leaders, journalists and politicians. He found conclusively that this planet is prominent in the charts of individuals engaged in these professions. In terms of character traits, the typical Jupiter type is extroverted, proud, authoritarian, humorous, ambitious and independent, among other Jovian qualities.

When researching charts that contain a stationary Jupiter, I was interested to discover that these occupations and traits cropped up time and again. In terms of both profession and personality, people born when Jupiter was stationary, or travelling at less than 30% of its average speed, strongly embodied the Jupiter archetype. The list of well-known people below includes a number of evangelists, politicians, actors, performers, activists and other larger-than-life characters. Several people on this list are also given to hubris, a symptom of a hyper-functioning Jupiter.

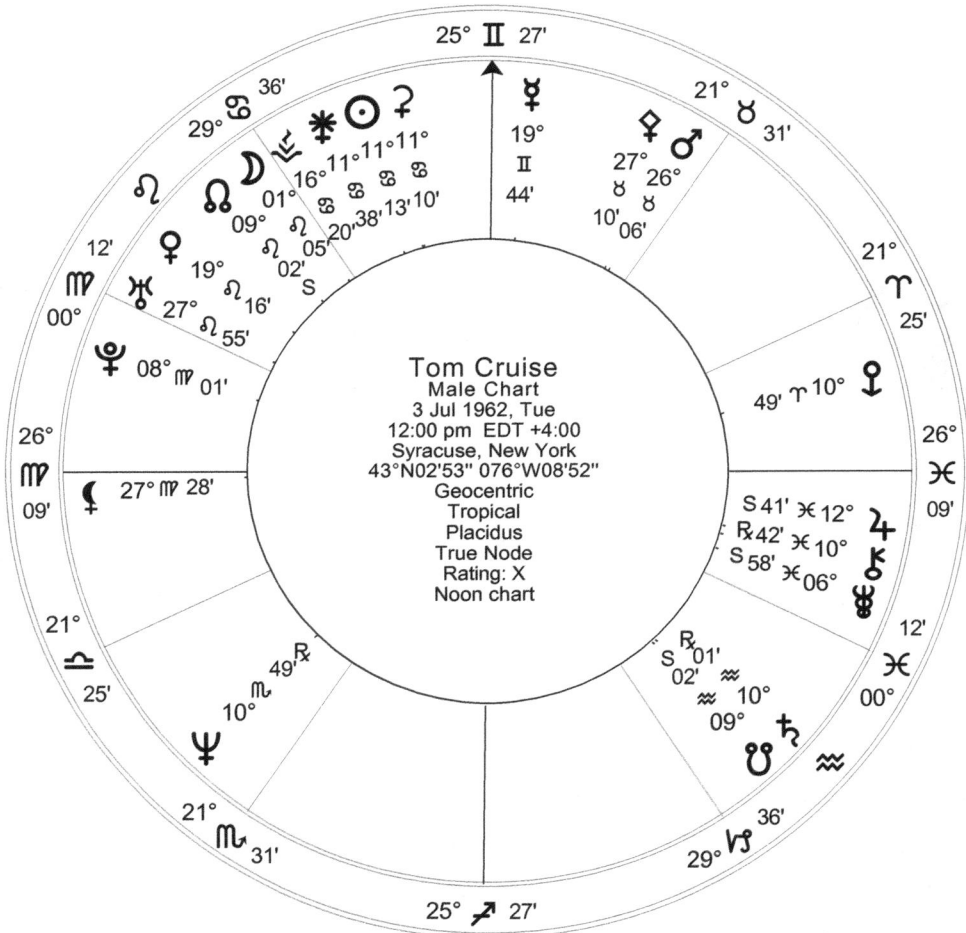

Tom Cruise (birth time unknown) is a good example of the stationary Jupiter type. He is an actor as well as a scientology enthusiast. Cruise is also known for his daredevil antics, often performing his own stunts. These include hanging off the side of a plane during take-off, sky diving from a height of 25,000 feet and holding his breath underwater for over six minutes.[49] His SR Jupiter (12PI41) is part of a powerful water

Grand Trine involving his Sun-Juno-Ceres conjunction in Cancer, and Neptune in Scorpio.

Excesses of all kinds are often part of the life experience of those with a stationary Jupiter. This excess can manifest in different ways. With Jim Morrison, Keith Richards, Judy Garland and Whitney Houston we see excessive drug and alcohol use. Jupiter can also represent material excess, as we see with Onassis, Getty, Reinhart, Murdoch and Trump.

Rupert Murdoch built an enormous media empire and is known for his ruthlessness and political influence. In Murdoch's chart we see SD Mars (27CN29) and SD Jupiter (10CN28). The midpoint of these two stationary planets is 18CN58 which is tightly aligned with his natal Pluto (18CN47). Pluto is itself, 21 days away from its station direct. Rupert was aged 21 when his father died, so Rupert's Pluto was SR by progression when his father passed away on 4 October 1952.

Rupert Murdoch's first media venture came about when he inherited the *Adelaide News* from his father. When his father died, transiting Uranus was located at 18CN21, directly activating this Mars-Jupiter midpoint and his natal Pluto. In addition, transiting Saturn, Mercury and Neptune were all squaring it. We also see that Juno was stationary at the time of his father's death, activating Rupert's 2nd house and natal Venus.

Murdoch became known as a ruthless media tycoon. The forceful energy associated with his stationary Mars and Jupiter, with Pluto at the midpoint, clearly has wide ranging implications. This is a powerful signature of political influence, money and excess. Aged 90 at the time of writing, Murdoch continues to control much of the world's media and manipulate political messages.

We also see stationary Jupiter in the charts of a number of evangelists, preachers and religious zealots including Queen Mary I. Known as Bloody Mary, she tried to re-establish the Catholic faith in England after the death of her younger brother, King Edward VI. She ordered the execution of around 280 so-called 'heretics' during her five years as Queen, the vast majority of whom were burned at the stake.

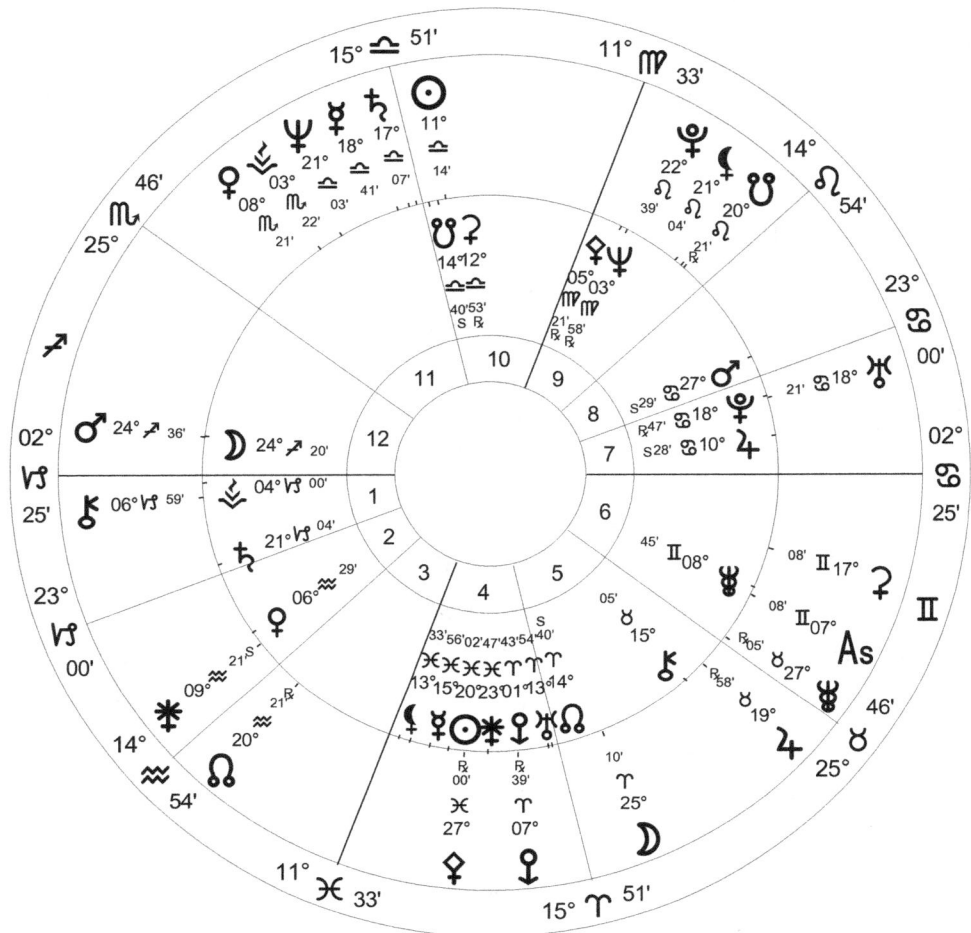

Inner Wheel: Rupert Murdoch. 11 March 1931. 11.59pm, Melbourne, Australia. (B)

Outer Wheel: Death of Keith Murdoch. 4 October 1952. Melbourne, Australia. (X) 11pm chart.

Modern day evangelists Billy Graham, Jimmy Swaggart and Hillsong leader, Brian Houston also have stationary Jupiter. A more moderate and jovial spiritual leader is the 14th Dalai-Lama.

Stationary Jupiter is also seen in a number of political leaders, notably Adolf Hitler and Donald Trump. A number of commentators have noted their similarities, which is reflected in their charts. Apart from stationary Jupiter, there are other astrological factors they share.

Hitler's Jupiter opposes Chiron, while Trump's Jupiter is conjunct Chiron. Hitler's Jupiter is conjunct Hygiea, while Trump's Jupiter opposes Hygiea. In both cases cardinal signs are involved. Trump's SD Jupiter is only about three hours away from its exact station.

A large number of entertainers have stationary Jupiter. I was curious to see if there was a higher percentage of entertainers with stationary Jupiter compared to the general population. Jupiter will be travelling at less than 30% of its average speed for around 15-16 days at each station. Therefore, every synodic cycle of Jupiter (which is 399 days), we would expect to find Jupiter flagged S for about 30 days. This equates to about seven or eight percent of its synodic cycle.

I created a sample group of 509 charts. Jupiter was found to be stationary in 37 of these charts, or 7.27% which is as expected. In another control group, I have the birth data of some Mensa members that I collected in the 1980s, which contains 241 individuals. Searching this group for stationary Jupiter, I found 17 charts, which is 7.05%.

However, for entertainers — a group within the Solar Fire database containing a total of 435 charts — there are 42 charts with a stationary Jupiter. This is 9.65%, a higher number than expected by chance (if it were 8% there would be only 34 charts). Looking at the Music & Dance database in Solar Fire — which contains many of the same charts as the Entertainment database, but also has a number of additional charts, 294 in all — we find that 32 of these individuals have Jupiter stationary, which is 10.88%. In this case, the expected number of charts, based on 8% is 23.

I then combined these two groups of entertainers, deleted any duplicates, and added a few notable performers whose charts I had collected previously, building a file of 678 entertainers, including dancers, musicians, actors, composers and directors. Charts containing a stationary Jupiter in this larger group totalled 65, or 9.58% — again, above average.

It's worth noting that Jupiter stations when making a trine to the Sun. But if you're calculating charts using the 30% rule, a slow Jupiter will not necessarily be making a trine to the Sun. In some cases where Jupiter is flagged S, the orb of the Jupiter–Sun trine stretches out to 11 degrees, which is too wide for a trine. In the following list of well-known people with a slow or stationary Jupiter, some have a Jupiter–Sun trine and others don't. This serves to illustrate that it seems to be the slow Jupiter, rather than the Jupiter–Sun trine, that is the key factor.

Jupiter SR

Spiro Agnew	15CN46 - see also Neptune
Justin Bieber	14SC39 - see also Juno & Pluto
Marlon Brando	19SG54
Jeanne Calment	01SC36 - see also Mercury & Ceres
Glenn Close	27SC31 - see also Mercury
Jimmy Connors	20TA54
Tom Cruise	12PI41 - (conjunct Chiron) see also Hygiea
Greta Garbo	16GE25 - (conjunct Asc)
Billy Graham	15CN47
Adolf Hitler	08CP14 - (conjunct Moon)
Whitney Houston	19AR28 - (conjunct Moon)
John Howard	08AR46 - see also Mercury
Bindi-Sue Irwin	27PI59 - (conjunct Asc) see also Pallas Athena
Karl Marx	12CP56
Jim Morrison	27LE00 - see also Pallas Athena
Mozart	18LI30 - see also Mars & Ceres
Charlotte Rampling	27LI18 - see also Juno & Chiron
Mark 'Chopper' Read	29CN56 - (conjunct Uranus)
Keith Richards	27LE01
George Bernard Shaw	09AR10
Paul Simon	21GE25 - see also Mercury
Jimmy Swaggart	23SC15

Events

1600 British East India Company	22VI10 - (conjunct Juno)
1781 Uranus Discovery	27SC25
1865 Lincoln Assassination	29SG00 - see also Venus
1996 Port Arthur Massacre	17CP35 - see also Neptune
2021 Florida Building Collapse	02PI09 - see also Mercury and Neptune

Jupiter SD

Kathleen Battle	19SG06 - see also Juno
Chuck Berry	17AQ20 - see also Juno & Pluto
Judy Garland	08LI59 - see also Ceres
John Paul Getty	15AR02 - see also Chiron & Hygiea
Julia Gillard	27CP22 - see also Ceres, Vesta & Saturn
Mikhail Gorbachev	10CN29 - see also Mars
Brian Houston	16GE29 - see also Ceres & Saturn
Evel Knievel	22AQ23 - see also Chiron
14th Dalai Lama	13SC28 - see also Mercury
Groucho Marx	02AQ21
Queen Mary I	09CN44 - see also Ceres
Henri Matisse	11TA01 - see also Ceres
Rupert Murdoch	10CN28 - see also Mars
Aristotle Onassis	26TA27
Camilla Parker-Bowles	17SC41
Robert Plant	19SG07 - see also Juno
Robert Redford	14SG40 - see also Uranus
Gina Rinehart	16GE24 - see also Ceres
Peter Sellers	12CP41
O.J. Simpson	17SC45 - see also Pallas Athena
Donald Trump	17LI27 - see also Ceres, Juno, Chiron & Neptune
Tina Turner	28PI52
H.G. Wells	22CP26
John Wilkes Booth	08VI50 - see also Neptune
Prince William	00SC29 - see also Ceres, Vesta & Saturn

Events

1962 Cuban Missile Crisis	02PI49 - (conjunct Chiron) see also Venus
1977 Granville Train Disaster	21TA11 - see also Mercury, Hygiea & Pluto
1788 Lord Howe Island Discovery	16GE30 - see also Mars & Chiron
2014 MH370	10CN26 - see also Mars, Vesta, Ceres, Saturn

SATURN

More than any other planet, Saturn represents our greatest 'test of time'. The Roman lord of time, in the Greek tradition he was known as Cronus, which is the origin of words like chronic and chronology that reference the passage of time.

Before the unexpected discovery of Uranus in 1781, Saturn was the most remote planet from the Sun which gave rise to its interpretation. Just like the mythic Saturn who was a stern father figure, Saturn is cold and distant. These qualities, and the fact that Saturn is surrounded by a vast ring system, informed its traditional meaning which still holds true today. Saturn governs boundaries and systems, and as the lord of time, he governs all aspects of the dimension in which we live. There is a time and a place for everything. In this life there is no escape from time.

Serious and slow, it takes time to develop the qualities associated with Saturn. You need to be patient and work within Saturn's rules. Saturn can be frustrating, but as in the tale of the tortoise and the hare, slow and steady often wins the race.

As we grow and develop over time, it's Saturn that provides the framework for us to construct and build our lives. From time to time we outgrow certain aspects of life and the structures we have built need to be remodelled, sometimes even torn down brick by brick. The 'building' that we have lived in up to that point might be familiar and even comfortable, but we have outgrown it and a new structure is needed.

Every seven years or so, when Saturn aspects its natal position by square, opposition, or by conjunction, we examine the reality of our lives and ask ourselves whether this external reality is a true representation of who we are and who we have become. Does our outer reality reflect our true self, and will it sustain us over the next seven years?

What are my goals in life? How do I make my goals a reality? What are my limitations and how can I reach my goals within these constraints? These are just a few of the questions that Saturn asks of us.

Some people will know their calling early in life, some will be content to follow the career advice of their parents, while others may change their career path several times, but Saturn is not just about our career. It's about marriage, parenthood and numerous other adult responsibilities. Whatever the journey, Saturn teaches us to be responsible and self-disciplined. It enables us to set goals and to know that reaching them takes hard work and time. Saturn teaches us how to make adult choices and not allow others to dictate the way our life is structured.

For everyone, the first Saturn Return at the age of 29 is a pivotal transit. It marks the threshold we cross into adulthood. Major life events and decisions often take place at the age of 29 as we transition towards a truer reflection of who we are.

If we somehow skip Saturn's developmental stage, juvenile behaviour can morph into emotional instability, poor impulse control and continued childish behaviour in adults.

Some people will remain in the adolescent stage well beyond the age of 30, but eventually Saturn will catch up to them. Others will have to take on a lot of responsibility at an early age, before they have the ability to make adult choices, and this can limit their options.

Saturn transits can be very challenging and transits to our Saturn placement can be equally difficult. But they teach us how to build the scaffolding and construct our life from the ground up, and rebuild it when that becomes necessary.

As they happen more frequently, stations of Saturn are a bit like miniature Saturn transits in that they ask us to examine our trajectory and compare it to our present life structure. Using the 30 percent rule, Saturn will appear stationary for around two weeks each time it alters direction. This equates to a period of about one month each year when Saturn can be considered to be at a virtual standstill as seen from Earth. These stations are opportunities to reflect on our progress and plan ahead.

For those born with stationary Saturn, the ringed planet will often play a key role in their early development. The family structure, or lack thereof, is of particular importance. Do we fit within this framework, or do we need to escape from it and build a new construction?

Consistent with the mythic Saturn, who swallowed his offspring to prevent them from taking over his role, those with stationary Saturn may encounter feelings of frustration at the hands of a parent who prevented them from expressing themselves creatively or following their natural calling. A parent may have forced the child to follow in their footsteps, or to take up a particular vocation not in keeping with their true nature. Material hardship can play a role too. Children may have to take on adult responsibilities at an early age, which can thwart the natural development of Saturn.

Those with stationary Saturn may have a fear of authority figures, or become stuck in situations because they do not feel they have the authority to speak up. But over time, Saturn helps us recognise that we are ultimately in control of our own choices.

Some people with stationary Saturn may break the law out of frustration, or think they are above the law. An example of this is drug cheat Lance Armstrong who chose to break the rules in order to reach the sporting goals he set himself. Saturn will eventually catch up with those who overstep Saturn's boundaries and regulations. Whether stationary or not, Saturn has a way of making us pay our dues.

Saturn stationed direct five days after I was born. I remember my first Saturn Return was incredibly stressful, which was compounded by the fact that transiting Uranus was moving over my natal Saturn at the same time. While under intense pressure to take on extra responsibilities and a huge workload in my regular job, Uranus was asking me to break free and establish my own business. By the end of my Saturn Return I had started working for myself, but soon after that a recession hit, and I struggled financially for many years. It wasn't easy. It took a long time to work through my Saturn issues. My second Saturn Return was largely uneventful, and much easier. It was around that time that I decided to cease client work, started art classes and took up golf.

'If you fail to plan, then you plan to fail.' Benjamin Franklin.

This saying by Benjamin Franklin is widely quoted in the field of project management. Our plans may change as circumstances change, but in order to build one's life, some kind of plan is needed.

What is the project? Who is in charge? What does it cost? When is the deadline? What are the risks of the plan failing? In what sequence do things need to be done? These are some of the questions that need to be answered.

Benjamin Franklin was born with the Sun in Capricorn, and Saturn was stationary direct (12TA54). He also had SR Mercury (12AQ19), so his two stationary planets were in a tight fixed square.

Franklin was an inventor, statesman, publisher, diplomat, scientist and author. He was also a musician and composer. He helped draft the US constitution and was one of the founding fathers of the United States of America. He made a vast contribution across many fields. Not only did he build his own life, but he helped build a nation.

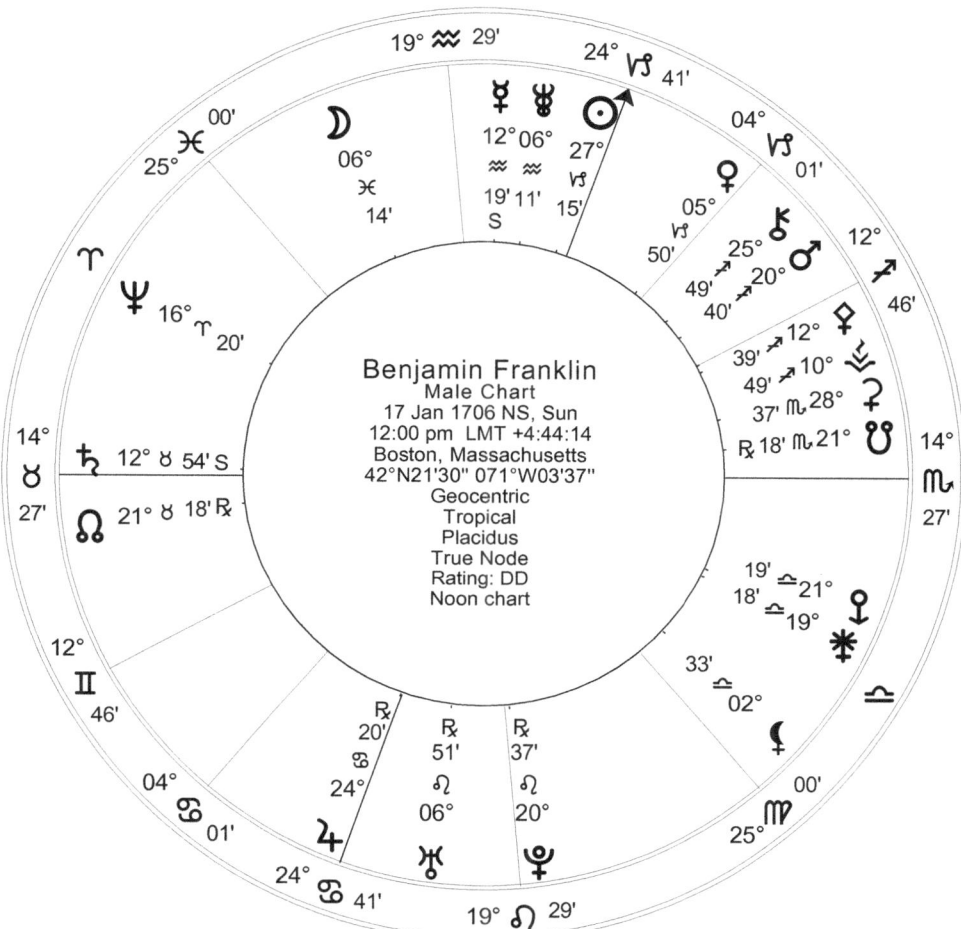

Franklin was the 15th child of 17. His father's first wife bore seven children, and his second wife had ten more. In the introduction to his autobiography we read:

> *'The youth who reads [this] fascinating story is astonished to find that Franklin in his early years struggled with the same everyday passions and difficulties that he himself experiences, and he loses the sense of discouragement that comes from a realization of his own shortcomings and inability to attain.'*[50]

With so many mouths to feed, his father put young Benjamin to work in his candle making business when he was aged just ten. Though having only about two years of formal education, Benjamin Franklin was fond of reading. His father noted his interest in books and encouraged him to become an apprentice in his brother's fledgling printing business. Benjamin started working with his brother at the age of 12. He learned the printing trade which would serve him well, but after several disagreements with his brother, Benjamin quit. His brother prevented him from obtaining work elsewhere in Boston, so 17 year-old Benjamin travelled to Philadelphia to start a new life on his own. He had to sell some of his books to afford the trip. He made his way in the world fending for himself from a young age and continued to educate himself, laying the foundation for his future achievements.[51] With Mercury and Saturn both stationary and in square aspect, through his early struggles he developed the life skills to establish himself in the world.

Interestingly, a very similar planetary pattern is seen in the chart of talented actor, Philip Seymour Hoffman. He also has both Saturn and Mercury stationary and in a tight square aspect. There is no known birth time available for Hoffman. In this 6am chart Saturn is SR (12AR27) conjunct Eris (12AR02) and square SD Mercury (12CN39). Hoffman was known for his 'ferocious' discipline and work ethic.[52]

Sadly, Hoffman died of a heroin overdose in 2014. At that time, transiting Pluto (12CP21) and transiting SD Venus (13CP36) were activating his natal stationary square aspect, opposing his Mercury and squaring his Saturn. Transiting Jupiter (12CN04) was also squaring his SR Saturn and was therefore conjunct his Mercury. These are immensely difficult transits with incredibly tight orbs.

Whether his death was accidental or suicide has not been fully determined. He had reportedly been free from drugs for many years but had relapsed in 2013 when his 14-year relationship (half a Saturn cycle) had broken down, and he and his partner Mimi O'Donnell separated.

Having both Saturn and Mercury stationary and in a tight square suggests a highly disciplined mind, as was the case with Benjamin Franklin. Hoffman was a great actor, often portraying troubled

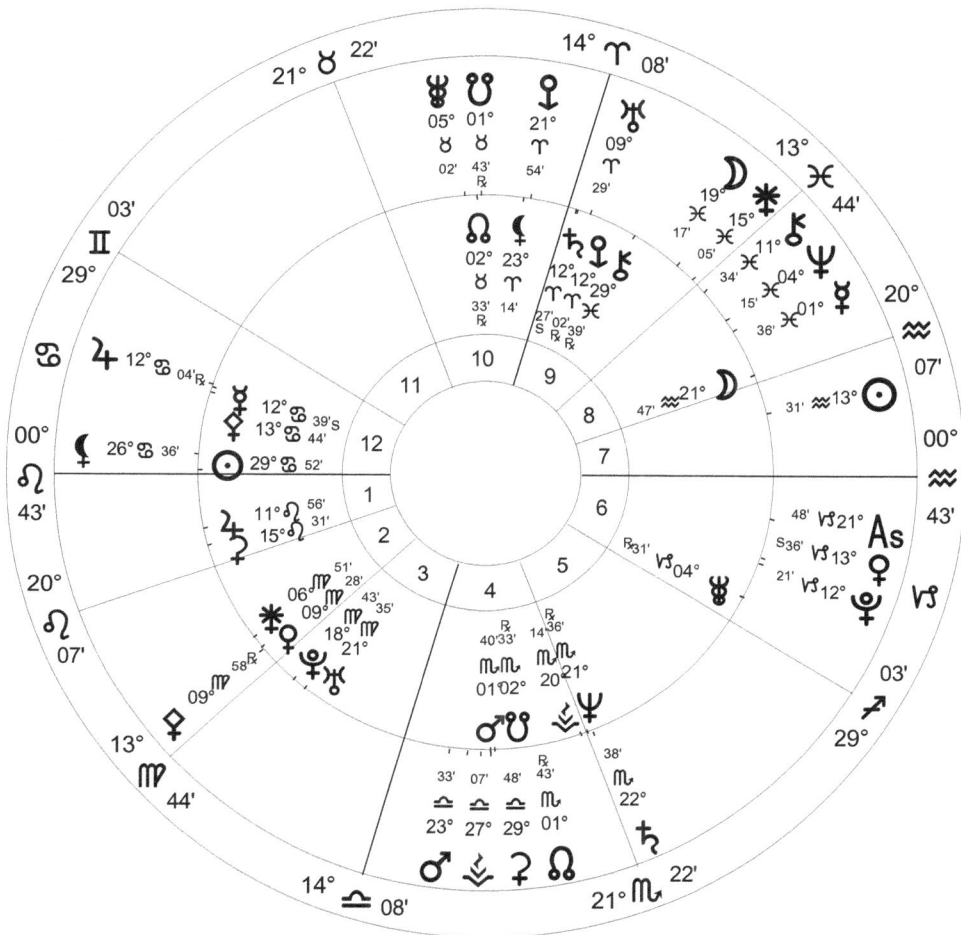

Inner Wheel: Philip Seymour Hoffman. 23 July 1967. Fairport, New York. (X) 6am chart.

Outer Wheel: His death. 2 February 2014. New York, New York. (X) 6am chart.

characters, but his inner demons and fears overwhelmed him. When transiting Pluto, transiting stationary Venus, and transiting Jupiter triggered his stationary Saturn and stationary Mercury, sadly it resulted in his death. Although Saturn is a tough taskmaster, these two examples show that we can always choose how we respond.

Saturn SR

Lance Armstrong	06GE31 - see also Mars
Ted Bundy	08LE52 - (opposite Ceres & conjunct Pluto)
George Clooney	29CP50 - (conjunct Moon) see also Venus
Patty Hearst	09SC20 - see also Mercury
Philip Seymour Hoffman	12AR27 - (conjunct Eris) see also Mercury
Brian Houston	09SC21 - see also Ceres & Jupiter
Steve Jobs	21SC09 - see also Mercury, Juno and Hygiea
Boris Johnson	05PI01 - see also Chiron
Frida Kahlo	27PI26 - see also Juno
Thomas Mann	26AQ05
John Travolta	09SC21 - see also Mercury
Johnny Weissmuller	21AQ00 - (conjunct Juno)
Betty White	07LI36

Events

1975 Whitlam Dismissal[53]	02LE57 - see also Mars, Pallas Athena & Vesta
1997 Thredbo Landslide	20AR21 - (opposite Mars)
2013 Pistorius kills Steenkamp	11SC30
2014 MH370	23SC17 - see also Mars, Vesta, Ceres, Jupiter.

Saturn SD

Muhammad Ali	21TA39 - see also Venus & Hygiea
Alois Alzheimer	11LI18 - (conjunct Moon) see also Chiron
William Bligh	10CP56 - see also Pallas Athena and Vesta
Charles Chaplin	13LE25 - see also Venus
Amelia Earhart	24SC07 - (conjunct Uranus)
King Edward VIII	18LI25 - see also Juno & Hygiea
Betty Ford	07LE376 - see also Pallas Athena
Benjamin Franklin	12TA54 - see also Mercury
Julia Gillard	23CP14 - see also Ceres, Vesta & Jupiter
Lenny Henry	19SG06 - (opposite Hygiea)
Michael Jackson	19SG07 - (opposite Hygiea)
Princess Mary Donaldson	29TA25 - see also Juno
Michelangelo	16CN57 - see also Venus
Joe Pesci	05GE35 - see also Uranus
Phil Spector	24AR25 - see also Neptune
Prince William	15LI30 - see also Ceres, Vesta & Jupiter

Events

1960 OPEC Founded   11CP49

CHIRON

Chiron has an orbit of around 50 years and marks another major milestone in life. It is at this age, at the Chiron Return, that most women reach menopause. Ageing and associated health issues, for women and for men, can develop, and at the same time we often have to deal with ageing parents. As in the myth of Chiron, our wounds, whether physical or psychological, can sometimes be incurable. Nevertheless, Chiron helps us to come to terms with our wounds and teaches us that they can be our most profound lessons in life.

Not surprisingly, a number of individuals born with Chiron stationary have endured long-term illness and disability. King Richard III who suffered from acute scoliosis, and the actor Michael J. Fox who was diagnosed with Parkinson's disease when quite young, both have Chiron stationary retrograde conjunct the South Node.

French artist, Henri Toulouse Lautrec had both Chiron and Hygiea stationary as well as Ceres and Eris. He broke both his thighs in two separate accidents in his early teens, leaving him with a permanent deformity. His legs ceased to grow after the breaks. This is a clear reference to the myth of the centaur Chiron, who was accidentally wounded in the thigh, an injury that did not heal.

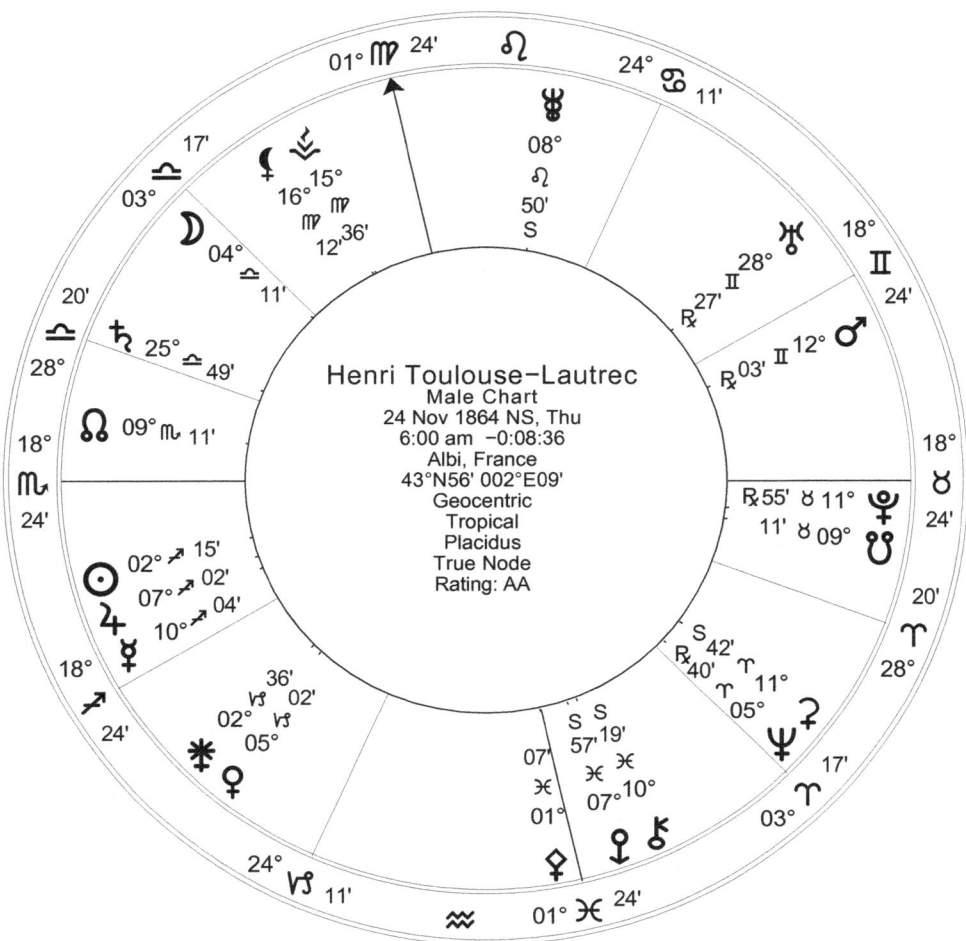

Lautrec's condition was attributed to in-breeding within his family as his parents were first cousins. He also suffered mental health issues and was an alcoholic. He died from the effects of syphilis and alcoholism at the age of 36.

A number of people with stationary Chiron have suffered physical trauma as a result of accidents. Golf champion Tiger Woods has been involved in numerous car accidents. His SD Chiron is in headstrong Aries (23AR35). When his car ran off the road in February 2021 causing serious damage to his leg, transiting Eris was within two minutes of arc of his stationary Chiron. Eris is also stationary in his natal chart.

Woods has Mars, ruler of Aries, in Gemini and it's retrograde. At the time of the 2021 accident the transiting North Node was crossing his Mars, and transiting Juno was opposing it. Gemini's ruler, Mercury, was stationary direct (11AQ23) as well. It's been reported that he was speeding, travelling at 87 MPH, which was 45 MPH above the speed limit.[54] His car spun out of control and crashed into a tree. Apparently, he did not hit the brakes before the accident.

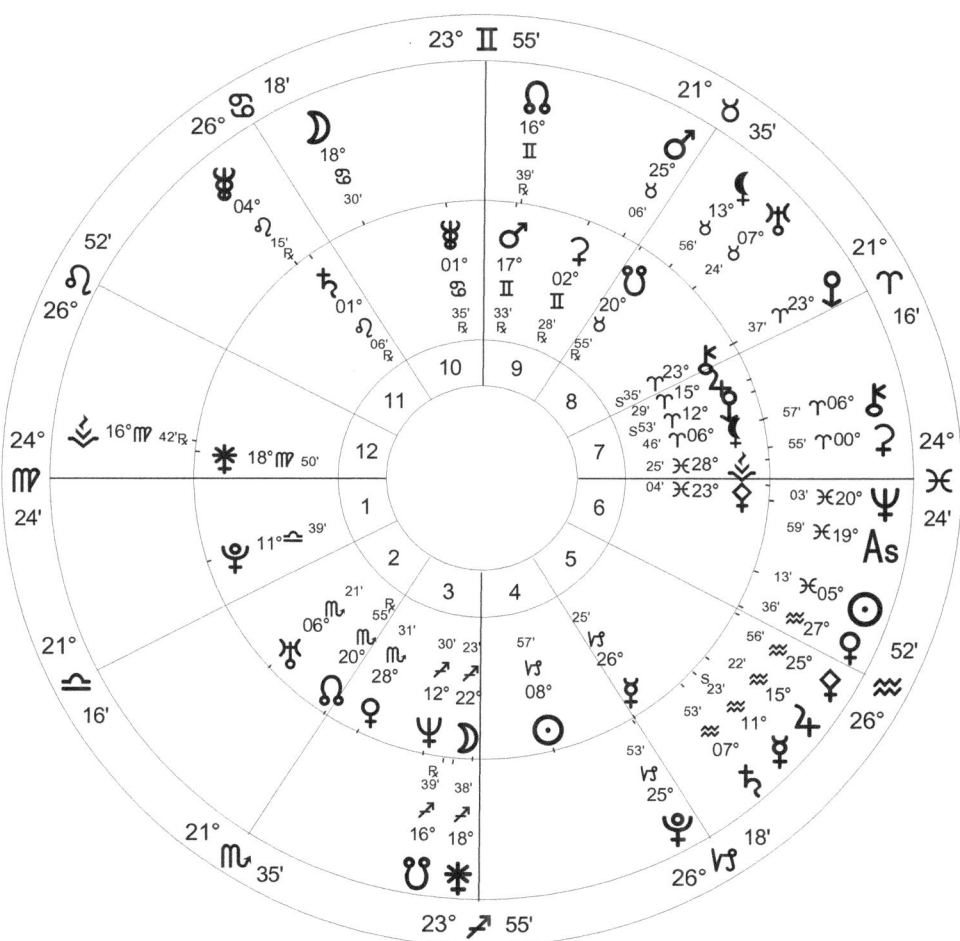

Inner Wheel: Tiger Woods. 30 December 1975. 10.50pm, Long Beach, California. (AA)
Outer Wheel: Car Accident. 23 February 2021. 7.12am, Los Angeles, California. (A)

Stunt motorbike rider Evel Knievel suffered acute trauma to his body in numerous accidents, but nevertheless, kept on performing his daredevil stunts. His Chiron is SR on the cusp of his 6th house of health. His Jupiter is SD in Aquarius, fuelling his capacity for risk taking.

In 1961 singer Patsy Cline was involved in a serious car accident. She suffered facial injuries and dislocated her hip. Less than two years later she died in a plane crash. Actor Eileen Brennan was seriously injured when she was hit by a car in 1982. It took her years to recover, then in 1989 she fell off stage and broke her leg. Interestingly, Cline and Brennan were born just a few days apart.

A number of healers and pioneers in the field of medicine have Chiron stationary in their charts. Nicholas Culpeper, noted 15th Century botanist, herbalist and astrologer, has Chiron stationary direct in Aquarius exactly opposite his Leo Moon. He also has Ceres and Uranus stationary retrograde. Culpeper was wounded when fighting against the Royalists in the English Civil War. Not long afterwards, he suffered another wound when fighting a duel. The wounds never completely healed, and he also developed tuberculosis.[55]

Alois Alzheimer was a German psychiatrist who pioneered research into senile dementia and many other diseases including epilepsy. Appropriately for a doctor studying diseases of the brain, he had stationary Chiron in Pisces conjunct Pallas Athena. His Saturn was stationary direct in a tight conjunction with his Moon. This Moon-Saturn conjunction in Libra opposes Mars, Ceres and Neptune. His health started to deteriorate in 1912, but he continued to work and teach. Alzheimer died of renal failure in 1915 at the age of 51 around the time of his Chiron Return. Pallas Athena was also making a return at the time of his death.

The charts of Carl Jung and Sigmund Freud both have Chiron stationary retrograde, and Mars stationary direct, which speaks to the pioneering work that both men undertook into psychology and mental health. Note that these stations are only evident if you use the 30 percent rule for chart calculation.

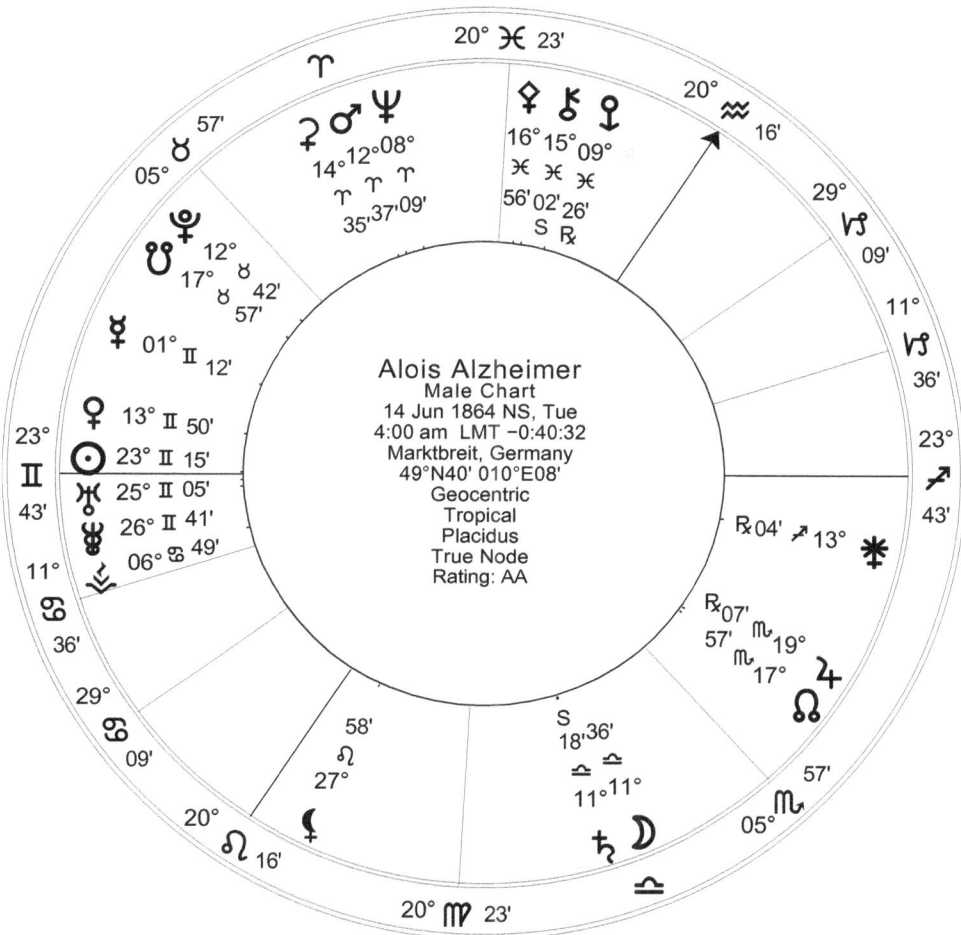

Two very long-lived actors, Kirk Douglas who lived to 103 and Olivia De Havilland who passed away at the age of 104, had Chiron stationary too. Perhaps this says something about the capacity to endure that we associate with Chiron. It's interesting that both actors at one time portrayed a number of people suffering mental illness and psychological problems. In *The Dark Mirror,* De Havilland played twins, one loving, and the other psychologically disturbed. She also starred in *The Snake Pit,* a film that documented the appalling treatment of the mentally ill in mental institutions.

Kirk Douglas played troubled artist Vincent Van Gogh in *Lust for Life.* Then in 1963 he played the role of Randle P. McMurphy in the first stage production of *One Flew Over the Cuckoo's Nest*. He also secured the film rights to the production. He wanted to play the role in the movie, but by the mid-1970s when the film was made, he was thought too old to play the part.[56]

Chiron SR

Alois Alzheimer	15PI02 - see also Saturn
Roald Amundsen	15AR04 - see also Hygiea
Eileen Brennan	28CP40 - see also Ceres
Fidel Castro	06TA05 - see also Venus
Mark David Chapman	05AQ30 - see also Ceres
Patsy Cline	28TA39 - see also Ceres
Salvador Dali	00AQ06
Olivia De Havilland	26PI20 - see also Juno
Blake Edwards	17AR29 - see also Mars & Hygiea
Michael J. Fox	06PI41 - (conjunct South Node)
Sigmund Freud	05AQ41 - see also Mars
John Paul Getty	03VI58 - see also Jupiter & Hygiea
John Glenn	13AR58 - see also Mercury
Mata Hari	00TA21 - see also Venus and Neptune
Prince Harry	08GE32 - see also Ceres & Hygiea
Boris Johnson	18PI47 - see also Saturn
Carl G. Jung	26AR24 - see also Mars
Evel Knievel	10CN02 - see also Jupiter
Monica Lewinsky	20AR54 - see also Ceres & Juno
Sophia Loren	09GE55 - see also Pallas Athena
Princess Margaret	18TA54
Charlotte Rampling	1LI29 - see also Juno & Jupiter
King Richard III	01CN50 - (conjunct South Node)

Events

1914 Assassination Arch Duke Ferdinand	18PI56 - see also Ceres
1966 First French Pacific Nuclear Test	26PI13 - (conjunct Saturn)

Chiron SD

Sam Cooke	14TA00 - see also Hygiea
Nicholas Culpeper	11AQ46 - see also Ceres & Uranus
Kirk Douglas	21PI48
Jodie Foster	06PI09 - (conjunct Jupiter)
Barbara Hutton	06PI25 - (conjunct Hygiea)
Martin Luther King Jr	05TA25 - (conjunct Jupiter) see also Mars
Martina Navratilova	06AQ26 - see also Pallas Athena
Franklin D. Roosevelt	17TA37 - (conj Jupiter and Neptune) see also Mars
Wallis Simpson	20LI35 - see also Mercury & Pallas Athena
Cat Stevens	18SC24 - see also Venus
Henri Toulouse Lautrec	10PI19 - see also Ceres, Hygiea & Eris
Pamela Travers	06SG49 - see also Juno & Uranus
Donald Trump	14LI54 - see also Juno, Ceres, Jupiter & Neptune
Tiger Woods	23AR35 - see also Eris

Events

1788 Lord Howe Island Discovery	8GE06 - see also Mars & Jupiter
1933 The Third Reich	23TA34 - (conjunct Vesta) see also Mars
1947 Roswell Alien Crash	02SC18 - see also Mercury & Pallas Athena
1963 JFK Assassination	10PI14 - (opposite Uranus & square Mercury)

URANUS

Uranus was discovered in 1781, and suddenly everything changed. First seen around the time of the French, the American and Industrial Revolutions, rebellious and unexpected Uranus called for freedom, equality and knowledge. The modern era was born. No longer was Saturn the boundary of our solar system, nor were we limited by the rules and traditions of the past. New inventions and scientific discoveries propelled us forward. The future was what mattered most.

The tremendous social changes that emerged at the time of its discovery, and the unusual facts we have subsequently learned about the planet itself, have become synonymous with its symbolic meaning.

The axis of this maverick planet is tilted at 98 degrees, completely at odds with all the other planets in our solar system. It's also unique in that its magnetic poles are in a totally different plane to this axis: 60 degrees away from its 98 degree tilt.[57] This arrangement generates a twisted magnetic field that stretches across millions of kilometres like a giant corkscrew. Uranus likes to do things its own way.

With an orbit of 84 years, Uranus corresponds to the approximate length of a human life. In symbolic terms, this means that we can potentially become conscious of the qualities Uranus represents. Similarly, Uranus is sometimes visible to the naked eye and so it lies at the limits of human consciousness. However, as there are vast numbers of people who are barely conscious of Saturn, let alone Uranus, there can be chaotic scenes and events when a Uranus transit comes along to wake us up. This is most evident at mid-life when the Uranus opposition heralds a crisis of consciousness.

Sometimes Uranus will create chaos if we have been stuck in a Saturn-like situation for longer than we need to be. It's been my experience that a Uranus transit is much easier to manage when we are no longer projecting Saturn onto external authority figures. The mythic Uranus was the father of Cronus (Saturn), and he will take control on the rare occasions when Saturn fails to act.

Stationary Uranus operates in a similar way to major transits of Uranus, but because stations happen more frequently, they are usually more subtle, unless of course the station happens to hit a planet or angle in your chart, in which case you are really going to know about it.

Using the 30% rule, Uranus is stationary for about 16 days each year, eight days at each station. Uranus can be unpredictable, but more often than not, its stations simply provide a different perspective that helps us see things in a new light. If we make the most of these stations, chances are we can minimise some of the really wild and chaotic effects of hard Uranus transits.

It stands to reason that those born with stationary Uranus want to change the status quo. They are keen to advance human knowledge. They are seekers of truth, want to advocate for human rights and are interested in shaping the future. They often personify the creative and eccentric qualities we associate with the most unusual planet in our solar system. Many of these individuals are unique and stand apart from the main herd.

Abraham Lincoln and Charles Darwin were astrological twins. Born on the same day, separated by the Atlantic Ocean, each man in his own way was an example of the Uranus archetype. They were born with SR Uranus in passionate Scorpio (09SC40) conjunct the

North Node. Despite widespread opposition and criticism, they each persisted in their attempts to change the future and open the minds of the masses.

Charles Darwin pioneered the science of natural selection and evolution, challenging the established thinking of the day and sparking a radical paradigm shift. Lincoln is best known as the US President who abolished slavery, giving millions their freedom and providing opportunities for countless future generations of African Americans. Lincoln was born around sunrise and Uranus stationed retrograde about 10 hours after his birth.

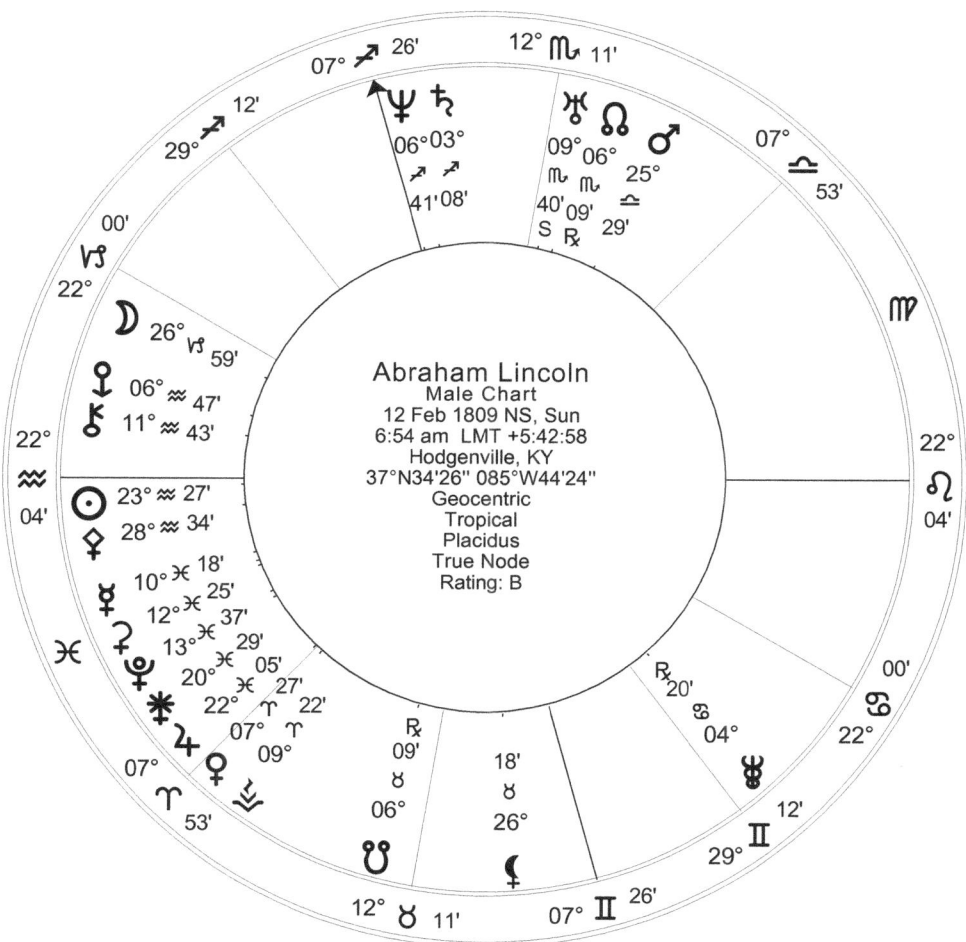

I have often cited the charts of Lincoln and Darwin to illustrate another important point regarding the traditional interpretation of planets that are said to be 'debilitated'. Both Lincoln and Darwin were born with the Sun, Moon, Mercury, Venus and Mars in opposite signs to the signs they are said to rule. According to classical astrology, all their personal planets are in 'detriment' and classified as afflicted. But here we have two men who despite the hardships they faced in life, persevered with their visions to change the status quo and laboured long and hard to do so.

Traditional astrology does not recognise Uranus (nor the planets beyond it) as having any 'rulership', but modern astrology has long associated Uranus with Aquarius, Neptune with Pisces, and Pluto with Scorpio. This issue of modern rulership has divided the astrological community for a long time. However, it should be noted that the traditional system of rulership and essential dignities, with its faces and terms, is not the same thing as the modern concept of rulership, which simply identifies the symbolic similarity shared by certain planets and signs.

When modern psychological astrologers talk about outer planet 'rulership', this acknowledges the similar symbolism shared by a planet and sign. For example, Neptune 'rules' Pisces because they share watery symbolism and are both imaginative and dreamy, among other shared qualities.

Born with the Sun in Aquarius and with stationary Uranus (its modern ruler) making a conjunction to the North Node, Lincoln and Darwin are good examples of the value of the modern symbolic rulership model.

It's interesting to note that the etymology of the word 'Uranus' (Greek, Ouranos) is linked to words like urine and urea, which references his mythic castration at the hands of Cronus. But it seems that it can be traced back even further. In Sanskrit, Uranus means 'rain maker'.[58] Therefore, Uranus shares the same symbolism as Aquarius, the 'water-bearer'.

Uranus

To help bridge the divide between traditional and modern approaches to rulership, perhaps modern astrologers should use another word instead of 'rulership'. Maybe, 'jurisdiction' would be a better term.

John F. Kennedy is another US President who challenged the establishment and looked to the future. Who can forget his iconic speech about sending man to the Moon? His Uranus was SD in Aquarius, where it has 'jurisdiction'. Stationary Mercury (20TA35) squares his stationary Uranus (23AQ43).

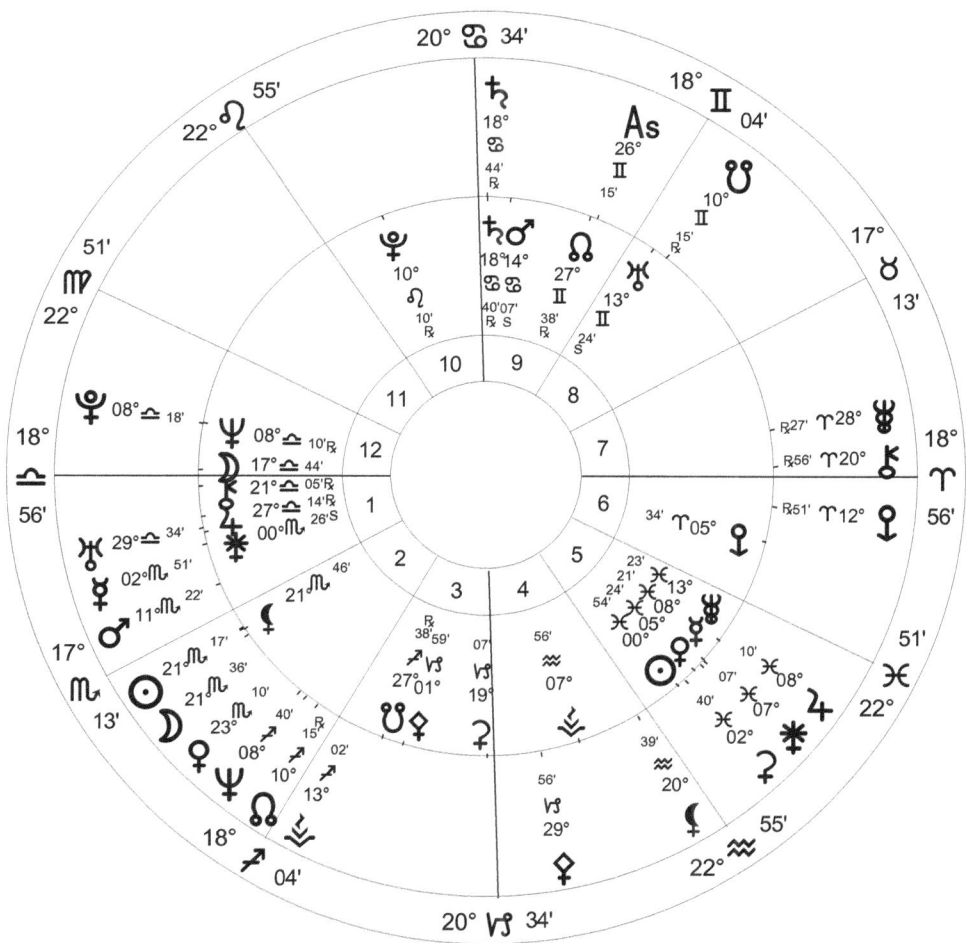

Inner Wheel: Karen Silkwood. 19 February 1946. 9.50pm, Longview, Texas. (AA)
Outer Wheel: Her death. 13 November 1974. 7.30pm, Midwest City, Oklahoma. (A)

Creative and highly original, others with Uranus stationary include a number of eccentric individuals such as Mary Poppins author, Pamela Travers, comedian Lily Tomlin, and innovative musicians Marc Bolan, Elvis Presley, Angus Young and Lady Gaga. Human rights advocate and QC, Geoffrey Robertson is another talented individual who embodies the Promethean themes associated with Uranus.

Union activist Karen Silkwood was born eight hours before Uranus stationed direct. She also had SD Mars and SR Juno. She was instrumental in exposing the dangerous practices at the nuclear power plant where she worked making plutonium pellets. Her story is told in the 1983 movie *Silkwood*, the title role played by Meryl Streep. After being exposed to radiation, either deliberately or negligently at the plant, she was killed in a car accident on her way to meet a journalist to provide evidence on multiple safety breaches at the Kerr-McGee facility. Despite evidence that her car was rammed from behind, her death was ruled an accident. Documents she had with her at the time were never found.[59] No conclusive evidence of foul play was ever established.

She died on her Saturn Return. In fact, Saturn was just four minutes of arc away from its exact return. Saturn had recently been crossing her SD Mars. When she died, transiting Uranus (29LI34) was conjunct her SR Juno (00SC26), the transiting South Node (10GE15) had recently crossed her SD Uranus (13GE24) plus transiting Vesta (13SG02) opposed her natal Uranus. The Kerr-McGee plant closed down in 1975.[60]

Uranus SR

Charles Baudelaire	03CP07 - see also Mercury & Ceres
Marc Bolan	26GE10
Bob Crane	07AR23 - see also Mercury & Ceres
Nicholas Culpeper	14CN21 - see also Ceres & Chiron
Charles Darwin	09SC40 - (conjunct North Node)
Cadel Evans	11SC47 - see also Ceres
Lady Gaga	22SG22 - see also Mercury & Juno
John F. Kennedy	23AQ43 - see also Mercury, Juno & Hygiea
Abraham Lincoln	09SC40 - (conjunct North Node)
Prince Philip Duke of Edinburgh	09PI38
Brad Pitt	10VI04 - see also Pluto
Robert Redford	09TA35 - see also Jupiter
Geoffrey Robertson	21GE47 - see also Ceres
Lily Tomlin	21TA57 - see also Mars & Vesta

Events

1939 WWII first shot	21TA57 - see also Mars & Vesta

Uranus SD

Peter Allen	04GE49 - see also Ceres
William Blake	19Pl17 - (opposite Juno)
Lindy Chamberlain	22GE06 - see also Mercury & Vesta
Robert Graves	15SC51 - see also Pallas Athena
Alfred Hitchcock	03SG59 - see also Juno
Jeff Kennett	22GE06 - see also Mercury & Vesta
Joe Pesci	00GE34 - see also Saturn
Elvis Presley	27AR29 - (conjunct Pallas Athena)
Karen Silkwood	13GE24 - see also Mars & Juno
Pamela Travers	03SG59 - see also Chiron & Juno
Harvey Weinstein	09CN54 - see also Mars
Angus Young	23CN35 - (conjunct Jupiter)

Events

2020 Saturn-Pluto   02TA39 - see also Hygiea & Eris

NEPTUNE

Neptune is mysterious and enigmatic. Well beyond the reaches of human consciousness, at its heart it represents the desire to connect with something beyond ourselves and beyond reality. Whether this feeling of spiritual union is provided by art, music, religion, romance, drugs or another means, our souls yearn to experience transcendence. The key thing with Neptune is to immerse ourselves in something universal that's meaningful, where we can experience a state of bliss.

While Uranus awakens consciousness, Neptune represents the mysteries of the unconscious. Neptune can devolve and take us on a downward spiral where we lose all sense of who we are. Equally, it can inspire the most profound feelings of euphoria.

Neptune has modern 'jurisdiction' over Pisces because they share the same watery symbolism, universal themes and imagery. Like the ocean depths, Neptune is deep and mysterious, and it's also blue. If we float in Neptune's realm for too long, we may dissolve, be washed out to sea, or drown. Like the unconscious and deepest oceans on Earth, Neptune can't be fathomed.

Spending time near the water, communing with nature and appreciating its majestic beauty is one of the best ways we can experience the sense of spiritual renewal Neptune can provide.

From time to time we can all experience disillusionment and depression. The Neptune square at age 41 is often a key time for questioning the meaning of life. Mid-life is often a time of acute stress due to the Uranus opposition, but with the Neptune square, this is often accompanied by a feeling of disillusionment that can take us on a downward spiral.

Because Neptune moves so slowly, whether at mid-life or when passing over a personal planet, transits of Neptune can linger. We may feel disconnected from ourselves, or as if we are lost in a fog. But as Neptune is stationary for just two weeks each year, we can use stationary Neptune days to contemplate, meditate and daydream.

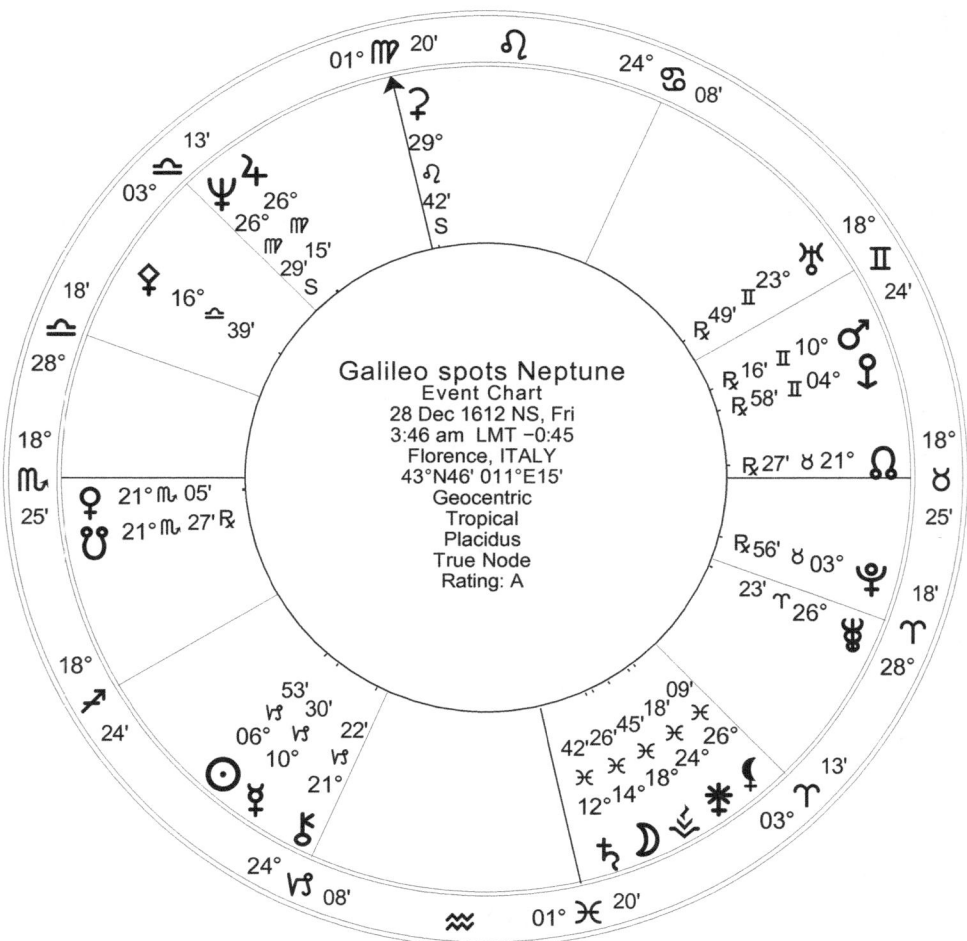

Regularly nourishing our soul, in however we choose to go about it, may mitigate some of the negative effects that can accompany longer transits of Neptune.

In 1612, Galileo was observing Jupiter and its moons through his telescope when he actually saw Neptune, recording the observation in his notes.[61] [62] [63] But as Neptune was just hours away from its exact station at the time, and typical of elusive Neptune, Galileo mistook it for a fixed star. It was another 234 years before Neptune was officially discovered.

An interesting example that illustrates the symbolism of stationary Neptune is seen in the chart for the Proclamation of Hollywood. On 1 February 1887, a real estate developer by the name of Harvey Wilcox officially registered the district of Hollywood in Los Angeles. His vision was to create a moral and Christian community.[64] Unfortunately for Wilcox, Neptune had a different vision for the area. On the day he registered Hollywood at the County Records Office in Los Angeles, Neptune was at a virtual standstill (25TA01). Far from the devout religious community he envisioned, Hollywood would become the hub of glamour where the movie industry had its genesis, fuelled by an excess of drugs, alcohol and debauchery.

Individuals with stationary Neptune include a number of people who developed drug and alcohol dependency, like Billie Holiday and F. Scott Fitzgerald. Others have been embroiled in scandals, Byron, Hari, Spector and Trump. Some others have become icons in the media and arts, Hanks, Streep and Winfrey. Writers, musicians, actors and political leaders are key members of this group. So too are cult leaders like Marshall Applewhite and Jim Jones who were born just a few days apart.

A fascinating example of stationary Neptune is Mata Hari who was born with three stationary planets, Venus (14CN02), Chiron (00TA21) and Neptune (05TA19). Notorious exotic dancer, prostitute and convicted spy, Mata's Neptune stationed retrograde around 10 hours after her birth.

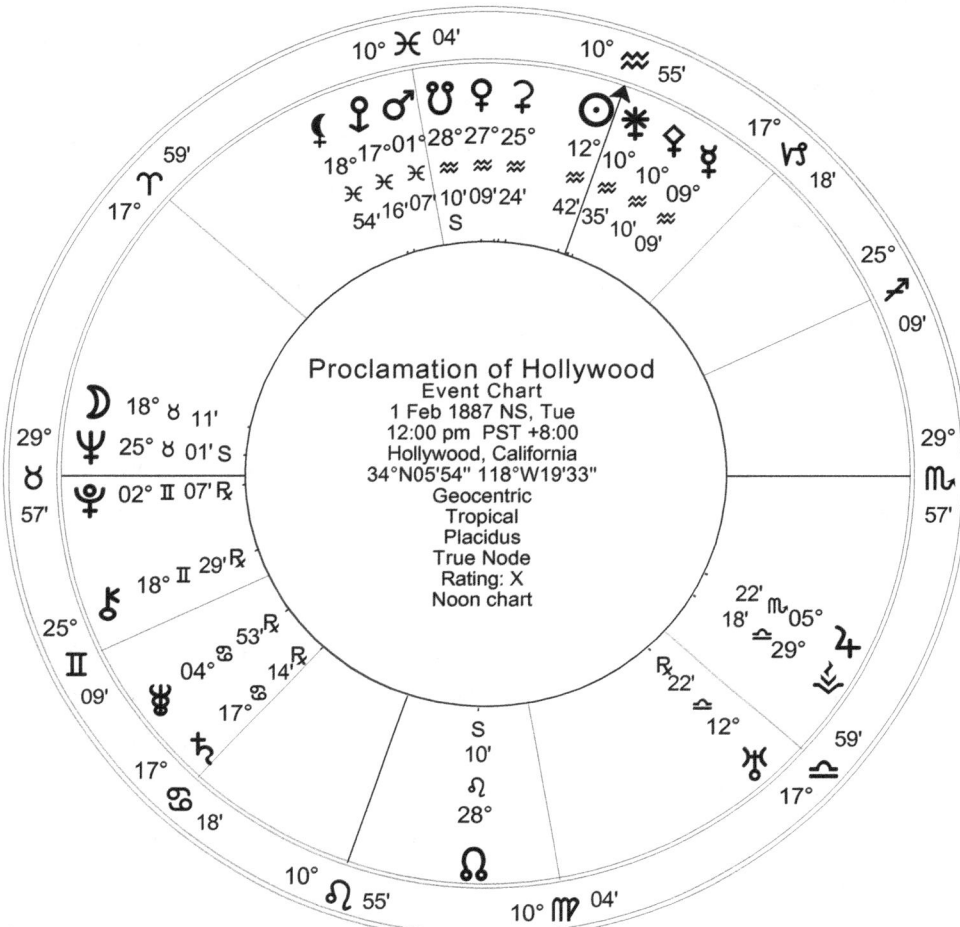

At age 15, after a prosperous childhood, her father was bankrupted when his haberdashery business failed. Her parents divorced and her mother died not long afterwards. Margaretha (her birth name) was handed around to distant relatives while her younger brothers stayed with their father and his new wife. Around this time, she was expelled from school for having sex with the headmaster. She was labelled a seductress.

The sudden rejection by her previously loving father led 18 year-old Margaretha to hastily marry a military officer named MacLeod who was twenty years her senior. The couple moved to Indonesia where MacLeod was stationed. He turned out to be a violent alcoholic, a gambler and womaniser. It's likely that he infected her with syphilis. MacLeod was born on 1 March 1856 with his Sun at 10 Pisces, exactly on Margaretha's Moon, so it's easy to see why they were initially attracted to one another.

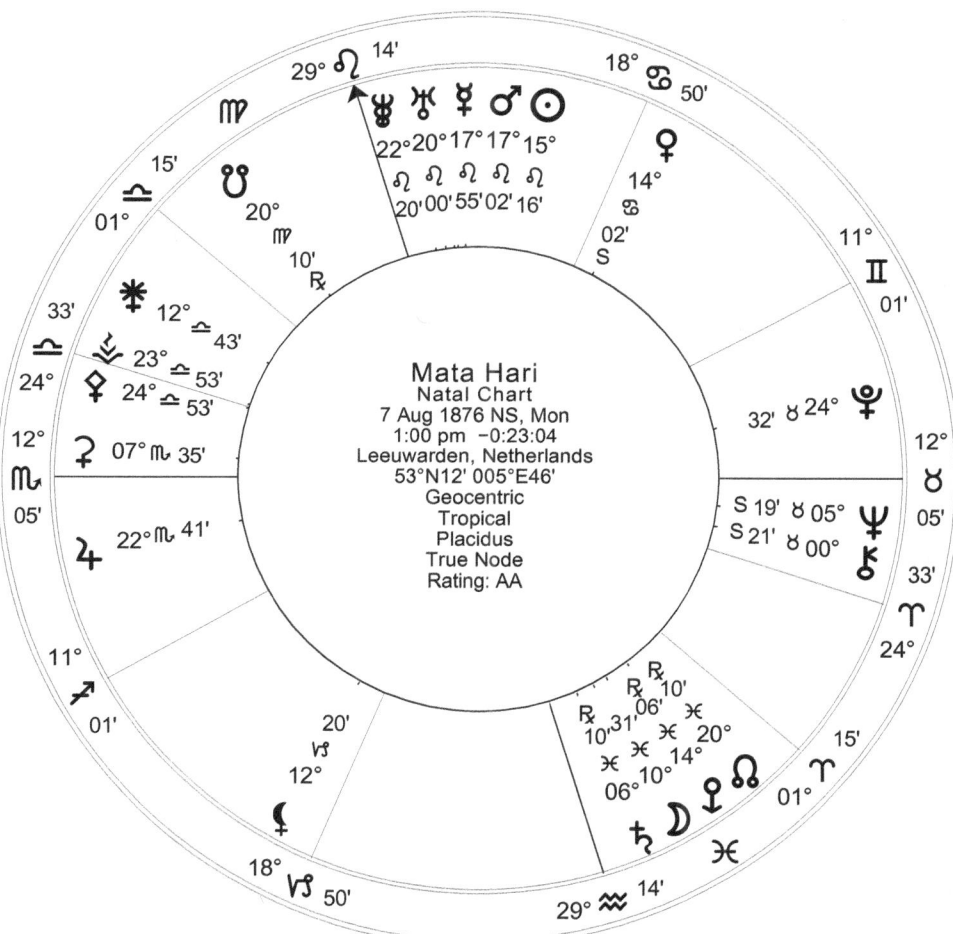

In Indonesia, Margaretha was ostracised by the European community because although she was Dutch, she had naturally dark skin and people assumed she was MacLeod's native concubine. Indeed, MacLeod continued to keep a concubine after their marriage, a common practice in the Dutch East Indies at that time. They had two children, one of whom died mysteriously, possibly from an overdose of mercury that was routinely used to treat syphilis. The children contracted the disease at birth.[65] The marriage went from bad to intolerable and in 1902, the couple divorced after returning to Holland. Although she was granted legal custody, MacLeod withheld financial support and forced her to leave their daughter with him.

Margaretha changed her name to Mata Hari and moved to Paris, reinventing herself as an exotic dancer and courtesan. She found immediate success in pioneering new forms of expressive dance. Travelling widely, she had many wealthy clients. Despite the harrowing ordeal of her marriage, Mata loved men and true to her Leo Sun and Pisces Moon, she has been described as self-centred, vain and deceptive. She probably needed to be in order to survive.

On 13 February 1917 she was arrested and placed on trial for treason. Found guilty of spying for Germany, she was executed by firing squad at 5am on 15 October 1917 in Vincennes, France. In the years since her death, several biographers have attested that the French officials falsified evidence at her trial and have concluded that she was simply a naïve exotic dancer and not a spy.[66]

Her vulnerability, extraversion and adventurous spirit is consistent with Venus having stationed direct two and a half days before her birth. Her stationary Neptune, which has 'jurisdiction' over her Pisces Moon, is in Venus ruled Taurus which fostered her alluring mystique, lack of discrimination and capacity for deception. But does that mean she was a spy? Her vulnerable Venus rules her 7th house and squares Juno, goddess of marriage. At her trial one of her lovers failed to support her and instead denounced her. Devastated at his betrayal, Mata Hari was executed at the age 41, at the time of her Neptune square. She refused to be blindfolded and faced her fate with dignity.

Neptune SR

Spiro Agnew	09LE19 - see also Jupiter
Beethoven	13VI59 - (conjunct Juno) see also Venus
Lord Byron	21LI07 - see also Vesta
F. Scott Fitzgerald	20GE18 - see also Mercury
Jane Fonda	21VI09 - see also Mercury & Eris
George Gershwin	24GE47
Mata Hari	05TA19 - see also Venus & Chiron
Bob Hawke	03VI35 - see also Vesta
Nick Kyrgios	25CP33 - see also Juno
Jimmy Page	04LI15 - see also Mars
Phil Spector	25VI30 - see also Saturn
John Wilkes Booth	10AQ25 - see also Jupiter
Oprah Winfrey	26LI03

Events

1612 Galileo first spots Neptune	26VI30 - see also Ceres
1996 Port Arthur Massacre	27CP45 - see also Jupiter
2021 Florida Building Collapse	23PI11 - see also Mercury and Jupiter

Neptune SD

Marshall Applewhite	02VI59 - see also Mercury, Vesta & Ceres
Oliver Cromwell	22LE59 - (opposite Uranus) see also Pallas Athena
Adolph Eichmann	07CN36 - see also Juno
Tom Hanks	27LI38 - see also Venus
Billie Holiday	27CN39
Jim Jones	02VI59 - see also Mercury & Ceres
Spike Milligan	04LE18 - see also Mercury, Mars & Pallas Athena
Cardinal George Pell	24VI54 - (conjunct North Node)
J.K. Rowling	17SC14 - see also Mercury & Ceres
Robert Louis Stevenson	04PI15 - (conjunct Moon) see also Ceres
Meryl Streep	12LI23
Donald Trump	05LI510 - see also Ceres, Juno, Jupiter & Chiron
George Washington	14GE40 - see also Eris

Events

1887 Proclamation of Hollywood   25TA02

PLUTO

Pluto is a very small world. Discovered in 1930, Pluto held planetary status until 24 August 2006 when the International Astronomical Union (IAU) downgraded Pluto to a dwarf planet. At the same time, Ceres was upgraded from asteroid to dwarf planet. This perfectly reflects the compromise that Pluto (Hades) and Ceres (Demeter) reached in the myth of the abduction of Proserpina (Persephone).

In the classic tale, Ceres and Pluto eventually agreed that that Proserpina would share her time equally between Pluto's Underworld and her mother's realm. Ceres who had withdrawn her care and oversight of nature in protest and grief, then restored and rejuvenated the fertility of the Earth. With Pluto and Ceres now having equal status in the planetary hierarchy, many hope this means that we are starting to have respect for the living Earth and greater gender balance.

Lord of the Underworld, Pluto operates under the cover of darkness. Death, rebirth and survival are Pluto's main themes. Power and control are his methods. When we perceive that our very survival is under threat, human beings are capable of just about anything.

As with all planets with an elliptical orbit, the length of time Pluto spends stationary depends on which part of its orbit these stations occur. Using the 30% rule, Pluto will station for between four and seven days at each station. Pluto is closest to the Sun (perihelion) and moves most swiftly when in Scorpio, and is furthest away (aphelion) and slowest in the opposite sign, Taurus. So, Pluto stations for around four days when in Scorpio and about seven days in Taurus.

Like the other planets that have long orbital cycles, Pluto stations can be used to honour the role Pluto plays in our lives. This may help us manage and process events that can accompany intense Pluto transits. Pluto often asks us to make some kind of sacrifice or to let go of an attachment before something new can be created. Perhaps making small sacrifices when Pluto is stationary can prepare us for the impact of major transformative events.

Themes of resurrection and rebirth are common among those born with stationary Pluto, and just as common are reversals of fortune and descents into the Underworld.

A number of powerful people are included in this group. Former UK Prime Minister Margaret Thatcher and L. Ron Hubbard, founder of Scientology, embody the powerful controlling influence and intensity of Pluto.

Falling from high positions of influence are figures such as member of the House of Lords, politician and writer Jeffrey Archer and convicted paedophile, entertainer Rolf Harris.

The infamous Kray twins, Reggie and Ronnie, were ruthless gangsters active in London in the 50s and 60s. Reggie became a born-again Christian.

There was hardly a more dramatic reversal of fortune than the fall of Louis XVI, King of France who was overthrown and executed during the French Revolution. During his rule, France was virtually bankrupt, but the monarchy enjoyed the lavish comfort of the court until the revolution swept across France.

The word 'revolution' refers to both the cyclic motion of the planets, as well as revolutionary forces that overthrow an established political or social system.[67] With its long orbital cycle of 248 years and themes

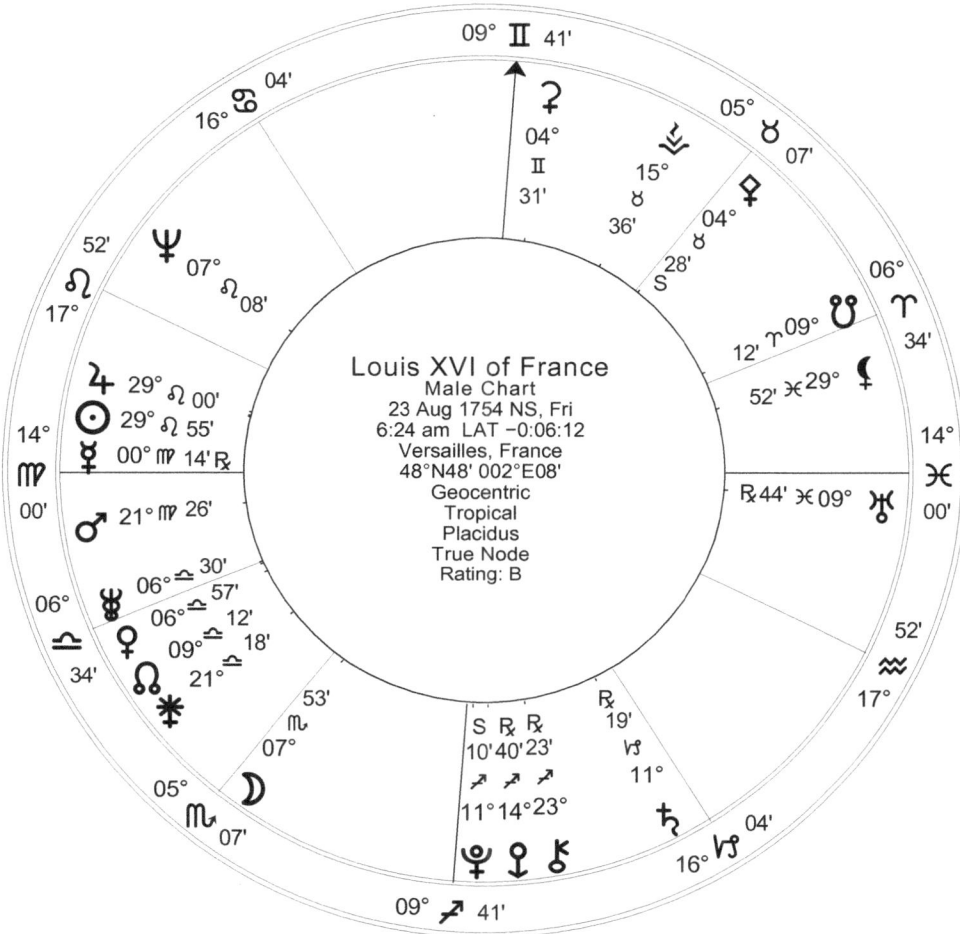

of death and rebirth, Pluto is the main agent of these revolutionary forces.

King Louis XVI has SD Pluto close to the I.C., in essence, literally in the Underworld, with Eris close by. Jupiter is tightly conjunct the Sun and located at the royal degree of fixed star Regulus. Jupiter has 'jurisdiction' over his stationary Pluto in Sagittarius, further inflaming the excess for which he was known.

Another King, namely Edward VI, the only son of Henry VIII, was another royal figure with stationary Pluto. He too was associated with revolutionary change. Edward ascended the English throne at the age of nine, during the Protestant Reformation, but died from respiratory disease at age 15. Being so young, he was subject to the control of a Council of Regency, and never had any real power of his own. When Edward died, members of the council attempted to keep their own power base intact by installing the young Lady Jane Grey as Queen. The coup backfired and soon Mary I (Bloody Mary) ascended the throne, resurrecting the Catholic religion across England.

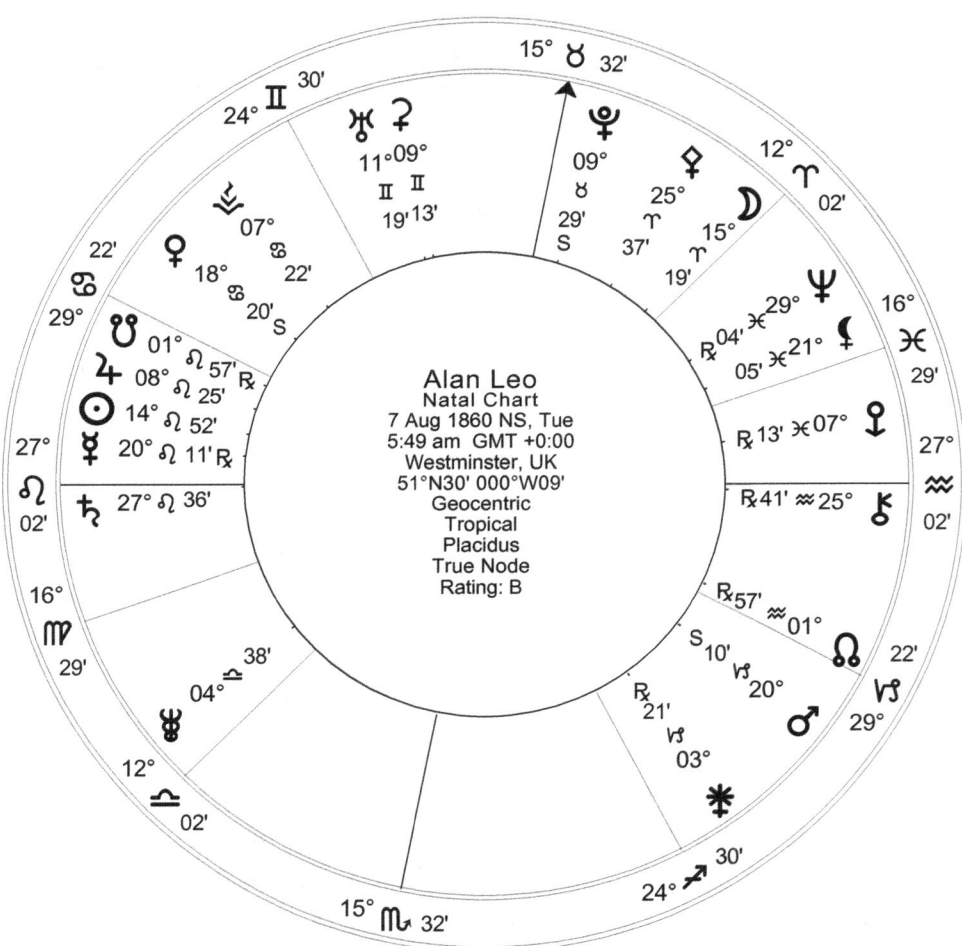

Astrologer Alan Leo (real name William Frederick Allan) rose from humble beginnings to establish a thriving astrology business. He was responsible for a resurgence of interest in astrology by popularising Sun signs and reinventing many astrological principles, focusing more on analysis than prediction.[68] His SR Pluto is in Taurus, where stations last seven days.

His chart also includes a Venus-Mars opposition and both planets are SD. This is a passionate aspect, but this passion must have been directed towards his work, as he was said to be celibate and his marriage to his wife Bessie, a platonic union.[69]

Venus and Mars are in opposition once every two years. Mars is always either retrograde, or at a virtual standstill when in opposition to Venus, but it is exceedingly rare that Venus is also stationary when this opposition occurs.

Pluto SR

Chuck Berry	15CN56 - see also Juno & Jupiter
Justin Bieber	28SC04 - see also Juno & Jupiter
Kenneth Branagh	08VI07 - (conjunct North Node and Moon)
Art Garfunkel	05LE47 - see also Mercury & Mars
Reginald & Ronald Kray	24CN45
Alan Leo	09TA29 - see also Venus & Mars
Brad Pitt	14VI13 - see also Uranus
Margaret Thatcher	14CN44 - (opposite Jupiter)

Events

1977 Granville Train Disaster	14LI11 - see also Mercury, Hygiea & Jupiter

Pluto SD

Jeffrey Archer	00LE36 - see also Ceres
King Edward VI	06AQ57 - (opposite Mars-Uranus)
Rolf Harris	17CN26 - (square Venus)
L. Ron Hubbard	25GE53
Jay Leno	15LE46 - see also Mars, Juno & Hygiea
King Louis XVI	11SG10 - see also Pallas Athena

Events

1917 Czar Nicholas II Abdication	02CN19 - see also Pallas Athena

ERIS

There are a number of small worlds in the outer reaches of the solar system, beyond the orbit of Pluto. I have not examined them all with regard to any influence they may have when stationary, but I thought it was worth a look at Eris.

Eris was discovered on 5 January 2005 and orbits the Sun in 557 Earth years. Initially, Eris was called Xena, but the IAU renamed the dwarf planet Eris after the Greek goddess of strife and discord. She was known for causing conflict and for her enjoyment of war and bloodshed.

In her mythic tale, Eris was upset when she wasn't invited to the wedding of Peleus and Thetis. In spite, she tossed a golden apple into the wedding party, addressed "to the fairest". The goddesses Hera (Juno), Athena (Minerva) and Aphrodite (Venus) quarrelled about who should claim it. Zeus appointed the Trojan Prince, Paris, to decide. All three goddesses offered him bribes to get his vote. Paris eventually chose Aphrodite (Venus) as the most beautiful goddess, because she had offered him the most beautiful mortal woman in the world, Helen of Troy. Unfortunately, Helen happened to be married to Menelaus, the King of Sparta. The dispute led to the Trojan War.

Dwarf planet Eris has a very small Moon called Dysnomia, named after the mythic daughter of Eris, the demon goddess of lawlessness.[70]

It might be helpful if the IAU had a serious rethink about the names they choose for new discoveries and select gods and goddesses who symbolise positive, uplifting and hopeful qualities. Doing so might help to restore peace and harmony to our world.

Eris moves so slowly that her stations only last a day or two. In 2020, stations of Eris took place around 11-12 January (SD) and 20-21 July (SR). Each year Eris stations move forward by a day or so.

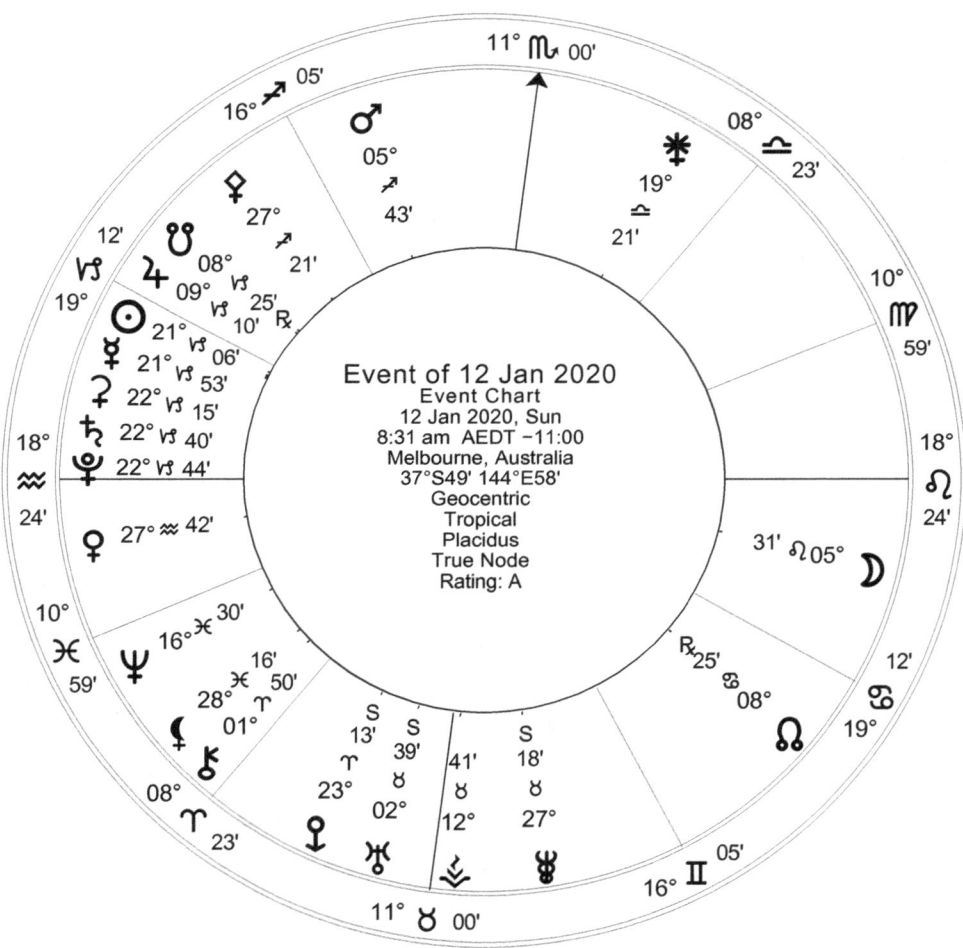

It's notable that Eris was stationing direct just when COVID-19 was about to cause strife and discord across the world.

Saturn and Pluto were making a conjunction at the time, which closely aligned with Ceres, Mercury and the Sun. Hard Saturn-Pluto aspects are well known to symbolise difficult times. Tough restrictions and economic pain often accompany these aspects. January 2020 was when horrific fires destroyed so much of Australia's precious flora and fauna, not to mention the human toll they took on people and their livelihoods.

Knowing that this conjunction of Pluto and Saturn was imminent, astrologers were fully aware that 2020 was going to be a tough gig, but as this chart shows, all these Capricorn planets are in a very tight square to SD Eris (23AR13). In addition, Hygiea, goddess of health and healing, is also stationary direct, voicing her concerns about personal hygiene and a pure and healthy environment. Plus, wild-card Uranus is also SD (02TA39), giving a shout out to do things differently in the future and to listen to science.

More research is needed to determine the significance of Eris in the birth chart, whether or not it's stationary. Watching events unfold on the days when Eris stations each year may offer some clues to its possible influence.

Stationary Eris may speak to the way we respond to life altering events that are beyond our control, like pandemics, wars and other global threats. It's interesting that a number of individuals born with stationary Eris have played pivotal roles in major conflicts.

George Washington was the commander of the colonial forces in the US War of Independence. His SR Eris (22SC54) is in a tight conjunction with Mars (23SC13). Winston Churchill led Britain to victory in WWII. His SD Eris (12PI13) trines Ceres (12CN58). Actor Jane Fonda campaigned against the Vietnam War. Travelling to Hanoi in 1972, she drew widespread criticism but was a major player in the anti-war movement. Her SD Eris (03AR06) is conjunct Saturn (28PI41) and squares her Sun (29SG18).

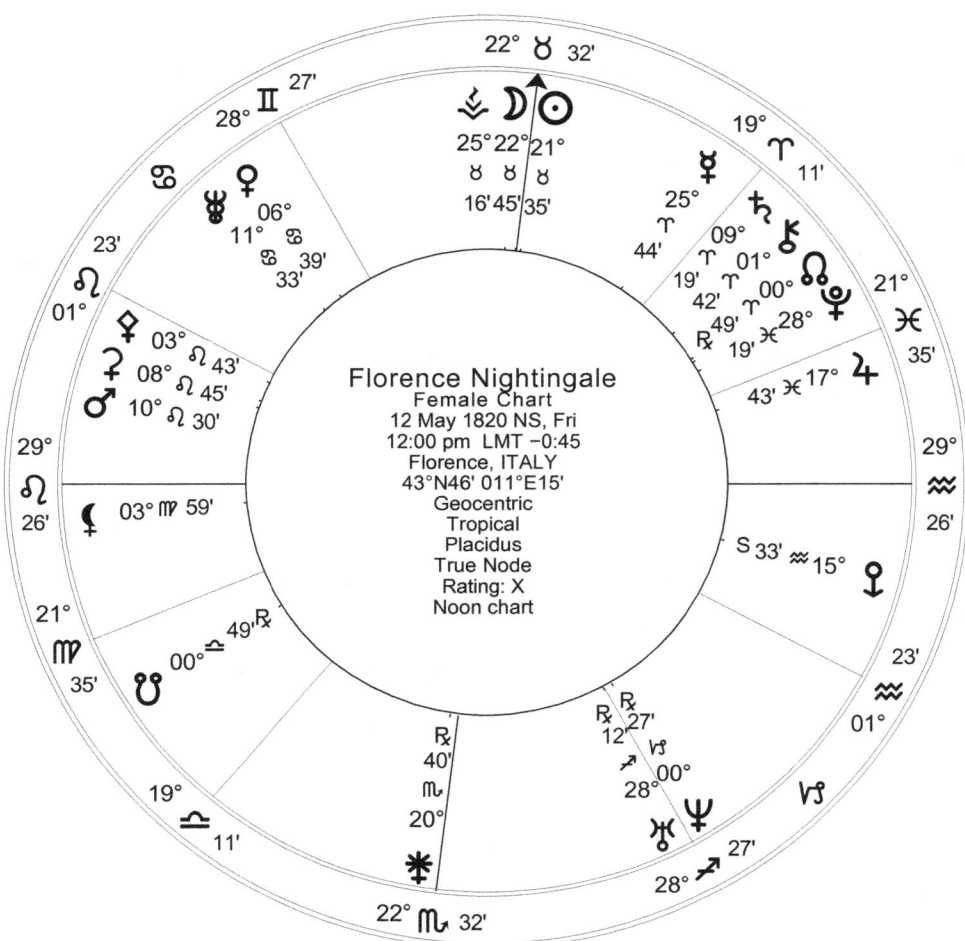

Florence Nightingale, founder of modern day nursing, made her name during the Crimean War. Her SR Eris (15AQ33) is opposite Mars. She trained volunteer nurses and publicised the appalling conditions she found among the wounded. Medical supplies were scant, and infection and disease were far more likely to kill than battle wounds. Appropriately, Chiron is conjunct her North Node. I was fascinated to discover that the midpoint of her Chiron and Hygiea, symbols of health and healing, is 21TA38, which is a breath away from her Sun. Florence Nightingale died peacefully in her sleep at the age of 90.

Eris SR

Robert Browning	09AQ58 - see also Juno
Schapelle Corby	14AR30 - see also Juno
John Dillinger	24PI10 - (conjunct Jupiter)
Florence Nightingale	15AQ33
Sissy Spacek	06AR19
George Washington	22SC54 - (conjunct Mars) see also Neptune

Eris SD

Winston Churchill	12PI13
Jane Fonda	03AR06 - see also Mercury & Neptune
Annie Lennox	07AR38
Henri Toulouse Lautrec	07PI57 - see also Hygiea, Ceres, Chiron
Tiger Woods	12AR53 - (opposite Pluto) see also Chiron

Events

2020 Saturn-Pluto	23AR13 - see also Hygiea & Uranus

SECTION THREE

DISASTERS AND ACCIDENTS

DISASTER (NOUN)

> *"anything that befalls of ruinous or distressing nature; any unfortunate event," especially a sudden or great misfortune, 1590s, from French désastre (1560s), from Italian disastro, literally "ill-starred," from dis-, here merely pejorative, equivalent to English mis- "ill" (see dis-) + astro "star, planet," from Latin astrum, from Greek astron "star" (from PIE root *ster- (2) "star").*

> *The sense is astrological, of a calamity blamed on an unfavorable position of a planet, and "star" here is probably meant in the astrological sense of "destiny, fortune, fate." Compare Medieval Latin astrum sinistrum "misfortune," literally "unlucky star," and English ill-starred.*[71]

The word 'disaster' has astrological origins. The inference is that when disasters happen, it's because there is an unfavorable aspect in the heavens and conditions are unlucky. However, the etymology also suggests that disasters take place when there's a 'disconnect' from the collective.

As the word 'universe' implies, we are all united. Everything and everyone is connected and an integral part of creation. If there is a 'disconnect' and people do things without regard for the wider implications of their actions, then it's this attitude that creates the conditions for disasters to strike.

A variety of decisions and human oversights can play a key role in disasters. Many accidents happen in just this way. The chain of events that lead to a catastrophe cannot be pinpointed in time, and since many people are often involved, these precursors can't be examined astrologically. Nevertheless, it's worth looking at charts for disasters to see what astrological factors might be at play. As timing can be a critical factor in disasters, I was interested to see what role stationary planets might play in these tragedies.

That being said, there were no stationary planets at the time of the Chernobyl nuclear accident in 1986, nor when the Concorde crashed on take-off in 2000, nor at the time of the more recent explosion in Beirut, Lebanon on 4 August 2020. There were no stationary planets at the time of the 11 September terrorist attacks in 2001, nor when the Exxon Valdez Oil spill happened in 1989. Just as there are multiple indicators to consider in birth charts, there are numerous astrological points to take into account in event charts.

MH370

When ill-fated flight MH370 departed Kuala Lumpur, many astrologers observed that Neptune, planet of mystery, was located exactly on the I.C. This chart also has five stationary planets, the most I have ever seen in any chart with the exception of Donald Trump. The five stationary planets here are Mars, Saturn, Ceres and Vesta which are stationing retrograde, and Jupiter which is stationary direct. All were still stationary hours later when the plane disappeared. While some debris was recovered months later, the mystery of what happened to MH370 endures.

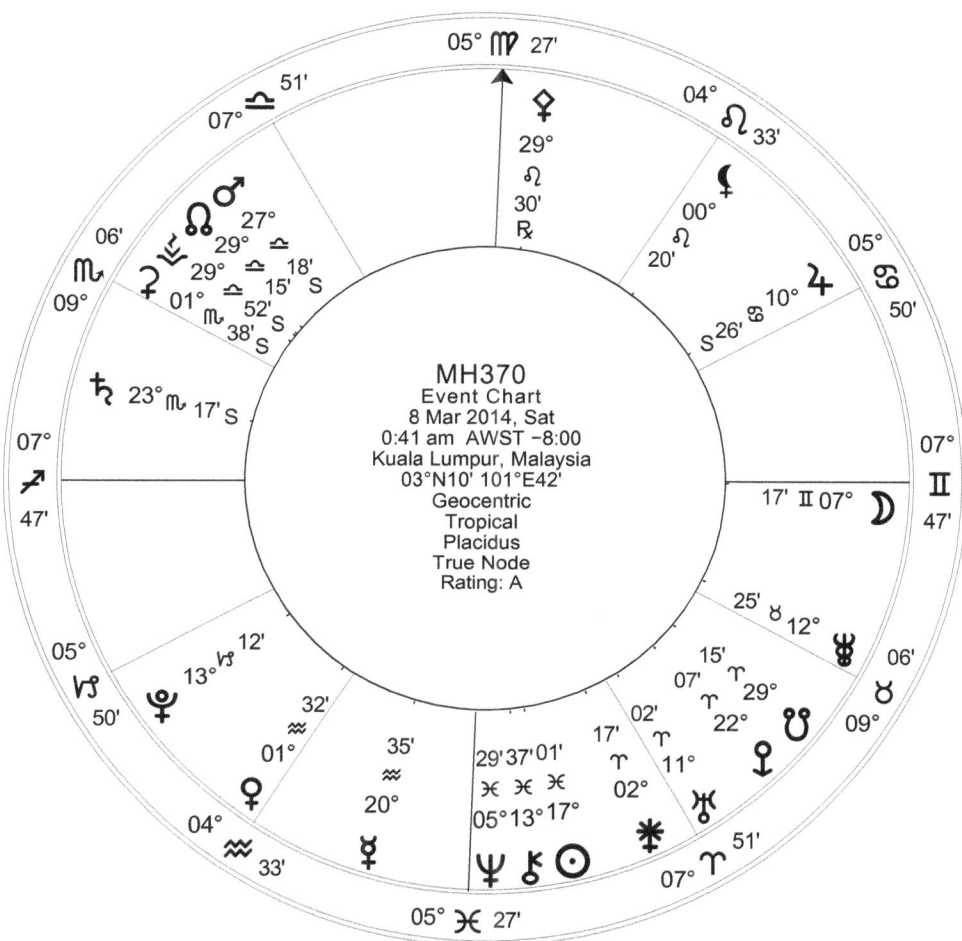

It's worth noting that the midpoint of SD Jupiter (10CN26) and SR Vesta (29LI52) is 05VI09, with the Jupiter-Ceres midpoint nearby (06VI02). These midpoints align exactly with the MC/IC axis and with Neptune.

After the authorities examined all the available data and eliminated most theories about what may have happened, it is widely thought that the pilot took control of the flight and deliberately ditched it into the Indian Ocean, perhaps first flying the plane to an extreme altitude and rendering all the passengers and himself unconscious.[72]

The pilot, Zaharie Ahmed Shah was born on 31 July 1961 in Penang Malaysia. His birth time is unknown so we can't ascertain the transits

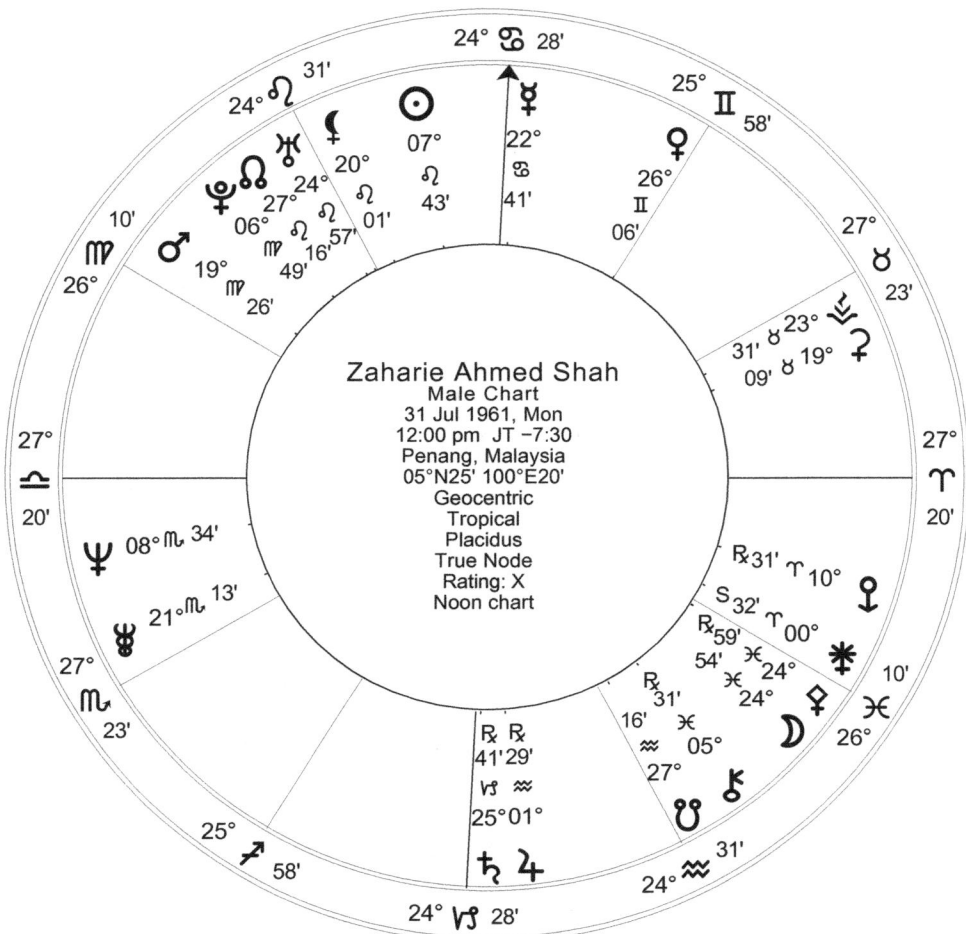

that might have been affecting the Moon or chart angles. However, it's worth mentioning that his natal Juno, goddess of marriage, is stationary retrograde (00AR32) and he had experienced a Juno Return a few days before MH370 disappeared. It's been reported that he had become very depressed as his marriage was falling apart. With Juno stationary, one's primary relationship is often particularly significant, which would be further amplified by its return.

At the same time, transiting Neptune (05PI29) was crossing his Chiron (05PI31). This can be quite a sad and depressing transit. In his birth chart, the Sun squares Neptune, which suggests that he may have been prone to bouts of depression.

While there are a number of possible scenarios to account for what happened to flight MH370, we will probably never know exactly what took place. However, in this case it seems likely that the tragedy was caused by the actions of just one individual.

GRANVILLE TRAIN DISASTER

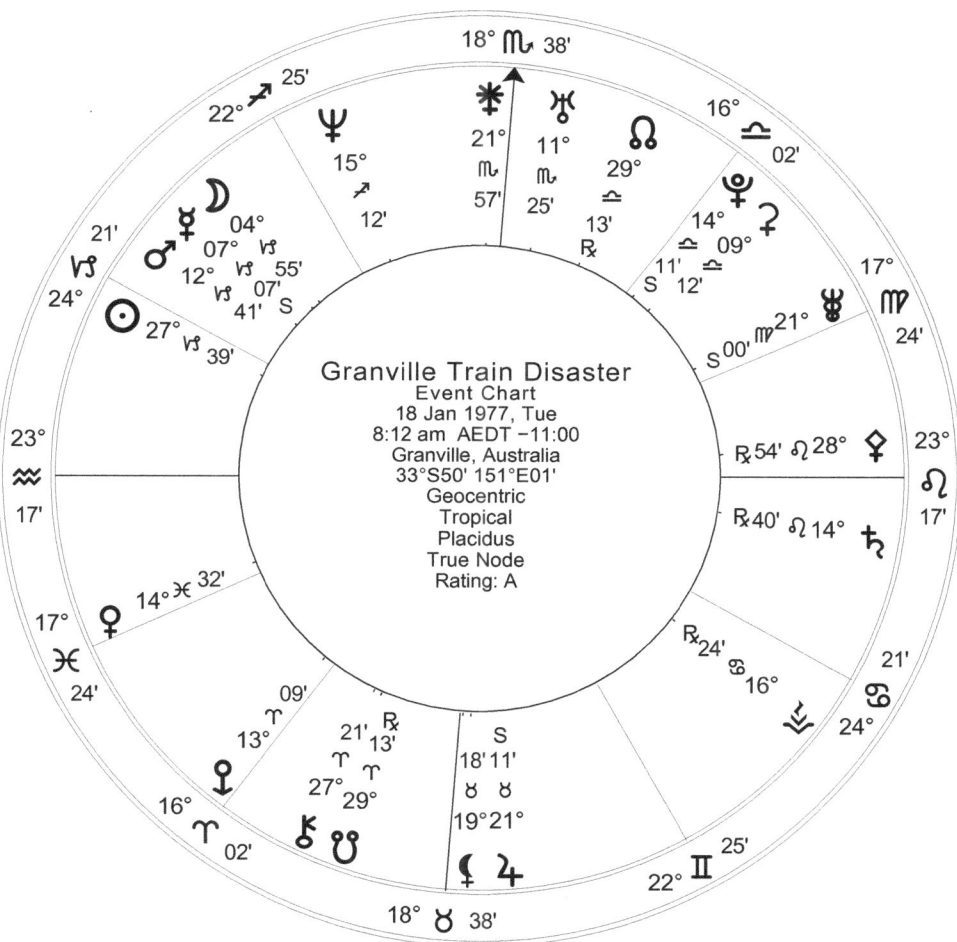

In January 1977 a city bound train jumped the tracks and hit the supporting pylons of an overhead bridge in Granville, in the western suburbs of Sydney. The concrete overpass collapsed onto several carriages, killing 83 people and injuring hundreds.

There were four stationary planets at the time of this tragic accident. Mercury, Hygiea, Jupiter and Pluto. The planets we associate with travel, namely Mercury and Jupiter, were both stationary direct. The exact midpoint of SD Mercury (07CP07) and SD Jupiter (21TA11) is 14PI09. This is incredibly close to Venus (14PI32) which is in turn, the apex of a tight yod involving Saturn (14LE40) and SR Pluto (14LI11). SR Hygiea is in a wide opposition to Venus. Note that Juno sits close to the Midheaven and opposes Jupiter.

An enquiry into this accident determined that there were a number of contributing factors, including a history of poor track and train maintenance. The poor design of the bridge was also noted. This issue had been identified earlier, but nothing had been done to fix the problem.[73] With SD Mercury, SD Jupiter and their midpoint activating Venus, the focal point of a yod, the time had come for this accident to occur.

In addition, the Sun (27CP39) squares Chiron (27AR21). The midpoint of this square also activates Venus, and the Mercury-Jupiter midpoint.

KLM-PAM AM COLLISION

Just two months after Granville came the worst aviation disaster in history when two Boeing 747s collided on the runway at Tenerife in the Canary Islands. There were 583 fatalities.

I remember when this accident happened, as I had just started working in the advertising agency that handled the KLM account. Not surprisingly, all KLM advertising was immediately cancelled.

As with many accidents, multiple decisions and events conspired to create the conditions for this accident. That day, flights had been diverted from Gran Canaria airport to Tenerife because of a terrorist incident. Neither plane was meant to be at Tenerife. The accident happened in thick fog (Neptune) that reduced visibility. Neptune had stationed retrograde about nine days earlier.

Disasters and Accidents

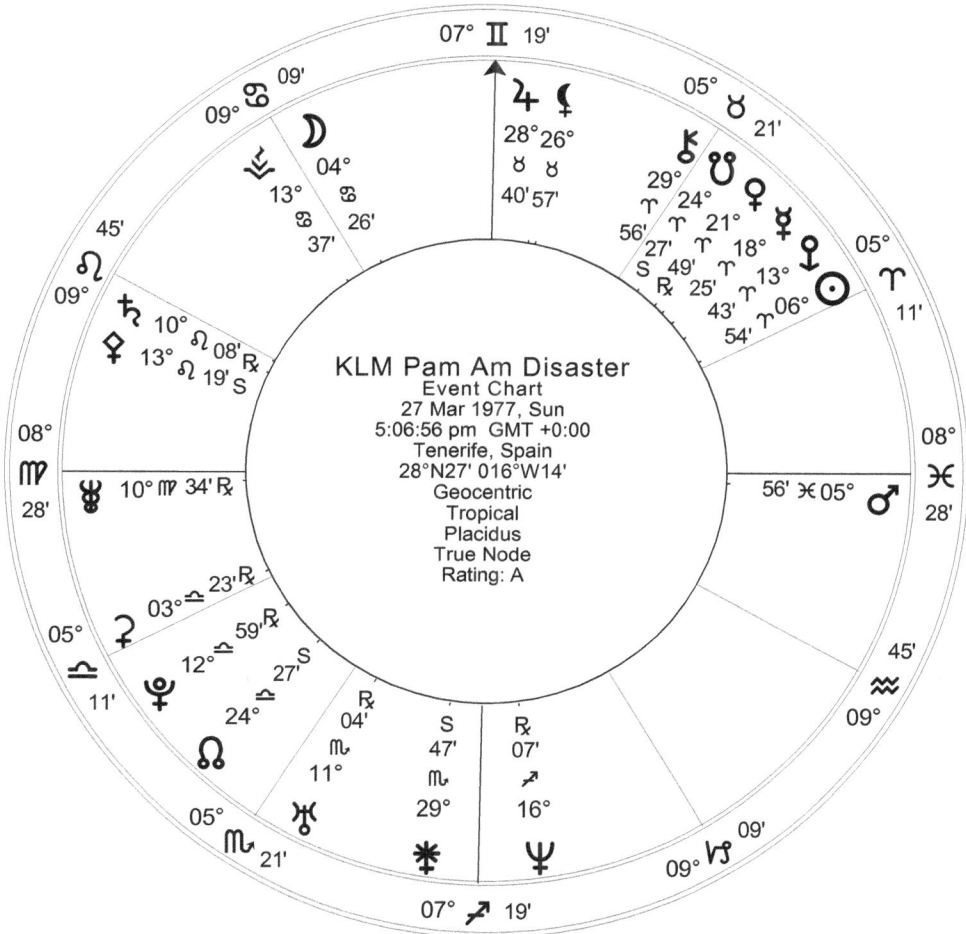

The horrific crash was due to a misunderstanding. After waiting a long time to depart, and believing he had received the go ahead, the KLM pilot commenced take off. Tragically, the Pam Am craft was taxiing across the runway ahead of them. There were 61 survivors, all of them were on the Pam Am 747.

In this chart we see SR Juno (29SC47) and SD Pallas Athena (13LE19). The midpoint of stationary Juno and Athena (06LI33) is opposite the 8th house Sun (06AR54). SR Juno is in a tight quincunx with Chiron and their midpoint (14AQ51) opposes SD Athena. There may not be as many obvious accident aspects or stationary planets in this chart as there are in the Granville chart, but once again we see Juno (29SC47) involved in an opposition with Jupiter (28TA40).

UNION CARBIDE GAS LEAK - BHOPAL

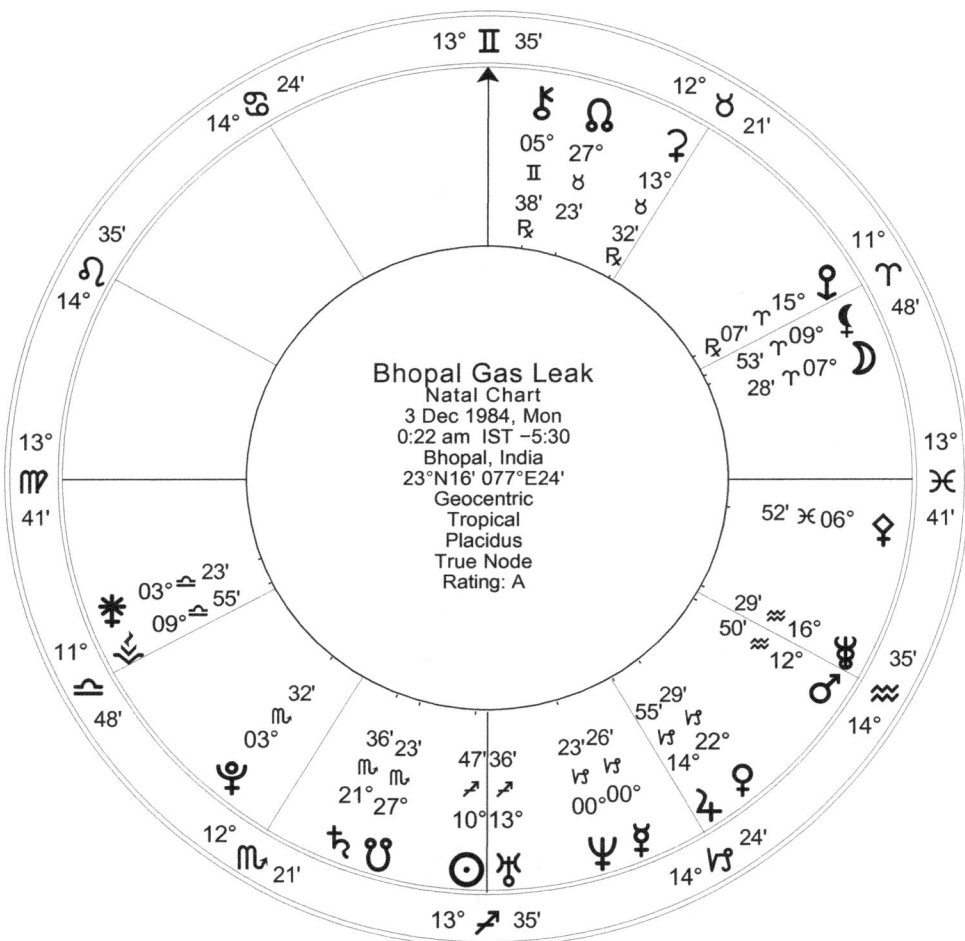

One of the worst industrial accidents to ever take place happened in India in 1984 when there was a gas leak at the Union Carbide pesticide plant in Bhopal. Over half a million people were exposed to methyl isocyanate (MIC) suffering severe and permanent injuries. Death toll estimates vary. Thousands of animals and trees also perished.

To this day, many people continue to suffer from a range of medical problems including birth defects, cancer and nerve damage, and people continue to die.[74]

In this chart[75] you will notice that no planets are flagged S; however, upon further investigation this chart may be a useful guide to help establish the exact percentage we should use for station settings.

Neptune (gas) and Mercury are in an extremely tight conjunction at the start of Capricorn. Mercury stationed retrograde 2.1 days after this horrific event. The exact station took place at 00CP48. If you animate this chart forward in time by just seven hours, Mercury is flagged S.

If you tweak the average percentage for stations up to 33 percent, Mercury is still not flagged S, but if you make it 34 percent, it is. This suggests that one third of average speed, 33.3% might be a better overall setting for stationary planets, although you can only enter whole numbers in this field. However, for the time being I have decided to stick with 30 percent.

It's telling that Mercury was so close to its station retrograde and so tightly aligned with Neptune when this devastating gas leak killed so many and caused horrific injuries to thousands more in the Bhopal district. The disaster was most likely caused by the cumulative effect of safety breaches and insufficient attention to maintenance over many years. In short, details (Mercury) were overlooked (Neptune). The gas leak (Neptune) happened when water (Neptune) entered a storage tank causing a chemical reaction that converted the liquid chemical to gas. Pressure built up, leading to an explosion.

MORE ACCIDENTS AND DISASTERS

The Titanic was launched on 31 May 1911 when Juno was stationary direct (07LI26). Juno was also stationary, but turning retrograde on 14 April 1912 (24SG59) when the ill-fated ship struck an iceberg in the mid-Atlantic and sank, killing more than 1,500 people. At both the launch and the time of accident, Juno was within just hours of its

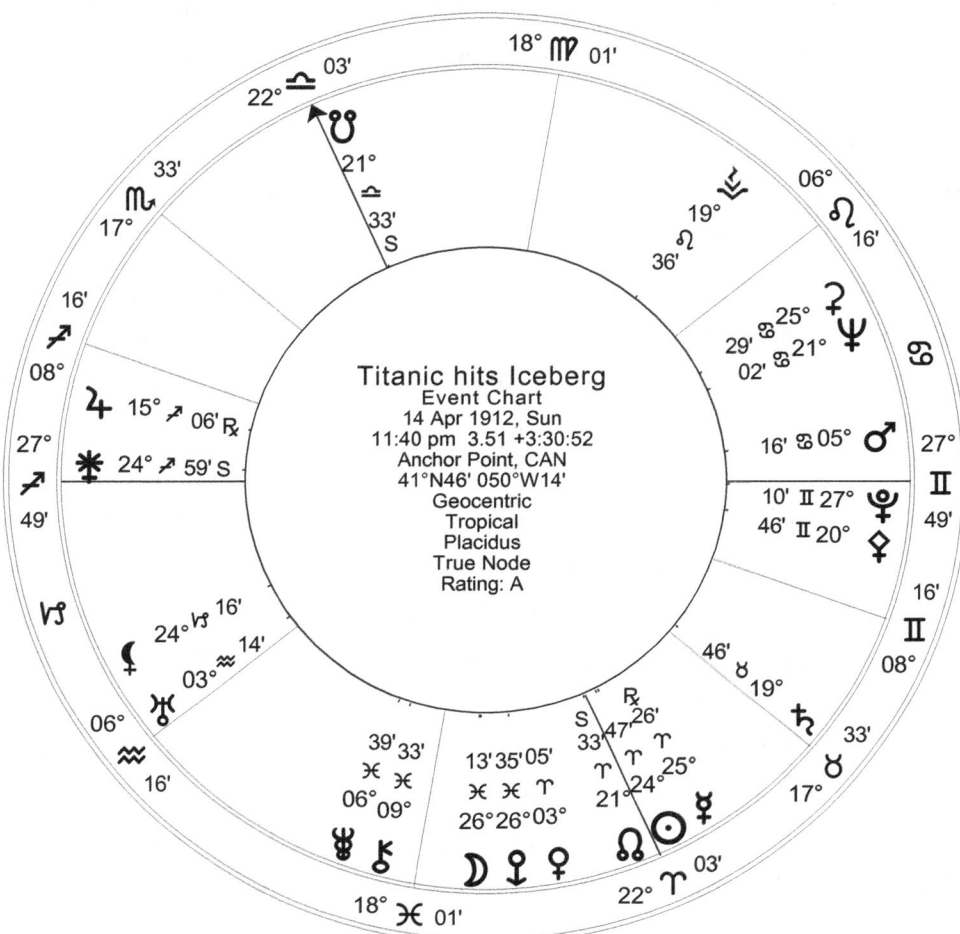

exact station. At the time of the collision, stationary Juno was rising, squaring the Moon and Eris and opposing Pluto.

I'm not sure of the astrological significance (if any) of stationary Juno at moments of accidents, but it's worth noting that she features in a number of these disasters. Apart from the charts I have already mentioned, there are a number of other major accidents where Juno is prominent, or stationary.

On 15 October 1970 Juno was stationary retrograde (26TA11) when the West Gate Bridge in Melbourne collapsed during its construction. 2000 tonnes of concrete and steel crashed into the Yarra River and 35 workers died. In this chart, stationary Juno is conjunct Saturn

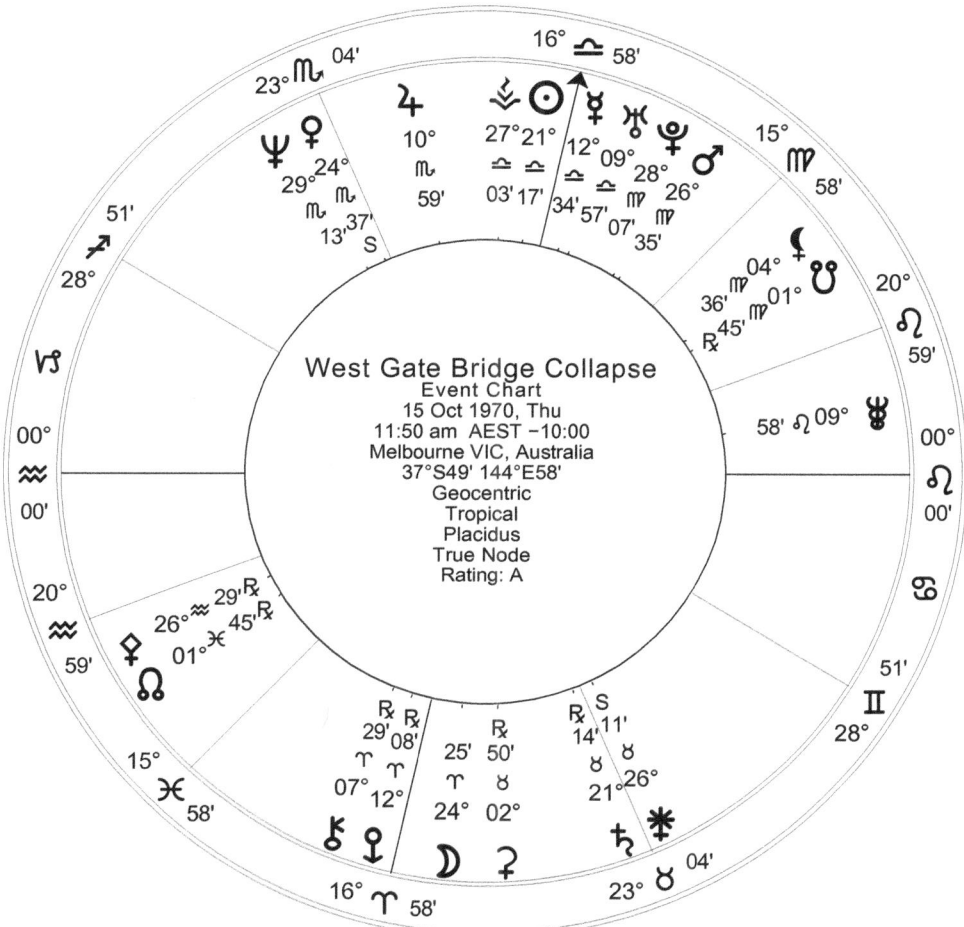

and opposite both Neptune and SR Venus (24SC37). There is also an awkward yod in this chart involving SR Venus, Mars in Virgo and the Moon in Aries. In addition, the Moon is opposite the Sun-Vesta midpoint.

In May 1937 when the Hindenburg airship burst into flames, Juno was stationary direct (25VI27) with the Moon in opposition (26PI10). Juno was involved in a yod with Pluto (26CN39) and Ceres (24AQ09). Jupiter opposes Pluto and trines Juno. Venus is SD (19AR32). The exact cause of this disaster has never been established. 36 people lost their lives.

The Test of Time

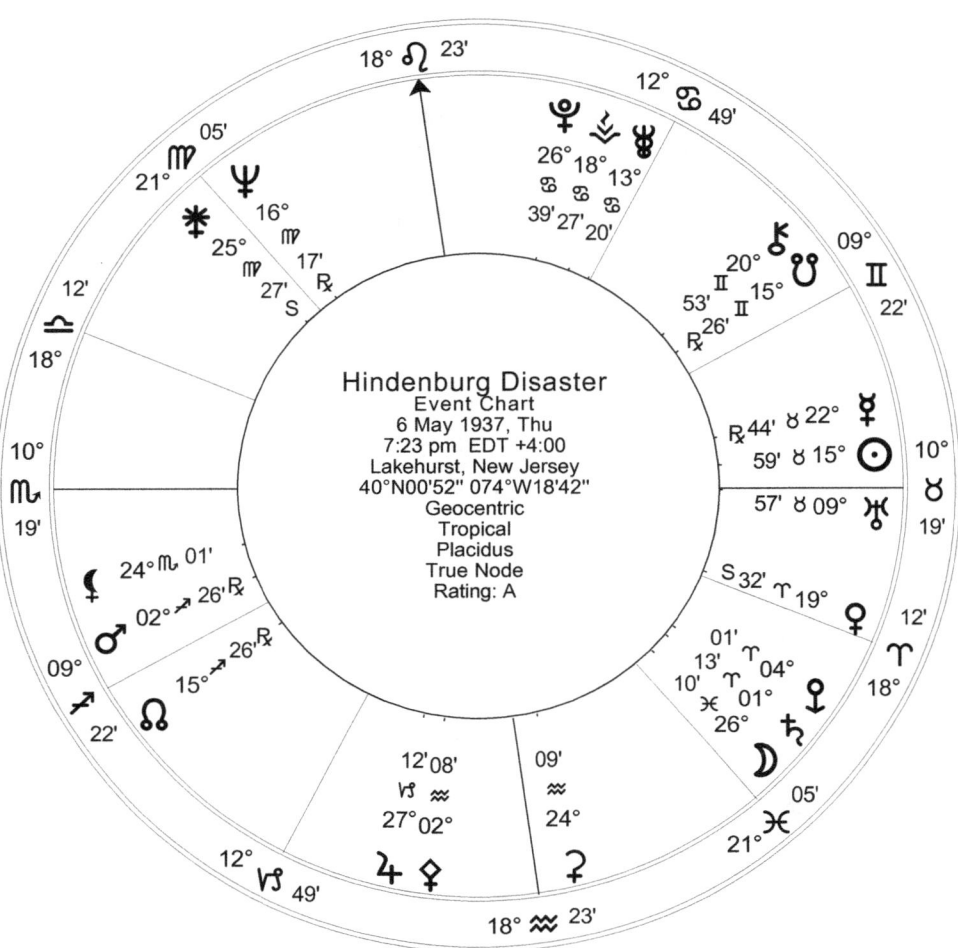

LUNAR PHASE RETURNS

Some years ago, when I was preparing for a presentation about the Metonic cycle, I decided to calculate some Lunar Phase Returns to illustrate the fact that the Sun and Moon both return to their natal positions every 19 years. In the process, I stumbled across a fascinating astrological congruence concerning stationary planets.

For those who are not familiar with the Metonic cycle, every 19 years New Moons, Full Moons, Eclipses, indeed all Moon phases, recur on the same day of the year at the same zodiac degrees. This is because 19 solar years and 235 lunar months is the same length of time, 6939 days, give or take a few hours.

Lunar Phase Return charts can be calculated for any month of any year to replicate the same Sun-Moon angle as in the birth chart. However, only those Lunar Phase Returns calculated for the ages of 19, 38, 57 and 76 will have the Sun and Moon located at the same positions as in the birth chart.

So, whose natal charts to use? I started looking for people who did something amazing at the age of 19. I was keen to see what other factors might be revealed in the Lunar Phase Return that illustrated why that time was so significant for them.

MARY SHELLEY

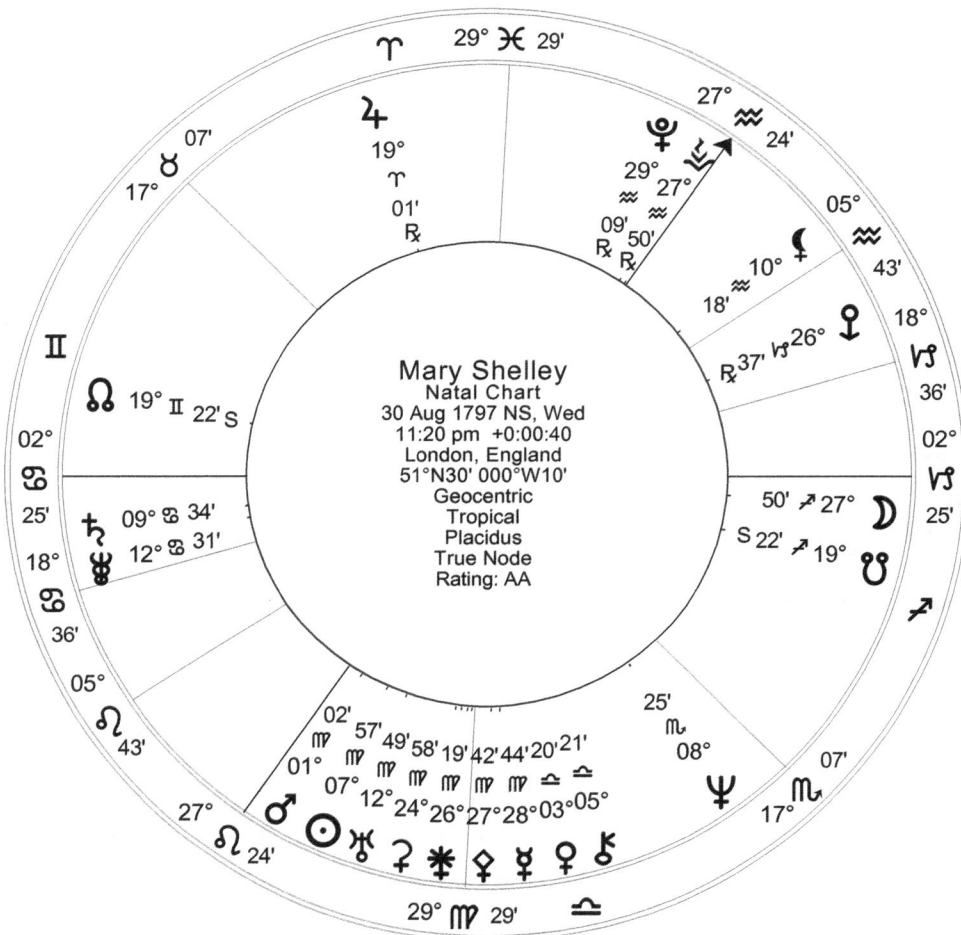

My first thought was Mary Shelley, who at the age of 19, penned the novel *Frankenstein* which immediately became a sensation. The story of how the novel came to be written is itself a mythic tale.

On 5 April 1815 Mt Tambora in Indonesia erupted. Five days later, the eruption intensified and a massive blast shattered the whole mountain. The eruption was so big it caused the weather around the world to go haywire. Rated seven on the Volcanic Explosivity Index (VEI), it's the biggest eruption in recent history and one of the most significant of all time. Death toll estimates vary. Around 100,000 people died initially, and perhaps up to one million perished in the aftermath. The eruption caused a global catastrophe that resulted in widespread disease and famine. The following year, 1816, became known as 'the year without a summer'.

That summer Mary Godwin Wollstonecraft, Percy Bysshe Shelley (Mary's husband to be) and Mary's step-sister, Claire Clairmont, travelled to Geneva Switzerland to stay with Lord Byron. Another guest of Lord Byron's was John William Polidori, a physician and writer. Owing to the poor weather conditions, the group spent much of the summer indoors. According to Mary,

'It proved a wet, ungenial summer and incessant rain often confined us for days to the house'.[76]

Sitting around the log fire at Byron's villa, the group amused themselves by telling ghost stories, which prompted Byron to propose they each write their own. Byron's doctor, William Polidori, wrote *The Vampire*, for which Byron would take credit. Sadly, a few years later the doctor took his own life.

At first Mary couldn't think of anything to write, but then Mary's idea for *Frankenstein* came to her in a dream.

It's thought that Mary's dream took place in the early morning of 16 June 1816 between 2 and 3am.[77] This was about two months before her 19th birthday. So, although her dream happened before her Lunar Phase Return for age 19, most of the story was written after her birthday. *Frankenstein, a Modern Prometheus* was published early in 1817. Her Lunar Phase Return for age 19 naturally shows the Sun and Moon at the same positions as in her natal chart, but also reveals a couple of other noteworthy points.

Mercury, planet of communication and writing is on the Midheaven (19VI53) along with Venus and Mars. Clearly this was a pivotal year. Most extraordinary is the fact that Neptune, planet of dreams and imagination, was within two minutes of her natal South Node (19SG22).

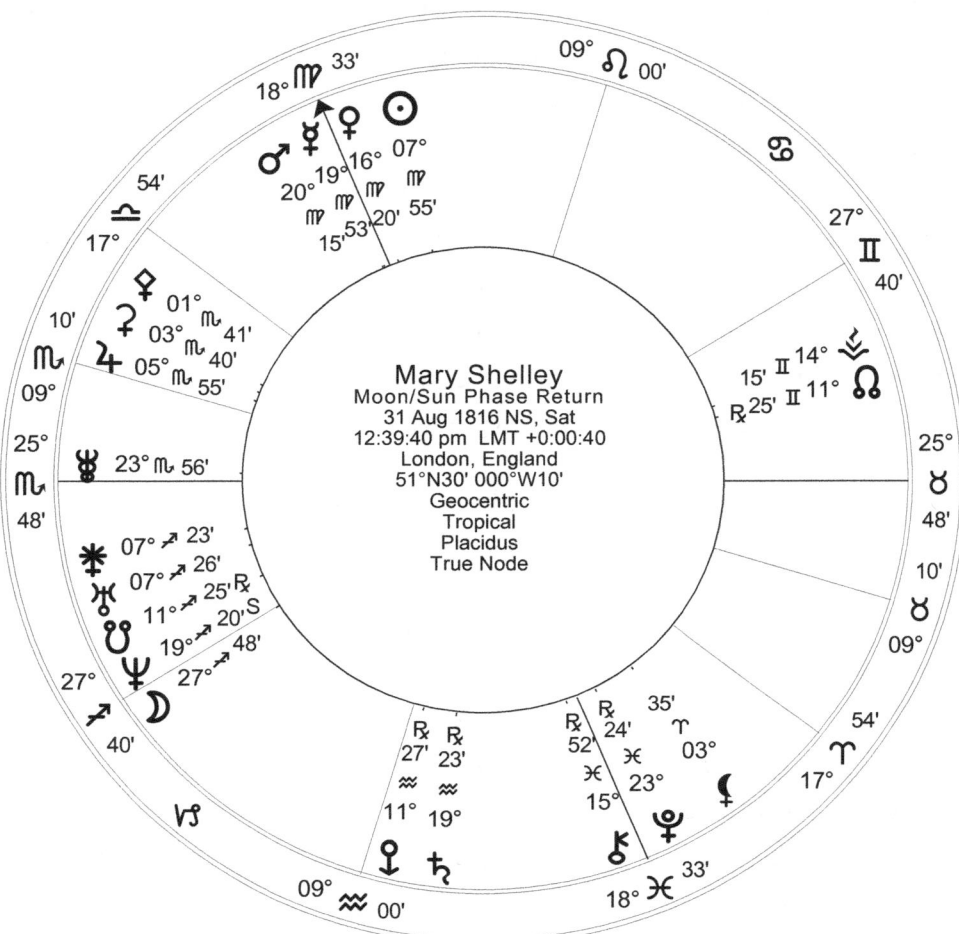

It would be difficult to find a more perfect astrological description for a dream arising from the depths of the unconscious. What is even more astounding is that same transiting Neptune (19SG20) was within two hours of its exact station.

Neptune is associated with the collective unconscious. It resonates with mystery and imagination. Mary's novel was an instant sensation. Neptune provided Mary with access to universal symbols and themes that spoke to the masses. Her tale of Dr Frankenstein and his monster has endured through the ages, appearing in numerous films and adaptations since her dream awakened her that cold summer morning in Switzerland in 1816.

MARK ZUCKERBERG

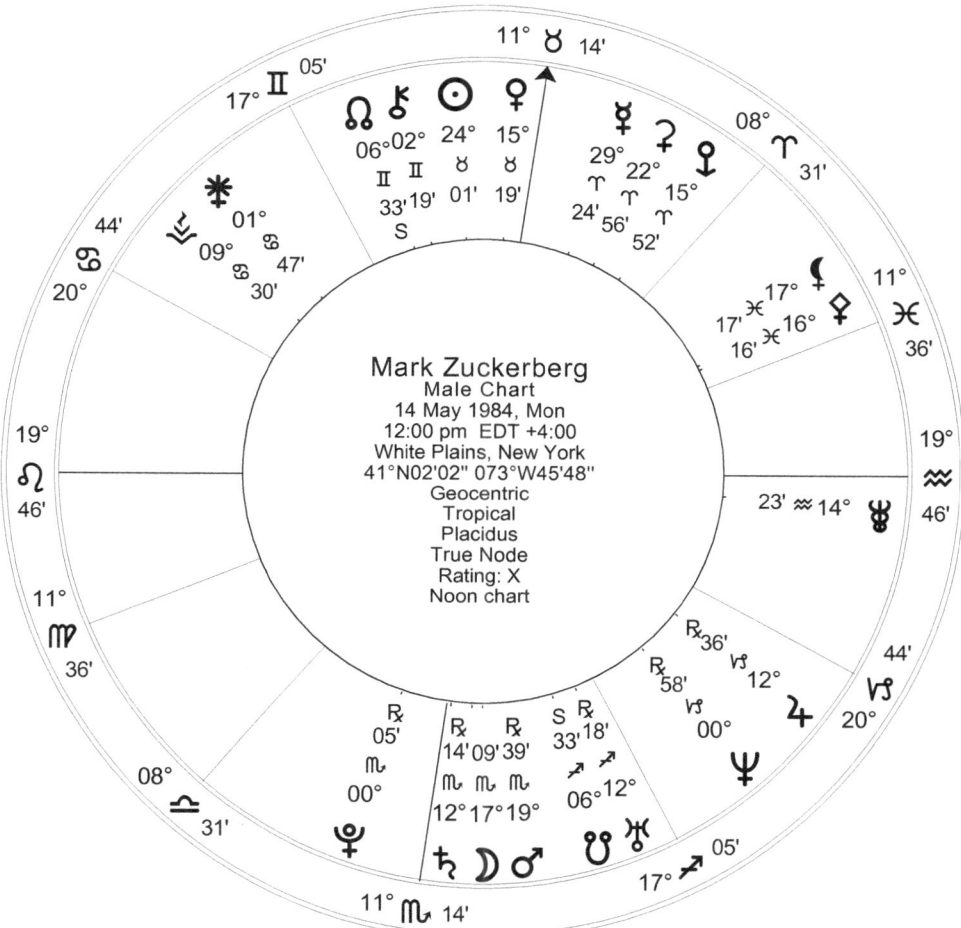

It's rare that people achieve global success that endures over time, and far less common for it to happen at the age of 19. But another example is Mark Zuckerberg who created Facebook at this age. Unfortunately, we don't have a birth time for Zuckerberg, which could affect the accuracy of the Lunar Phase Return in terms of its exact Moon position, chart angles and houses, but it does not affect stationary planets which have a minimum orb of several days.

Zuckerberg created the first version of Facebook (Facesmash) in 2003. It was an immediate success and quickly evolved into the

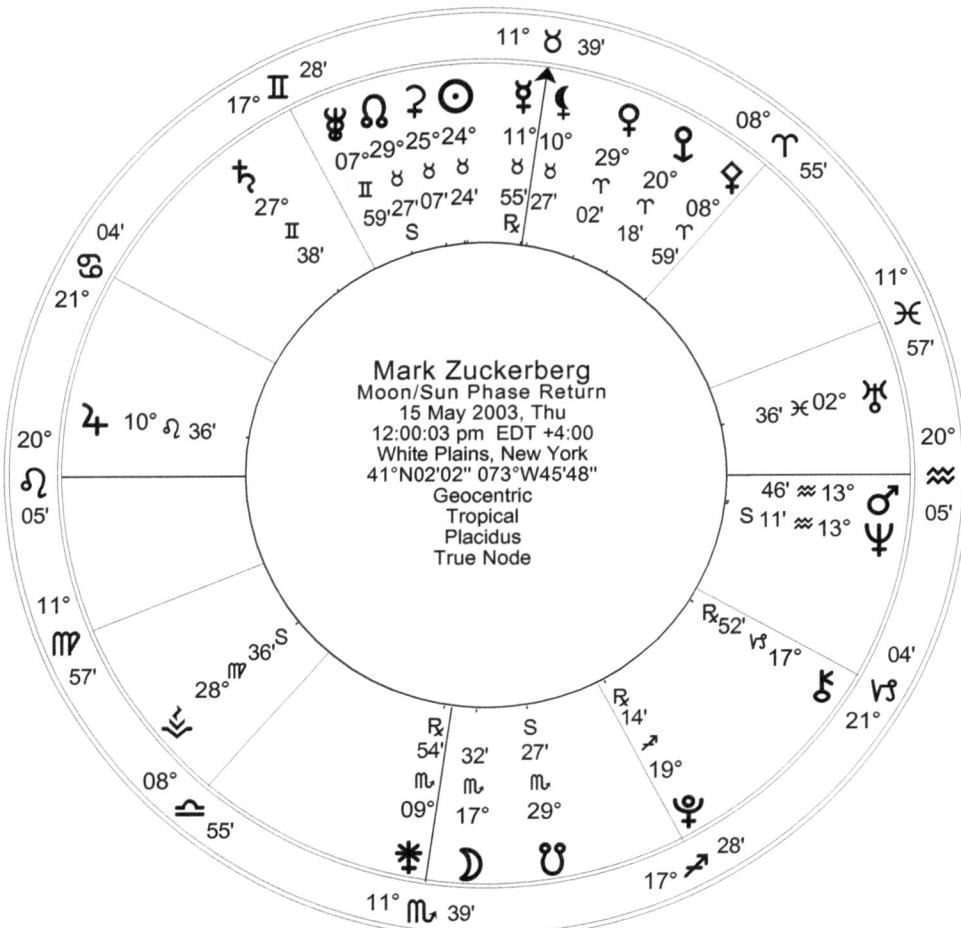

Facebook we know today. In his Lunar Phase Return for 2003, you'll notice that Neptune is once again marked with an S to indicate it's stationary. In fact, based on a noon natal chart, it's about nine hours away from its exact station. So whatever time of day he was born, Neptune is still going to be within hours of its exact station in this Lunar Phase Return.

Mars (13AQ46) is in a tight conjunction with SR Neptune (13AQ11). Interestingly, both planets are located in Aquarius, the sign we associate with friendship. Helping friends to connect was the reason that Zuckerberg created Facebook.

As we know, Facebook has become a global phenomenon with billions of users. Once again, we see the power of Neptune. Clearly both Shelley and Zuckerberg were able to tap into the collective unconscious and create something with universal appeal. Like Frankenstein's monster, Facebook links together various people who are remote from one another. Some would argue that it too, is a monster.

NEIL ARMSTRONG

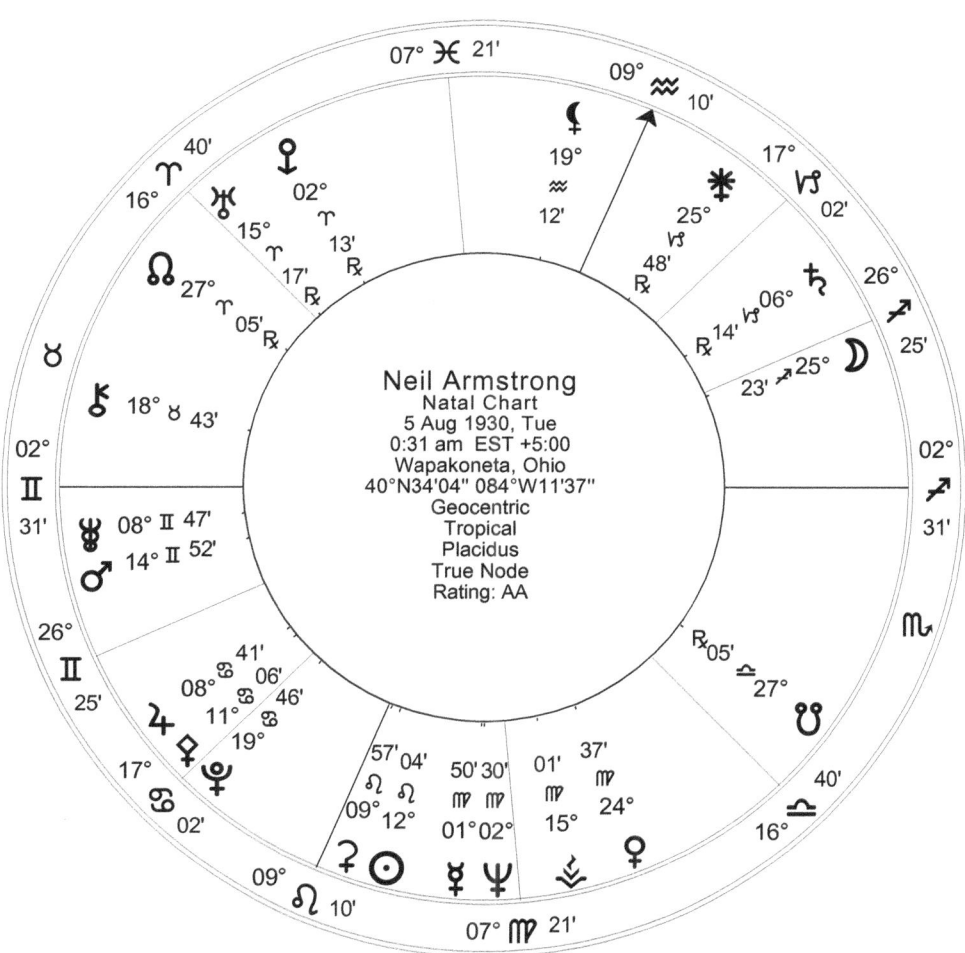

Neil Armstrong captured the world's imagination when he became the first man to set foot on the Moon at the age of 38. It was, and is, a landmark event in human history. Armstrong was having his second Metonic Cycle Lunar Phase Return. Fortunately, we have a very precise birth time for him.

In Armstrong's Lunar Phase Return for his 38th birthday in August 1968, Neptune could not be more prominent. It's on the Midheaven, and again it's stationary. In this case it's turning direct and is within just 58 minutes of its exact station. SR Saturn (25AR32) and SR Hygiea (10AR09) are also seen in this Lunar Phase Return. Significantly, SR Saturn is making a conjunction to his natal North Node (27AR05).

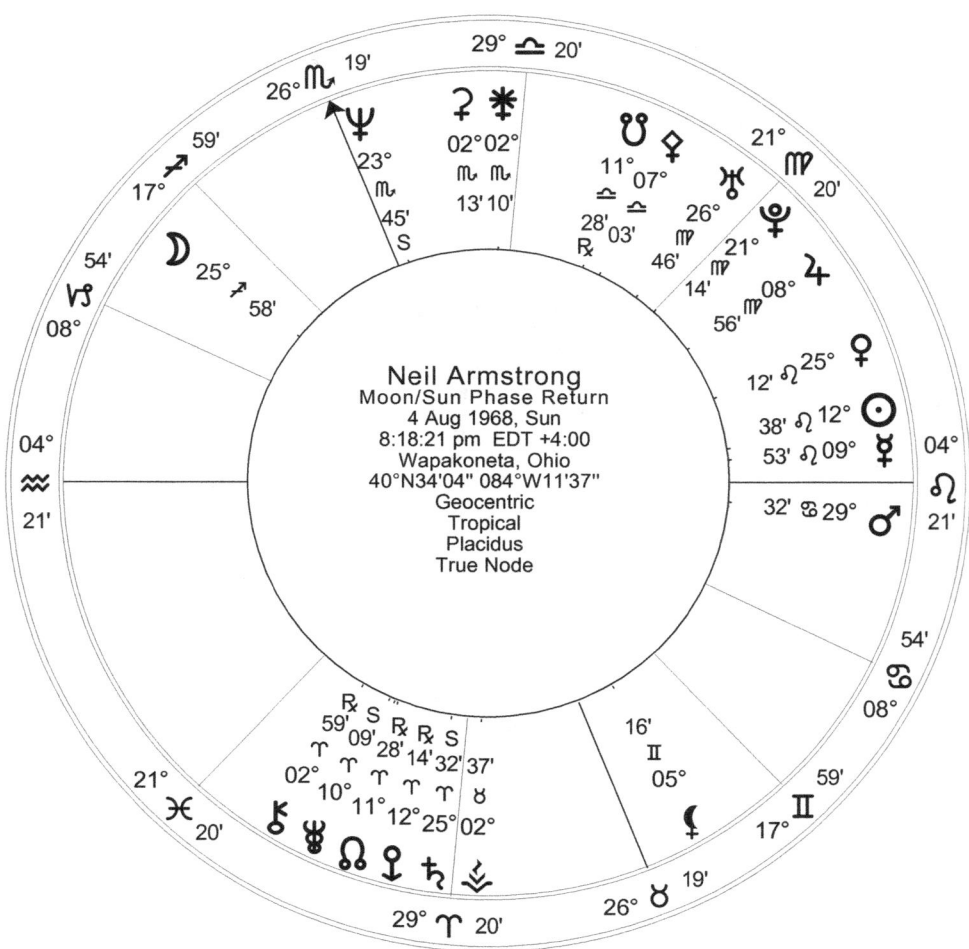

Eleven months later the whole world watched in awe when Neil Armstrong set foot on the Moon and uttered those immortal words.

Neptune's symbolism is evident in all three of these stories and not just because of their powerful global resonance. No one believed that 19 year old Mary Shelley had penned Frankenstein. In keeping with Neptune's theme, it seemed beyond belief. Similarly, Mark Zuckerberg was challenged by fellow students from Harvard who accused him of misleading them to believe he would help build a social network called ConnectU.[78] Was this a Neptunian deception by Zuckerberg, or a fraudulent accusation? We may never know the full story. That's the way it is with Neptune. Even with the Moon landing in 1969, conspiracy theories abound that it never actually happened and was staged.

Not many people do something amazing at the age of 19, 38, 57 or 76. But since first discovering the incredible sphere of influence of stationary Neptune in these Lunar Phase Returns, I have managed to identify a couple of other people whose Lunar Phase Returns for the age of 19 have stationary planets other than Neptune.

PRINCESS DIANA

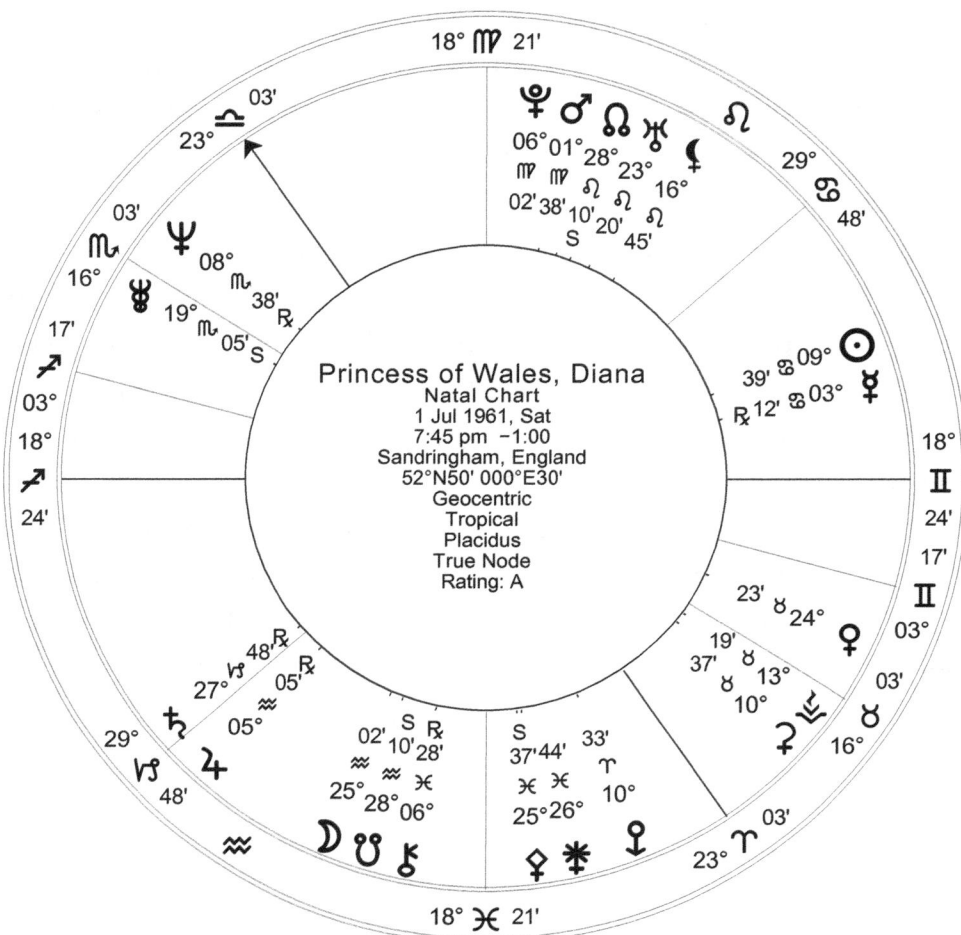

Looking for other individuals who might fit this theme of widespread global attention, I was keen to see whether Neptune was stationary in the Lunar Phase Return for Princess Diana. Diana was 19 when Prince Charles proposed to her on 3 February 1981 and when the Royal engagement was officially announced on 24 February 1981. They married that same year, just after Diana's 20th birthday.

Diana's Lunar Phase Return for her 19th birthday in 1980 shows not Neptune, but Venus stationing direct. This perfectly symbolises her engagement. Venus was stationing direct (16GE32) which is indicative

Lunar Phase Returns

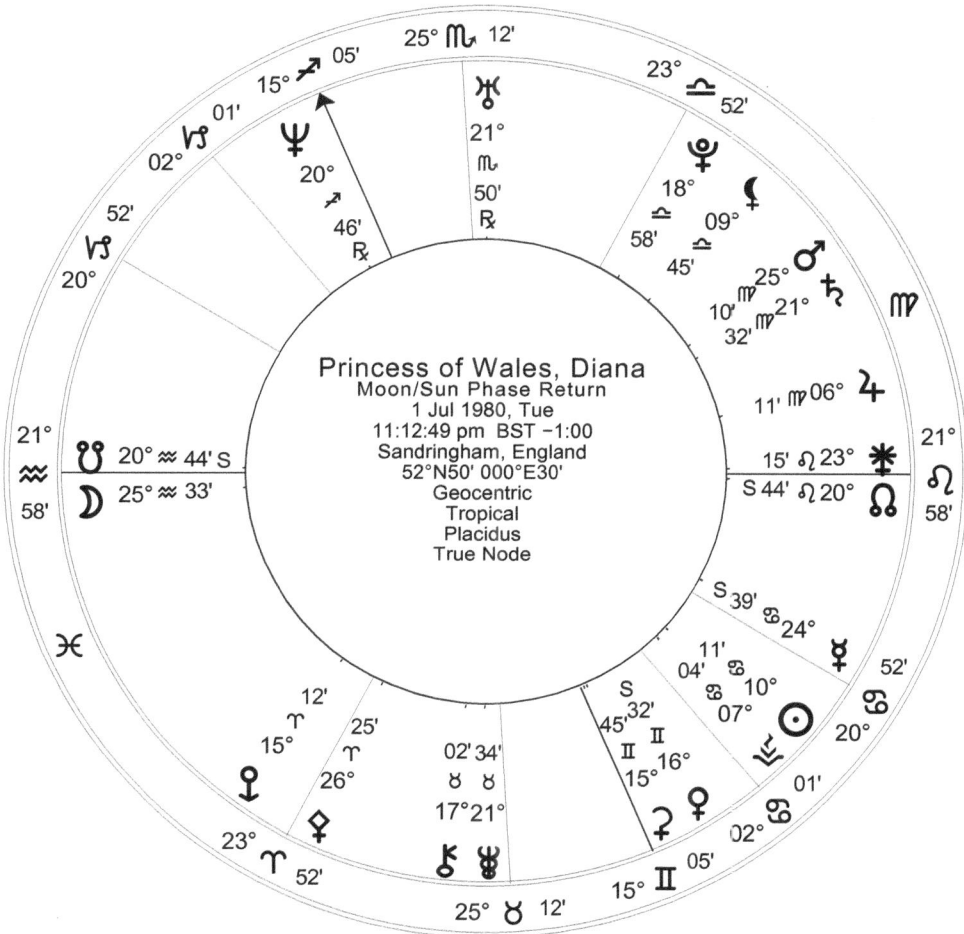

of a new relationship commitment. Venus was conjunct Ceres. Note that the North Node (20LE44) and the goddess of marriage Juno (23LE15) are not only in the royal sign of Leo, but also significantly located in this chart, straddling the Descendant, with the Moon in opposition. These are key indicators of her betrothal.

Looking at the bi-wheel, we can see a number of additional powerful alignments. Significantly, stationary Venus (16GE32) is within a couple of degrees of her natal Descendant (18GE24). You could not get a more apt description for marriage. With Ceres close by, motherhood would play a major role in her new life.

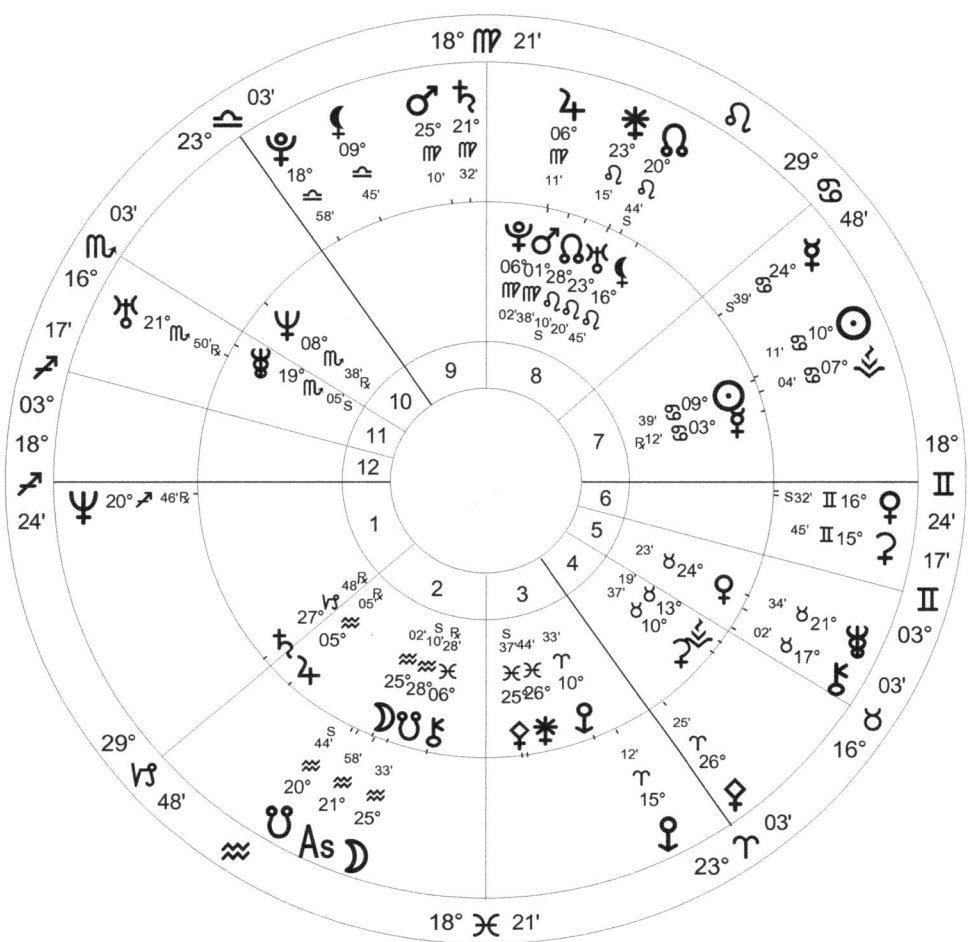

Inner Wheel: Diana.
Outer Wheel: Her Lunar Phase Return.

Transiting Juno (23LE15) sits right on her natal Uranus (23LE20) and activates her natal Moon-Uranus opposition. This speaks to the conflict she would face between being loyal to her marriage vows, versus being free to be herself.

In her Lunar Phase Return, Mercury too is stationary, turning retrograde (24CN39). This station sextiles Mars (25VI10) and Saturn (21VI32) and activates an awkward yod that focuses on her Moon-Uranus complex.

The engagement was officially announcement on 24 February at 11am.[79] Transiting Juno had stationed retrograde the previous day. In the chart for the announcement, stationary Juno (07SC47) sits with the Moon (07SC28), and they were making a conjunction to Diana's natal Neptune (08SC38). There was no backing out now.

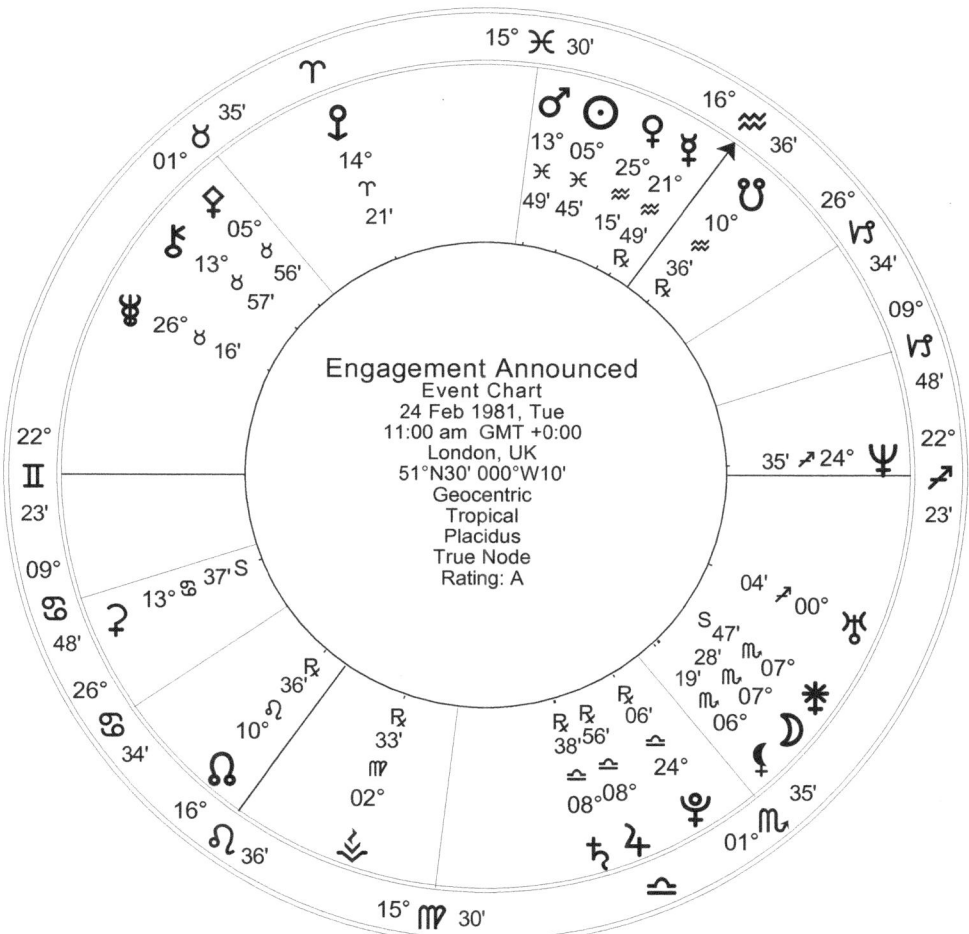

HELEN KELLER

Many people have no stationary planets in their birth charts. Whether we do have a stationary planet or not, when transiting planets station and 'hit' a sensitive point it in our chart, it can have a dramatic impact.

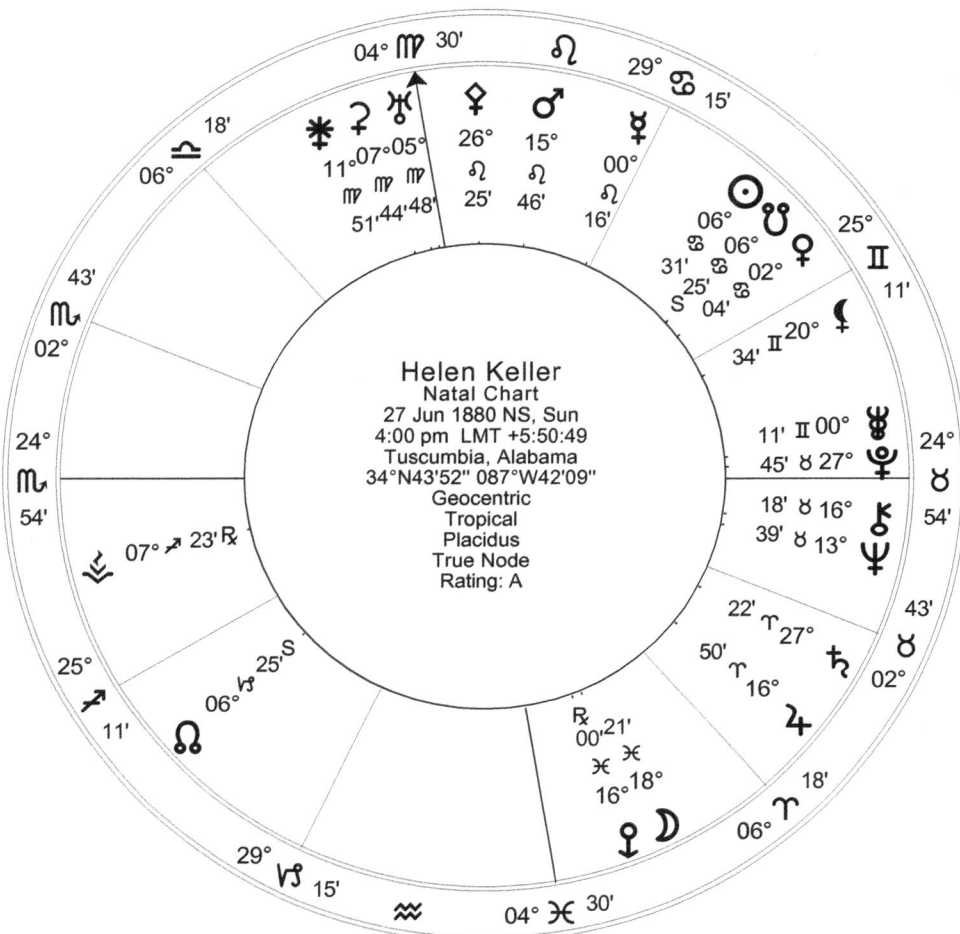

We can see an example of this in the chart of Helen Keller.[80] When Helen was 19 months old she contracted a fever which left her blind and deaf.

In her autobiography,[81] Helen writes that in February 1882 she was struck down by a strange fever that would leave her unable to see or hear. Unfortunately, we don't know the exact date she fell ill, but around that time there were a number of stationary transits, all of them turning direct. On 10 January transiting Jupiter stationed direct (16TA12) within just six minutes of arc of her natal 6th house Chiron (16TA18). On 23 January transiting Neptune stationed direct (13TA46) having barely moved from its natal position, also in her 6th house of health. Three days later, Chiron stationed direct at 17TA36, it too having barely moved from its natal position in her 6th house. Chiron and Neptune were travelling in tandem and stationing in tandem throughout 1880 and 1881. Turning direct again shortly before she fell ill, the midpoint of these two stations (15TA41) is just a few minutes of arc away from an exact square to her natal Mars (15LE46). Then, in early February, transiting Mars stationed direct close to her 8th house cusp and Pluto turned direct too.

Date 1882	Transiting Station	Location
6 January	SD Saturn	05TA32
10 January	SD Jupiter	16TA12
23 January	SD Neptune	13TA46
26 January	SD Chiron	17TA36
2 February	SD Mars	26GE57
10 February	SD Pluto	27TA20

Table 4. List of stations in the lead up to Helen's illness.

Helen was born with the South Node in a very tight conjunction with the Sun, five days after a lunar eclipse. There was a solar eclipse a few weeks later.

Helen was always a wilful and determined soul, and she used that passion to help her find a way to reach out through her darkness.

Before her teacher, Anne Sullivan, arrived on 3 March 1887,[82] Helen had devised her own crude type of sign language that she used to communicate her basic needs. Over time she became more and more frustrated at not being able to express herself and her temper would often flare. Helen's father was a newspaper editor, and he understood his daughter's need to communicate. He sought the advice of Alexander Graham Bell. Through various channels, Anne Sullivan came to be recommended. She would become Helen's constant companion and teacher.

When Anne first arrived at the Keller household on 3 March 1887, healing planets Chiron and Hygiea had both recently stationed direct. Chiron stationed direct at 18GE01 squaring Helen's Moon, and Hygiea at 03CN06, between Helen's Sun-North Node conjunction and her Venus.

It's worth noting that on 12 March 1887 when Helen's lessons first began, Mercury stationed retrograde (06AR22) while squaring her Sun (06CN31) and Nodal Axis (06CN25).

On 17 March 1887 transiting Saturn stationed direct at 15CN34 in sextile aspect to Helen's Chiron-Neptune, providing new opportunities for her to learn through the daily discipline of Anne's instruction. According to Anne Sullivan's notes which accompany Helen's autobiography, she first won Helen's trust at this time.

Date 1887	Transiting Station	Location
16 January	SR Uranus	12LI29
4 February	SD Neptune	25TA01
14 February	SD Pluto	02GE05
19 February	SR Jupiter	05SC52
22 February	SD Chiron	18GE01
23 February	SD Hygiea	03CN23
5 March	SR Vesta	03SC06
12 March	SR Mercury	06AR22
17 March	SD Saturn	15CN34
4 April	SD Mercury	23PI31

Table 5. Stations in early 1887.

It was on the 4th or 5th of April 1887[83] when Helen first knew that words had meaning. As recounted in the movie *The Miracle Worker*, the light dawned when Helen realised that the sign for water was not just a word game, but actually meant water. With her Sun in Cancer, her Moon in Pisces and Scorpio rising, it seems that 'water' was something that Helen intrinsically understood.

At that time, on 4 April at 11.46am in Tuscumbia, Alabama, Mercury stationed direct in water sign Pisces (23PI31).

What an extraordinary learning curve she managed to climb. Helen was highly intelligent, and she learnt sign language quickly. She learnt Braille and how to write. By 1890, at the age of ten, Helen was learning to speak. Incredibly, she wrote a brief account of her experiences at the age of 12 which was published in *Youth's Companion*.

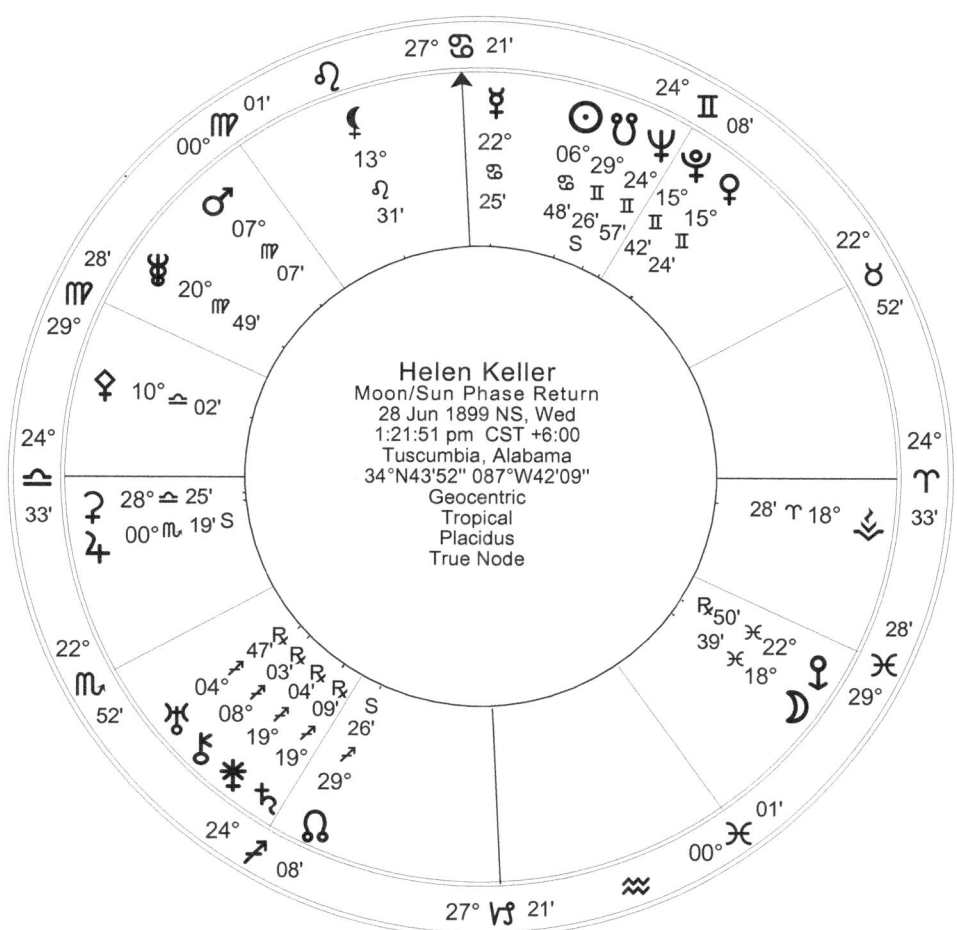

On 27 June 1899 Helen turned 19. Just days later, on the 29th and 30th of June 1899 she took her entrance examinations for Radcliffe College.[84] She excelled and was enrolled.

Helen's Lunar Phase Return for age 19 has the planet of higher education, Jupiter, stationary direct (00SC19). Jupiter stationed direct exactly on Helen's 19th birthday and it was in an extremely tight square to her natal Mercury (00LE16). This is highly significant given that both Mercury and Jupiter are naturally associated with learning and education. This fixed square no doubt signifies the challenges she faced to be accepted into college, as well as her determination to succeed.

> *'Trying to write is very much like trying to put a Chinese puzzle together. We have a pattern in mind which we wish to work out in words; but the words will not fit the spaces, or, if they do, they will not match the design. But we keep on trying because we know that others have succeeded, and we are not willing to acknowledge defeat'. Helen Keller.*[85]

Helen's dedication to the challenge of learning was never in question. She graduated from college with honours. She wrote her autobiography while at Radcliffe which was published in 1902 when she was just 22.

Helen not only learned to communicate, but incredibly went on to write numerous books and essays. She learned several languages, translated books, gave lectures and travelled extensively. Her amazing healing journey is a compelling example of the Chiron myth. Though she never regained her sight or hearing, Helen was healed through the support and guidance of her teacher, Anne Sullivan.[86]

Helen Keller led a remarkable life. She overcame monumental challenges and made an incredible contribution, helping to heal others and inspiring people across the world. Despite being deaf and blind, she led a full, productive and successful life. Helen Keller passed away in 1968 just before her 88th birthday.

These stories illustrate the powerful influence of stationary planets in terms of transits to our natal chart. Lunar Phase Returns are a potent astrological tool in themselves, but if you happen to spot a stationary planet in one of these returns, whether for the age of 19, 38, 57 or 76, these examples suggest the most incredible life altering events can transpire.

Whatever challenges we face in life, there is no doubt that stationary planets, wherever they are found, in the birth chart, in returns, when transiting, or when progressing, provide us with enormous opportunities. All we have to do is take the time to master them.

FINAL WORDS

Appendices one and two that follow, list all the zodiacal positions of the stationary planets I have examined. There is an alphabetical list and the other is listed according to zodiac degree. All 15 planetary bodies that I have explored are included.

In total, there are 522 stationary planets. These were identified in 302 birth charts. I have not included any of the event or return charts I have covered, only stationary planets found in the birth charts are listed. All charts have been calculated using the 30 percent rule.

When I was compiling these lists, I was immediately struck by the fact that there are relatively few stationary planets in Leo, so I decided to take a closer look. It turns out that there is a corresponding spike in the opposite sign, Aquarius. It seems odd that stationary bodies seem to prefer to be located in Aquarius and to avoid being in Leo, at least in the charts of the famous and infamous people I have so far examined.

To verify and check whether or not something statistically significant is at work here, I consulted Associate Professor John O'Byrne at Sydney University who was kind enough to assist me and provide his advice. John was most helpful and guided me in working out the significance of these findings. While 522 is not a huge sample size, it is potentially big enough to provide some meaningful statistical results.

The first thing he said was that it did seem strange to have such an emphasis in Aquarius and corresponding lack in Leo, especially given there were 15 different planetary bodies included, but he said that seasonal birth data could possibly account for this.

Most of the 302 people are born in the northern hemisphere, in Europe and the US where births more usually happen in August and September.[87] However, when I looked at the distribution of my 302 birth charts there was no real emphasis in any particular Sun sign, so we can rule this out. The p value for the distribution of Sun signs is 0.849 which is not significant.

However, the distribution of stationary planets is significant at the 0.5 level and with the extra zeros in front, it's even more so. This could just be a fluke, but equally there could be something going on here that we cannot account for.

Category	Observed	Expected		
Aries	44	43.5		
Taurus	46	43.5		
Gemini	50	43.5		
Cancer	46	43.5		
Leo	24	43.5		
Virgo	33	43.5		
Libra	47	43.5		
Scorpio	55	43.5		
Sagittarius	35	43.5		
Capricorn	36	43.5		
Aquarius	62	43.5		
Pisces	43	43.5		
Total	521		0.005811	p value

Table 6. Stationary planet distribution by sign.

Category	Observed	Expected		
Aries	18	25.1666		
Taurus	25	25.1666		
Gemini	29	25.1666		
Cancer	30	25.1666		
Leo	30	25.1666		
Virgo	21	25.1666		
Libra	27	25.1666		
Scorpio	21	25.1666		
Sagittarius	23	25.1666		
Capricorn	24	25.1666		
Aquarius	29	25.1666		
Pisces	24	25.1666		
Total	301		0.849426	p value

Table 7. Sun sign distribution.

I should mention that of the 302 individuals, around ten percent were born in the southern hemisphere, which is around the same distribution as global population; that is, around 90 percent of people are born in the northern hemisphere.

From an astrological point of view, I find it incredibly interesting that stationary planets prefer to be located in Aquarius and avoid being in Leo, at least as far as these famous and infamous people are concerned.

The Sun is the ruling planet of Leo, and since stationary planets are a by-product of their relationship to the Sun (consciousness), these findings seem to support my theory that stations provide us with an opportunity to integrate their message into consciousness. It's only by experiencing those things that are unfamiliar (opposite) and being tested by them, that consciousness grows. Of course, whether or not we pass the 'test of time' is another matter altogether.

At this stage I have not had the opportunity to replicate these findings, but I did a quick check of a random sample group of mostly southern hemisphere, 20th Century births for comparison. These were taken from my client files, so the people were not famous, nor infamous. I looked at over 500 charts and found 436 stationary planets. This is fewer overall stations for the number of charts examined, but it did not show up any significant sign emphasis.

If anyone is interested to do further follow up research into stationary planets, please get in touch.

~~~~~

Life is a bit like the game of golf. Some golf courses are more difficult than others. Even if people are playing on the same course, with similar sets of clubs, there's an infinite number of different routes to take. Some people will try really hard but end up in the rough or a bunker, others might get lucky and sink a hole in one. In life, as in golf, we each have different handicaps too. It helps to have a map of the course we are playing and to learn the rules of the game. It takes time, you need patience and lots of practice. Hopefully, we learn from our mistakes and improve over time.

~~~~~

APPENDIX ONE

ALPHABETICAL LISTING OF INDIVIDUALS WITH STATIONARY PLANETS

Surname	First Name	Degrees	Stationary Planet	SR/SD
14th Dalai Lama		25GE35	Mercury	SD
14th Dalai Lama		13SC28	Jupiter	SD
Abbott	Tony	18GE15	Juno	SR
Agnew	Spiro	15CN46	Jupiter	SR
Agnew	Spiro	09LE19	Neptune	SR
Alexander	Jason	29LE53	Venus	SD
Ali	Muhammad	21TA39	Saturn	SD
Ali	Muhammad	25TA17	Hygiea	SD
Ali	Muhammad	20AQ40	Venus	SR
Allen	Peter	04GE49	Uranus	SD
Allen	Peter	24GE25	Ceres	SD
Allen	Woody	20AR29	Juno	SD
Alzheimer	Alois	11LI18	Saturn	SD
Alzheimer	Alois	15PI02	Chiron	SR
Amundsen	Roald	15AR04	Chiron	SR
Amundsen	Roald	03SG07	Hygiea	SD
Andrews	Daniel	18GE24	Venus	SD
Andrews	Julie	06VI38	Venus	SD
Applewhite	Marshall	04TA07	Mercury	SD

Applewhite	Marshall	02VI59	Neptune	SD
Applewhite	Marshall	02LI13	Ceres	SD
Applewhite	Marshall	21CP57	Vesta	SR
Archer	Jeffrey	00LE36	Pluto	SD
Archer	Jeffrey	06VI31	Ceres	SD
Armstrong	Lance	06GE31	Saturn	SR
Armstrong	Lance	12AQ26	Mars	SD
Assange	Julian	21AQ32	Mars	SR
Bacall	Lauren	08TA10	Ceres	SR
Bacall	Lauren	21TA15	Hygiea	SR
Bacall	Lauren	25AQ35	Mars	SD
Bader Ginsburg	Ruth	07AR12	Mercury	SR
Battle	Kathleen	13AR33	Juno	SR
Battle	Kathleen	19SG06	Jupiter	SD
Baudelaire	Charles	08SG02	Ceres	SR
Baudelaire	Charles	03CP07	Uranus	SR
Baudelaire	Charles	27PI23	Mercury	SD
Beatty	Warren	05TA37	Venus	SR
Beethoven		13VI59	Neptune	SR
Beethoven		26CP46	Venus	SR
Belushi	John	20AQ10	Mercury	SR
Berry	Chuck	15CN56	Pluto	SR
Berry	Chuck	17AQ20	Jupiter	SD
Berry	Chuck	01PI38	Juno	SD
Biden	Joe	20PI05	Ceres	SD
Bieber	Justin	02SC31	Juno	SR
Bieber	Justin	14SC39	Jupiter	SR
Bieber	Justin	28SC04	Pluto	SR
Blair	Tony	15AR01	Venus	SD
Blake	William	19PI17	Uranus	SD
Bligh	William	04TA24	Pallas Athena	SR
Bligh	William	17TA05	Vesta	SR
Bligh	William	10CP56	Saturn	SD
Bolan	Marc	26GE10	Uranus	SR
Bolt	Usain	17AR25	Vesta	SR
Bolt	Usain	11CP59	Mars	SD
Bono	Sonny	23LI58	Mars	SR
Borg	Bjorn	00GE14	Mercury	SD
Borg	Bjorn	28LI05	Vesta	SD
Borg	Bjorn	08CN15	Venus	SR
Borg	Bjorn	00AQ03	Hygiea	SR

Appendix One

Borgia	Lucrezia	13VI01	Pallas Athena	SD
Borgia	Lucrezia	18VI03	Juno	SD
Branagh	Kenneth	08VI07	Pluto	SR
Brando	Marlon	19SG54	Jupiter	SR
Branson	Richard	06SG01	Ceres	SD
Branson	Richard	10SG57	Hygiea	SD
Brennan	Eileen	12CP28	Ceres	SD
Brennan	Eileen	28CP40	Chiron	SR
Brockovich	Erin	29AQ10	Ceres	SR
Browning	Robert	09AQ58	Eris	SR
Browning	Robert	15CP42	Juno	SR
Bryant	Martin	14CP23	Hygiea	SR
Bundy	Ted	08LE52	Saturn	SR
Calment	Jeanne	00CN23	Ceres	SD
Calment	Jeanne	01SC36	Jupiter	SR
Calment	Jeanne	16PI38	Mercury	SR
Campbell	Joseph	04SG48	Pallas Athena	SR
Capote	Truman	20AQ56	Vesta	SD
Capote	Truman	25AQ48	Mars	SD
Cardinal George Pell		24VI54	Neptune	SD
Carter	Jimmy	20AQ56	Vesta	SD
Carter	Jimmy	25AQ53	Mars	SD
Carter	Rubin	19AR34	Venus	SD
Carter	Rubin	25VI28	Juno	SR
Castro	Fidel	06TA05	Chiron	SR
Castro	Fidel	24VI02	Venus	SR
Catherine the Great		05CP04	Juno	SR
Cezanne	Paul	29VI16	Mars	SR
Chamberlain	Lindy	22GE06	Uranus	SD
Chamberlain	Lindy	14CN13	Vesta	SD
Chamberlain	Lindy	21AQ33	Mercury	SD
Chanel	Coco	22AR04	Pallas Athena	SR
Chaplin	Charles	18TA06	Venus	SR
Chaplin	Charles	13LE25	Saturn	SD
Chapman	Mark David	25CP04	Ceres	SR
Chapman	Mark David	05AQ30	Chiron	SR
Christie	Agatha	15LI13	Mercury	SR
Churchill	Winston	12PI13	Eris	SD
Cline	Patsy	28TA39	Chiron	SR
Cline	Patsy	12CP37	Ceres	SD
Clinton	Bill	01TA43	Hygiea	SR

Clinton	Bill	27SG57	Pallas Athena	SD
Clinton	Hillary	04CN19	Hygiea	SR
Clinton	Hillary	21SC23	Mercury	SR
Clinton	Hillary	28AQ28	Pallas Athena	SD
Clooney	George	29CP50	Saturn	SR
Clooney	George	13AR04	Venus	SD
Close	Glenn	27SC31	Jupiter	SR
Close	Glenn	09PI31	Mercury	SD
Connors	Jimmy	20TA54	Jupiter	SR
Cooke	Sam	14TA00	Chiron	SD
Cooke	Sam	04GE19	Hygiea	SD
Copernicus	Nicholas	26PI30	Mercury	SR
Corby	Schapelle	14AR30	Eris	SR
Corby	Schapelle	14SC20	Juno	SD
Court	Margaret	07SC42	Juno	SD
Coward	Noel	05SG49	Mercury	SD
Crane	Bob	07AR23	Uranus	SR
Crane	Bob	03CN32	Mercury	SD
Crane	Bob	17PI58	Ceres	SR
Cromwell	Oliver	22LE59	Neptune	SD
Cromwell	Oliver	17VI38	Pallas Athena	SD
Cruise	Tom	06PI57	Hygiea	SR
Cruise	Tom	12PI41	Jupiter	SR
Culpeper	Nicholas	20GE22	Ceres	SR
Culpeper	Nicholas	14CN21	Uranus	SR
Culpeper	Nicholas	11AQ46	Chiron	SD
Curie	Marie	11CN50	Vesta	SR
Dahmer	Jeffrey L.	17CP13	Vesta	SR
Dahmer	Jeffrey L.	29CP04	Pallas Athena	SR
Dali	Salvador	00AQ06	Chiron	SR
Darwin	Charles	09SC40	Uranus	SR
De Havilland	Olivia	17SC35	Juno	SD
De Havilland	Olivia	26PI20	Chiron	SR
Dean	James	15LI24	Ceres	SR
Dillinger	John	24PI10	Eris	SR
Douglas	Kirk	21PI48	Chiron	SD
Earhart	Amelia	24SC07	Saturn	SD
Eastwood	Clint	23TA48	Mercury	SD
Eastwood	Clint	06AQ19	Juno	SR
Edison	Thomas	19LI33	Vesta	SR
Edwards	Blake	17AR29	Chiron	SR

Edwards	Blake	03SG03	Hygiea	SD
Edwards	Blake	11SG44	Mars	SD
Eichmann	Adolph	07CN36	Neptune	SD
Eichmann	Adolph	09LE27	Juno	SD
Epstein	Jeffrey	03GE23	Ceres	SD
Evans	Cadel	10LI27	Ceres	SR
Evans	Cadel	11SC47	Uranus	SR
Faraday	Michael	16TA09	Pallas Athena	SR
Faraday	Michael	20LI08	Mercury	SR
Faraday	Michael	03SC20	Venus	SR
Farmer	Frances	04AQ01	Vesta	SD
Farmer	Frances	28TA51	Hygiea	SR
Fisher	Carrie	17AQ10	Pallas Athena	SD
Fisher	Carrie	14PI00	Mars	SD
Fitzgerald	F. Scott	20GE18	Neptune	SR
Fitzgerald	F. Scott	24LI48	Mercury	SR
Fleiss	Heidi	13AQ07	Venus	SR
Fleming	Alexander	10SG06	Ceres	SD
Fonda	Jane	03AR06	Eris	SD
Fonda	Jane	21VI09	Neptune	SR
Fonda	Jane	15CP33	Mercury	SR
Ford	Betty	07LE36	Saturn	SD
Ford	Betty	19SG13	Pallas Athena	SR
Ford	Harrison	07SC34	Juno	SD
Foster	Jodie	06PI09	Chiron	SD
Fox	Michael J.	06PI41	Chiron	SR
Franklin	Benjamin	12TA54	Saturn	SD
Franklin	Benjamin	12AQ19	Mercury	SR
Frazier	Joe	04GE16	Vesta	SD
Frazier	Joe	05GE11	Mars	SD
Freud	Sigmund	03LI22	Mars	SD
Freud	Sigmund	05AQ41	Chiron	SR
Fry	Stephen	21AR32	Vesta	SR
Fry	Stephen	24VI48	Mercury	SR
Gabriel	Peter	11LI01	Mars	SR
Gabriel	Peter	04AQ07	Venus	SD
Galileo		15CN48	Hygiea	SD
Galileo		02SC11	Vesta	SR
Gandhi	Indira	26PI38	Vesta	SD
Gandhi	Mohandas	03GE12	Ceres	SR
Garbo	Greta	16GE25	Jupiter	SR

The Test of Time

Garfunkel	Art	05LE47	Pluto	SR
Garfunkel	Art	11AR11	Mars	SD
Garfunkel	Art	26LI27	Mercury	SD
Garland	Judy	08LI59	Jupiter	SD
Garland	Judy	26LI02	Ceres	SD
Gauquelin	Michel	09CN16	Mars	SR
Gershwin	George	24GE47	Neptune	SR
Getty	John Paul	15AR02	Jupiter	SD
Getty	John Paul	17LE24	Hygiea	SR
Getty	John Paul	03VI58	Chiron	SR
Gillard	Julia	04GE28	Vesta	SR
Gillard	Julia	23CP14	Saturn	SD
Gillard	Julia	27CP22	Jupiter	SD
Gillard	Julia	26TA45	Ceres	SR
Glenn	John	11CN09	Mercury	SD
Glenn	John	13AR58	Chiron	SR
Goodman	Linda	02TA36	Mercury	SR
Goodman	Linda	20SG14	Juno	SR
Gorbachev	Mikhail	10CN29	Jupiter	SD
Gorbachev	Mikhail	27CN38	Mars	SD
Gould	Shane	06AR50	Ceres	SD
Graham	Billy	15CN47	Jupiter	SR
Grant	Ulysses S.	00CP50	Vesta	SR
Graves	Robert	15SC51	Uranus	SD
Graves	Robert	07SG52	Pallas Athena	SD
Hamilton-Byrne	Anne	09TA49	Vesta	SD
Hanks	Tom	22GE50	Venus	SD
Hanks	Tom	27LI38	Neptune	SD
Hanson	Pauline	08CP26	Mars	SR
Hari	Mata	00TA21	Chiron	SR
Hari	Mata	05TA19	Neptune	SR
Hari	Mata	14CN02	Venus	SD
Harris	Rolf	17CN26	Pluto	SD
Hawke	Bob	16LE16	Vesta	SR
Hawke	Bob	03VI35	Neptune	SR
Hawking	Stephen	20AQ46	Venus	SR
Hearst	Patty	09SC20	Saturn	SR
Hearst	Patty	16PI04	Mercury	SR
Henry	Lenny	19SG06	Saturn	SD
Hitchcock	Alfred	03SG59	Uranus	SD
Hitchcock	Alfred	14SG22	Juno	SD

Appendix One

Hitler	Adolf	08CP14	Jupiter	SR
Hoffman	Philip Seymour	12AR27	Saturn	SR
Hoffman	Philip Seymour	12CN39	Mercury	SD
Holiday	Billie	27CN39	Neptune	SD
Holt	Harold	06CN32	Venus	SD
Houston	Brian	16GE29	Jupiter	SD
Houston	Brian	13LI03	Ceres	SR
Houston	Brian	09SC21	Saturn	SR
Houston	Whitney	19AR28	Jupiter	SR
Howard	John	08AR46	Jupiter	SR
Howard	John	24LE02	Mercury	SR
Hubbard	L. Ron	25GE53	Pluto	SD
Hutton	Barbara	06PI25	Chiron	SD
Irwin	Bindi-Sue	02AR11	Pallas Athena	SR
Irwin	Bindi-Sue	27PI59	Jupiter	SR
Jackson	Michael	19SG07	Saturn	SD
Jobs	Steve	21SC09	Saturn	SR
Jobs	Steve	19LI51	Hygiea	SR
Jobs	Steve	14AQ21	Mercury	SD
Jobs	Steve	18SC07	Juno	SR
Johnson	Boris	05PI01	Saturn	SR
Johnson	Boris	18PI47	Chiron	SR
Johnson	Lyndon B.	04CP27	Juno	SD
Jones	James Earl	18VI50	Pallas Athena	SR
Jones	James Earl	06CP03	Mercury	SD
Jones	Jim	02VI59	Neptune	SD
Jones	Jim	03TA35	Mercury	SD
Jones	Jim	02LI14	Ceres	SD
Jones	Tom	13CN15	Venus	SR
Jung	Carl G.	26AR24	Chiron	SR
Jung	Carl G.	21SG22	Mars	SD
Kahlo	Frida	00SC41	Juno	SD
Kahlo	Frida	27PI26	Saturn	SR
Keating	Paul	04GE15	Vesta	SD
Keating	Paul	05GE14	Mars	SD
Keating	Paul	08CP54	Mercury	SD
Keaton	Buster	16AQ17	Hygiea	SD
Keaton	Buster	18VI43	Venus	SD
Keaton	Buster	25AQ40	Vesta	SD
Keeler	Christine	05AQ31	Venus	SD
Keeler	Christine	11AQ36	Mercury	SD

Kennedy	Ethel	01VI14	Juno	SD
Kennedy	John F.	20TA36	Mercury	SD
Kennedy	John F.	09AQ51	Hygiea	SR
Kennedy	John F.	13AQ06	Juno	SR
Kennedy	John F.	23AQ43	Uranus	SR
Kennedy	John F. Jnr	18CN30	Mars	SR
Kennedy	Robert	23CN39	Hygiea	SR
Kennedy	Ted	12CN13	Juno	SD
Kennedy Onassis	Jacqui	12AR42	Pallas Athena	SR
Kennett	Jeff	22GE06	Uranus	SD
Kennett	Jeff	14CN12	Vesta	SD
Kennett	Jeff	21AQ39	Mercury	SR
Kidman	Nicole	17SC56	Vesta	SD
King Charles II		05TA10	Venus	SD
King Edward VI		06AQ57	Pluto	SD
King Edward VIII		18LI25	Saturn	SD
King Edward VIII		05SC24	Juno	SD
King Edward VIII		07SC20	Hygiea	SD
King George III		25GE54	Mercury	SR
King Jr	Martin Luther	05TA25	Chiron	SD
King Jr	Martin Luther	21GE53	Mars	SD
King Louis XVI		04TA28	Pallas Athena	SR
King Louis XVI		11SG10	Pluto	SD
King Richard III		01CN50	Chiron	SR
Knievel	Evel	10CN02	Chiron	SR
Knievel	Evel	22AQ23	Jupiter	SD
Koresh	David	07LE51	Mercury	SD
Koresh	David	15VI14	Venus	SR
Kray	Reginald & Ronald	24CN45	Pluto	SR
Kyrgios	Nick	04CP28	Juno	SR
Kyrgios	Nick	25CP33	Neptune	SR
Lady Gaga		16SG28	Juno	SR
Lady Gaga		22SG22	Uranus	SR
Lady Gaga		18PI04	Mercury	SD
Lang	K.D.	22LI33	Mercury	SD
Lang	K.D.	07PI22	Pallas Athena	SD
Lang	K.D.	17PI24	Juno	SD
Lange	Jessica	03VI30	Hygiea	SD
Lange	Jessica	26SG23	Vesta	SR
Ledger	Heath	26PI09	Mercury	SD
Lennox	Annie	07AR38	Eris	SD

Appendix One

Leno	Jay	15LE46	Pluto	SD
Leno	Jay	18VI52	Juno	SD
Leno	Jay	22VI11	Mars	SD
Leno	Jay	22SG28	Hygiea	SR
Leo	Alan	09TA29	Pluto	SR
Leo	Alan	18CN20	Venus	SD
Leo	Alan	20CP10	Mars	SD
Lewinsky	Monica	20AR54	Chiron	SR
Lewinsky	Monica	03SG58	Ceres	SD
Lewinsky	Monica	06SG45	Juno	SD
Lincoln	Abraham	09SC40	Uranus	SR
Lord Byron		08GE30	Vesta	SD
Lord Byron		21LI07	Neptune	SR
Loren	Sophia	17TA17	Pallas Athena	SR
Loren	Sophia	09GE55	Chiron	SR
Love	Courtney	20GE24	Venus	SD
Love	Courtney	18SC25	Pallas Athena	SD
Love	Courtney	19SC26	Juno	SD
Love	Courtney	16PI46	Vesta	SR
Lovelock	James	05AR14	Ceres	SR
MacLaine	Shirley	21VI06	Vesta	SD
MacLaine	Shirley	07CP56	Juno	SR
Mandela	Nelson	00SG32	Pallas Athena	SD
Mann	Thomas	26AQ05	Saturn	SR
Mansfield	Jayne	01VI11	Mars	SD
Manson	Charles	02SC59	Mercury	SD
Marquez	Marc	08CN42	Mars	SD
Marx	Groucho	02AQ21	Jupiter	SD
Marx	Karl	12CP56	Jupiter	SR
Mary Queen of Scots		01TA32	Ceres	SD
Masters	Dr William	15TA30	Ceres	SD
Masters	Dr William	29LE43	Mars	SR
Matisse	Henri	11TA01	Jupiter	SD
Matisse	Henri	19TA09	Ceres	SD
McCartney	Paul	11AQ40	Vesta	SR
McCartney	Paul	26AQ07	Pallas Athena	SR
McGraw	Dr Phil	02LI14	Mercury	SR
Menendez	Erik	09SC56	Venus	SD
Michelangelo		24AR41	Venus	SR
Michelangelo		16CN57	Saturn	SD

Midler	Bette	03LE10	Mars	SR
Milk	Harvey	06AQ01	Juno	SR
Milligan	Spike	10TA23	Mercury	SR
Milligan	Spike	04LE18	Neptune	SD
Milligan	Spike	14VI27	Mars	SD
Milligan	Spike	19SG05	Pallas Athena	SR
Minogue	Kylie	23LI02	Ceres	SD
Morricone	Ennio	09CN16	Mars	SR
Morrison	Jim	05AR00	Pallas Athena	SD
Morrison	Jim	27LE00	Jupiter	SR
Mozart		00CN19	Mars	SD
Mozart		05LI54	Ceres	SR
Mozart		18LI30	Jupiter	SR
Murdoch	Rupert	10CN28	Jupiter	SD
Murdoch	Rupert	27CN29	Mars	SD
Musk	Elon	20AQ56	Mars	SR
Nadal	Rafael	22CP56	Mars	SR
Nash	John	12CN07	Mercury	SR
Navratilova	Martina	06AQ26	Chiron	SD
Navratilova	Martina	17AQ06	Pallas Athena	SD
Navratilova	Martina	13PI35	Mars	SD
Neal	Patricia	11GE09	Pallas Athena	SD
Neal	Patricia	25AQ56	Venus	SR
Newton	Matthew	01GE19	Ceres	SD
Newton	Matthew	14GE44	Mars	SD
Nicholson	Jack	05SG07	Mars	SR
Nightingale	Florence	15AQ33	Eris	SR
Nilsen	Dennis	02LE20	Mars	SR
Nostradamus		02AQ23	Venus	SR
Obama	Barack	00AR39	Juno	SR
Onassis	Aristotle	26TA27	Jupiter	SD
Ono	Yoko	05SC50	Juno	SR
Page	Jimmy	04GE51	Mars	SD
Page	Jimmy	04LI15	Neptune	SR
Pankhurst	Emmeline	26SC23	Pallas Athena	SD
Parker-Bowles	Camilla	17SC41	Jupiter	SD
Pavarotti	Luciano	07PI17	Vesta	SD
Pesci	Joe	00GE34	Uranus	SD
Pesci	Joe	05GE35	Saturn	SD
Piaf	Edith	28LE50	Mars	SR
Picasso	Pablo	24SC14	Mercury	SR

Appendix One

Pistorius	Oscar	02AR39	Vesta	SD
Pistorius	Oscar	05SC11	Venus	SD
Pistorius	Oscar	13SC05	Mercury	SD
Pitt	Brad	10VI04	Uranus	SR
Pitt	Brad	14VI13	Pluto	SR
Plant	Robert	13AR48	Juno	SR
Plant	Robert	19SG07	Jupiter	SD
Polanski	Roman	22AR13	Ceres	SR
Presley	Elvis	27AR29	Uranus	SD
Prince Charles		01AR29	Juno	SD
Prince Harry		25TA16	Ceres	SR
Prince Harry		08GE32	Chiron	SR
Prince Harry		04AQ23	Hygiea	SD
Prince Philip		09PI38	Uranus	SR
Prince William		15LI30	Saturn	SD
Prince William		00SC29	Jupiter	SD
Prince William		12SC56	Ceres	SD
Prince William		24AQ29	Vesta	SR
Princess Diana		19SC05	Hygiea	SD
Princess Diana		25PI37	Pallas Athena	SR
Princess Margaret		18TA54	Chiron	SR
Princess Mary Donaldson		29TA25	Saturn	SD
Princess Mary Donaldson		19LI45	Juno	SR
Putin	Vladimir	17GE17	Ceres	SR
Putin	Vladimir	09AQ29	Juno	SD
Queen Mary I		07CN34	Ceres	SD
Queen Mary I		09CN44	Jupiter	SD
Rampling	Charlotte	21LI29	Chiron	SR
Rampling	Charlotte	27LI18	Jupiter	SR
Rampling	Charlotte	00SC04	Juno	SR
Read	Mark 'Chopper'	29CN56	Jupiter	SR
Reagan	Ronald	23LI14	Juno	SR
Redford	Robert	09TA35	Uranus	SR
Redford	Robert	14SG40	Jupiter	SD
Redgrave	Vanessa	11LI03	Juno	SR
Reeve	Christopher	27TA36	Hygiea	SR
Reeve	Christopher	09AQ17	Juno	SD
Richards	Keith	27LE01	Jupiter	SR
Rinehart	Gina	16GE24	Jupiter	SD
Rinehart	Gina	13LI14	Ceres	SR

Rivers	Joan	20Ll09	Juno	SD
Robbins	Tim	02GE15	Mars	SR
Robbins	Tim	23GE11	Hygiea	SR
Robertson	Geoffrey	21GE47	Uranus	SR
Robertson	Geoffrey	29CP24	Ceres	SD
Roosevelt	Eleanor	24AQ50	Hygiea	SD
Roosevelt	Franklin D.	17TA37	Chiron	SD
Roosevelt	Franklin D.	27GE00	Mars	SD
Rowling	J.K.	02AR46	Ceres	SR
Rowling	J.K.	00Vl02	Mercury	SR
Rowling	J.K.	17SC14	Neptune	SD
Russell	Rosalind	18CP53	Mars	SR
Sellers	Peter	12CP41	Jupiter	SD
Shaw	George Bernard	09AR10	Jupiter	SR
Shepherd	Cybill	10Ll44	Mars	SR
Shepherd	Cybill	03AQ09	Venus	SD
Silkwood	Karen	13GE24	Uranus	SD
Silkwood	Karen	14CN07	Mars	SD
Silkwood	Karen	00SC26	Juno	SR
Simenon	Georges	01CN00	Pallas Athena	SD
Simenon	Georges	16Ll05	Mars	SR
Simenon	Georges	03AQ40	Mercury	SD
Simon	Paul	21GE25	Jupiter	SR
Simon	Paul	11SC52	Mercury	SR
Simone	Nina	05SC52	Juno	SR
Simpson	O.J.	17SC45	Jupiter	SD
Simpson	O.J.	16Pl51	Pallas Athena	SR
Simpson	Wallis	16GE04	Mercury	SD
Simpson	Wallis	20Ll35	Chiron	SD
Simpson	Wallis	03Pl58	Pallas Athena	SR
Spacek	Sissy	06AR19	Eris	SR
Spector	Phil	24AR25	Saturn	SD
Spector	Phil	25Vl30	Neptune	SR
Spielberg	Steven	18AR39	Hygiea	SD
Spitz	Mark	11Ll01	Mars	SR
Starr	Ringo	05LE12	Mercury	SR
Stevens	Cat	25GE08	Venus	SD
Stevens	Cat	18SC24	Chiron	SD
Stevenson	Robert Louis	04Pl15	Neptune	SD
Stevenson	Robert Louis	24Pl48	Ceres	SD
Stosur	Samantha	28SC05	Mars	SR

Appendix One

Streep	Meryl	12LI23	Neptune	SD
Sutcliffe	Peter	14LI44	Juno	SD
Sutcliffe	Peter	13AQ11	Ceres	SR
Swaggart	Jimmy	23SC15	Jupiter	SR
Temple Black	Shirley	01VI17	Juno	SD
Thatcher	Margaret	14CN44	Pluto	SR
Thomas	Dylan	22GE58	Vesta	SR
Thomas	Dylan	22SC57	Mercury	SR
Thunberg	Greta	08TA38	Hygiea	SD
Thunberg	Greta	28CP26	Mercury	SR
Tomlin	Lily	08TA47	Vesta	SR
Tomlin	Lily	21TA57	Uranus	SR
Tomlin	Lily	24CP23	Mars	SD
Toulouse Lautrec	Henri	11AR42	Ceres	SD
Toulouse Lautrec	Henri	08LE50	Hygiea	SR
Toulouse Lautrec	Henri	07PI57	Eris	SD
Toulouse Lautrec	Henri	10PI19	Chiron	SD
Travers	Pamela	03SG59	Uranus	SD
Travers	Pamela	06SG49	Chiron	SD
Travers	Pamela	14SG20	Juno	SD
Travolta	John	09SC21	Saturn	SR
Travolta	John	15PI56	Mercury	SR
Truman	Harry S.	01GE16	Mercury	SR
Trump	Donald	05LI510	Neptune	SD
Trump	Donald	14LI54	Chiron	SD
Trump	Donald	14LI48	Juno	SD
Trump	Donald	17LI27	Jupiter	SD
Trump	Donald	13AQ07	Ceres	SR
Turner	Tina	28PI52	Jupiter	SD
Van Gogh	Vincent	25AR36	Mercury	SR
Washington	George	14GE40	Neptune	SD
Washington	George	22SC54	Eris	SR
Weinstein	Harvey	09CN54	Uranus	SD
Weinstein	Harvey	18SC18	Mars	SR
Weissmuller	Johnny	21AQ00	Saturn	SR
Wells	H.G.	22CP26	Jupiter	SD
White	Betty	07LI36	Saturn	SR
Whitlam	Gough	17SC13	Juno	SD
Wilkes Booth	John	08VI50	Jupiter	SD
Wilkes Booth	John	10AQ25	Neptune	SR
Williams	Kenneth	10CN25	Hygiea	SD

The Test of Time

Williams	Kenneth	10AQ58	Venus	SD
Williams	Robin	23SC54	Juno	SD
Williams	Robin	16PI35	Ceres	SR
Wilson	Brian	07SC39	Juno	SD
Wilson	Brian	11AQ34	Vesta	SR
Wilson	Brian	26AQ02	Pallas Athena	SR
Winehouse	Amy	05TA31	Juno	SR
Winehouse	Amy	23LE12	Venus	SD
Winfrey	Oprah	26LI03	Neptune	SR
Woods	Tiger	12AR53	Eris	SD
Woods	Tiger	23AR35	Chiron	SD
Young	Angus	23CN35	Uranus	SD

APPENDIX TWO

ZODIAC DEGREE LISTING OF INDIVIDUALS WITH STATIONARY PLANETS

Degrees	Surname	First Name	Stationary Planet	SR/SD
00AR39	Obama	Barack	Juno	SR
01AR29	Prince Charles		Juno	SD
02AR11	Irwin	Bindi-Sue	Pallas Athena	SR
02AR39	Pistorius	Oscar	Vesta	SD
02AR46	Rowling	J.K.	Ceres	SR
03AR06	Fonda	Jane	Eris	SD
05AR00	Morrison	Jim	Pallas Athena	SD
05AR14	Lovelock	James	Ceres	SR
06AR19	Spacek	Sissy	Eris	SR
06AR50	Gould	Shane	Ceres	SD
07AR12	Bader Ginsburg	Ruth	Mercury	SR
07AR23	Crane	Bob	Uranus	SR
07AR38	Lennox	Annie	Eris	SD
08AR46	Howard	John	Jupiter	SR
09AR10	Shaw	George Bernard	Jupiter	SR
11AR11	Garfunkel	Art	Mars	SD
11AR42	Toulouse Lautrec	Henri	Ceres	SD
12AR27	Hoffman	Philip Seymour	Saturn	SR

The Test of Time

12AR42	Kennedy Onassis	Jacqui	Pallas Athena	SR
12AR53	Woods	Tiger	Eris	SD
13AR04	Clooney	George	Venus	SD
13AR33	Battle	Kathleen	Juno	SR
13AR48	Plant	Robert	Juno	SR
13AR58	Glenn	John	Chiron	SR
14AR30	Corby	Schapelle	Eris	SR
15AR01	Blair	Tony	Venus	SD
15AR02	Getty	John Paul	Jupiter	SD
15AR04	Amundsen	Roald	Chiron	SR
17AR25	Bolt	Usain	Vesta	SR
17AR29	Edwards	Blake	Chiron	SR
18AR39	Spielberg	Steven	Hygiea	SD
19AR28	Houston	Whitney	Jupiter	SR
19AR34	Carter	Rubin	Venus	SD
20AR29	Allen	Woody	Juno	SD
20AR54	Lewinsky	Monica	Chiron	SR
21AR32	Fry	Stephen	Vesta	SR
22AR04	Chanel	Coco	Pallas Athena	SR
22AR13	Polanski	Roman	Ceres	SR
23AR35	Woods	Tiger	Chiron	SD
24AR25	Spector	Phil	Saturn	SD
24AR41	Michelangelo		Venus	SR
25AR36	Van Gogh	Vincent	Mercury	SR
26AR24	Jung	Carl G.	Chiron	SR
27AR29	Presley	Elvis	Uranus	SD
00TA21	Hari	Mata	Chiron	SR
01TA32	Mary Queen of Scots		Ceres	SD
01TA43	Clinton	Bill	Hygiea	SR
02TA36	Goodman	Linda	Mercury	SR
03TA35	Jones	Jim	Mercury	SD
04TA07	Applewhite	Marshall	Mercury	SD
04TA24	Bligh	William	Pallas Athena	SR
04TA28	King Louis XVI		Pallas Athena	SR
05TA10	King Charles II		Venus	SD
05TA19	Hari	Mata	Neptune	SR
05TA25	King Jr	Martin Luther	Chiron	SD
05TA31	Winehouse	Amy	Juno	SR
05TA37	Beatty	Warren	Venus	SR
06TA05	Castro	Fidel	Chiron	SR
08TA10	Bacall	Lauren	Ceres	SR

Appendix Two

08TA38	Thunberg	Greta	Hygiea	SD
08TA47	Tomlin	Lily	Vesta	SR
09TA29	Leo	Alan	Pluto	SR
09TA35	Redford	Robert	Uranus	SR
09TA49	Hamilton-Byrne	Anne	Vesta	SD
10TA23	Milligan	Spike	Mercury	SR
11TA01	Matisse	Henri	Jupiter	SD
12TA54	Franklin	Benjamin	Saturn	SD
14TA00	Cooke	Sam	Chiron	SD
15TA30	Masters	Dr William	Ceres	SD
16TA09	Faraday	Michael	Pallas Athena	SR
17TA05	Bligh	William	Vesta	SR
17TA17	Loren	Sophia	Pallas Athena	SR
17TA37	Roosevelt	Franklin D.	Chiron	SD
18TA06	Chaplin	Charles	Venus	SR
18TA54	Princess Margaret		Chiron	SR
19TA09	Matisse	Henri	Ceres	SD
20TA36	Kennedy	John F.	Mercury	SD
20TA54	Connors	Jimmy	Jupiter	SR
21TA15	Bacall	Lauren	Hygiea	SR
21TA39	Ali	Muhammad	Saturn	SD
21TA57	Tomlin	Lily	Uranus	SR
23TA48	Eastwood	Clint	Mercury	SD
25TA16	Prince Harry		Ceres	SR
25TA17	Ali	Muhammad	Hygiea	SD
26TA27	Onassis	Aristotle	Jupiter	SD
26TA45	Gillard	Julia	Ceres	SR
27TA36	Reeve	Christopher	Hygiea	SR
28TA39	Cline	Patsy	Chiron	SR
28TA51	Farmer	Frances	Hygiea	SR
29TA25	Princess Mary Donaldson		Saturn	SD
00GE14	Borg	Bjorn	Mercury	SD
00GE34	Pesci	Joe	Uranus	SD
01GE16	Truman	Harry S.	Mercury	SR
01GE19	Newton	Matthew	Ceres	SD
02GE15	Robbins	Tim	Mars	SR
03GE12	Gandhi	Mohandas	Ceres	SR
03GE23	Epstein	Jeffrey	Ceres	SD
04GE15	Keating	Paul	Vesta	SD
04GE16	Frazier	Joe	Vesta	SD
04GE19	Cooke	Sam	Hygiea	SD

The Test of Time

04GE28	Gillard	Julia	Vesta	SR
04GE49	Allen	Peter	Uranus	SD
04GE51	Page	Jimmy	Mars	SD
05GE11	Frazier	Joe	Mars	SD
05GE14	Keating	Paul	Mars	SD
05GE35	Pesci	Joe	Saturn	SD
06GE31	Armstrong	Lance	Saturn	SR
08GE30	Lord Byron		Vesta	SD
08GE32	Prince Harry		Chiron	SR
09GE55	Loren	Sophia	Chiron	SR
11GE09	Neal	Patricia	Pallas Athena	SD
13GE24	Silkwood	Karen	Uranus	SD
14GE40	Washington	George	Neptune	SD
14GE44	Newton	Matthew	Mars	SD
16GE04	Simpson	Wallis	Mercury	SD
16GE24	Rinehart	Gina	Jupiter	SD
16GE25	Garbo	Greta	Jupiter	SR
16GE29	Houston	Brian	Jupiter	SD
17GE17	Putin	Vladimir	Ceres	SR
18GE15	Abbott	Tony	Juno	SR
18GE24	Andrews	Daniel	Venus	SD
20GE18	Fitzgerald	F. Scott	Neptune	SR
20GE22	Culpeper	Nicholas	Ceres	SR
20GE24	Love	Courtney	Venus	SD
21GE25	Simon	Paul	Jupiter	SR
21GE47	Robertson	Geoffrey	Uranus	SR
21GE53	King Jr	Martin Luther	Mars	SD
22GE06	Chamberlain	Lindy	Uranus	SD
22GE06	Kennett	Jeff	Uranus	SD
22GE50	Hanks	Tom	Venus	SD
22GE58	Thomas	Dylan	Vesta	SR
23GE11	Robbins	Tim	Hygiea	SR
24GE25	Allen	Peter	Ceres	SD
24GE47	Gershwin	George	Neptune	SR
25GE08	Stevens	Cat	Venus	SD
25GE35	14th Dalai Lama		Mercury	SD
25GE53	Hubbard	L. Ron	Pluto	SD
25GE54	King George III		Mercury	SR
26GE10	Bolan	Marc	Uranus	SR
27GE00	Roosevelt	Franklin D.	Mars	SD
00CN19	Mozart		Mars	SD

Appendix Two

00CN23	Calment	Jeanne	Ceres	SD
01CN00	Simenon	Georges	Pallas Athena	SD
01CN50	King Richard III		Chiron	SR
03CN32	Crane	Bob	Mercury	SD
04CN19	Clinton	Hillary	Hygiea	SR
06CN32	Holt	Harold	Venus	SD
07CN34	Queen Mary I		Ceres	SD
07CN36	Eichmann	Adolph	Neptune	SD
08CN15	Borg	Bjorn	Venus	SR
08CN42	Marquez	Marc	Mars	SD
09CN16	Gauquelin	Michel	Mars	SR
09CN16	Morricone	Ennio	Mars	SR
09CN44	Queen Mary I		Jupiter	SD
09CN54	Weinstein	Harvey	Uranus	SD
10CN02	Knievel	Evel	Chiron	SR
10CN25	Williams	Kenneth	Hygiea	SD
10CN28	Murdoch	Rupert	Jupiter	SD
10CN29	Gorbachev	Mikhail	Jupiter	SD
11CN09	Glenn	John	Mercury	SD
11CN50	Curie	Marie	Vesta	SR
12CN07	Nash	John	Mercury	SR
12CN13	Kennedy	Ted	Juno	SD
12CN39	Hoffman	Philip Seymour	Mercury	SD
13CN15	Jones	Tom	Venus	SR
14CN02	Hari	Mata	Venus	SD
14CN07	Silkwood	Karen	Mars	SD
14CN12	Kennett	Jeff	Vesta	SD
14CN13	Chamberlain	Lindy	Vesta	SD
14CN21	Culpeper	Nicholas	Uranus	SR
14CN44	Thatcher	Margaret	Pluto	SR
15CN46	Agnew	Spiro	Jupiter	SR
15CN47	Graham	Billy	Jupiter	SR
15CN48	Galileo		Hygiea	SD
15CN56	Berry	Chuck	Pluto	SR
16CN57	Michelangelo		Saturn	SD
17CN26	Harris	Rolf	Pluto	SD
18CN20	Leo	Alan	Venus	SD
18CN30	Kennedy	John F. Jnr	Mars	SR
23CN35	Young	Angus	Uranus	SD
23CN39	Kennedy	Robert	Hygiea	SR
24CN45	Kray	Reginald & Ronald	Pluto	SR

27CN29	Murdoch	Rupert	Mars	SD
27CN38	Gorbachev	Mikhail	Mars	SD
27CN39	Holiday	Billie	Neptune	SD
29CN56	Read	Mark 'Chopper'	Jupiter	SR
00LE36	Archer	Jeffrey	Pluto	SD
02LE20	Nilsen	Dennis	Mars	SR
03LE10	Midler	Bette	Mars	SR
04LE18	Milligan	Spike	Neptune	SD
05LE12	Starr	Ringo	Mercury	SR
05LE47	Garfunkel	Art	Pluto	SR
07LE36	Ford	Betty	Saturn	SD
07LE51	Koresh	David	Mercury	SD
08LE50	Toulouse Lautrec	Henri	Hygiea	SR
08LE52	Bundy	Ted	Saturn	SR
09LE19	Agnew	Spiro	Neptune	SR
09LE27	Eichmann	Adolph	Juno	SD
13LE25	Chaplin	Charles	Saturn	SD
15LE46	Leno	Jay	Pluto	SD
16LE16	Hawke	Bob	Vesta	SR
17LE24	Getty	John Paul	Hygiea	SR
22LE59	Cromwell	Oliver	Neptune	SD
23LE12	Winehouse	Amy	Venus	SD
24LE02	Howard	John	Mercury	SR
27LE00	Morrison	Jim	Jupiter	SR
27LE01	Richards	Keith	Jupiter	SR
28LE50	Piaf	Edith	Mars	SR
29LE43	Masters	Dr William	Mars	SR
29LE53	Alexander	Jason	Venus	SD
00VI02	Rowling	J.K.	Mercury	SR
01VI11	Mansfield	Jayne	Mars	SD
01VI14	Kennedy	Ethel	Juno	SD
01VI17	Temple Black	Shirley	Juno	SD
02VI59	Applewhite	Marshall	Neptune	SD
02VI59	Jones	Jim	Neptune	SD
03VI30	Lange	Jessica	Hygiea	SD
03VI35	Hawke	Bob	Neptune	SR
03VI58	Getty	John Paul	Chiron	SR
06VI31	Archer	Jeffrey	Ceres	SD
06VI38	Andrews	Julie	Venus	SD
08VI07	Branagh	Kenneth	Pluto	SR
08VI50	Wilkes Booth	John	Jupiter	SD

Appendix Two

10Vl04	Pitt	Brad	Uranus	SR
13Vl01	Borgia	Lucrezia	Pallas Athena	SD
13Vl59	Beethoven		Neptune	SR
14Vl13	Pitt	Brad	Pluto	SR
14Vl27	Milligan	Spike	Mars	SD
15Vl14	Koresh	David	Venus	SR
17Vl38	Cromwell	Oliver	Pallas Athena	SD
18Vl03	Borgia	Lucrezia	Juno	SD
18Vl43	Keaton	Buster	Venus	SD
18Vl50	Jones	James Earl	Pallas Athena	SR
18Vl52	Leno	Jay	Juno	SD
21Vl06	MacLaine	Shirley	Vesta	SD
21Vl09	Fonda	Jane	Neptune	SR
22Vl11	Leno	Jay	Mars	SD
24Vl02	Castro	Fidel	Venus	SR
24Vl48	Fry	Stephen	Mercury	SR
24Vl54	Cardinal George Pell		Neptune	SD
25Vl28	Carter	Rubin	Juno	SR
25Vl30	Spector	Phil	Neptune	SR
29Vl16	Cezanne	Paul	Mars	SR
02Ll13	Applewhite	Marshall	Ceres	SD
02Ll14	Jones	Jim	Ceres	SD
02Ll14	McGraw	Dr Phil	Mercury	SR
03Ll22	Freud	Sigmund	Mars	SD
04Ll15	Page	Jimmy	Neptune	SR
05Ll510	Trump	Donald	Neptune	SD
05Ll54	Mozart		Ceres	SR
07Ll36	White	Betty	Saturn	SR
08Ll59	Garland	Judy	Jupiter	SD
10Ll27	Evans	Cadel	Ceres	SR
10Ll44	Shepherd	Cybill	Mars	SR
11Ll01	Gabriel	Peter	Mars	SR
11Ll01	Spitz	Mark	Mars	SR
11Ll03	Redgrave	Vanessa	Juno	SR
11Ll18	Alzheimer	Alois	Saturn	SD
12Ll23	Streep	Meryl	Neptune	SD
13Ll03	Houston	Brian	Ceres	SR
13Ll14	Rinehart	Gina	Ceres	SR
14Ll44	Sutcliffe	Peter	Juno	SD
14Ll48	Trump	Donald	Juno	SD
14Ll54	Trump	Donald	Chiron	SD

The Test of Time

15Ll13	Christie	Agatha	Mercury	SR
15Ll24	Dean	James	Ceres	SR
15Ll30	Prince William		Saturn	SD
16Ll05	Simenon	Georges	Mars	SR
17Ll27	Trump	Donald	Jupiter	SD
18Ll25	King Edward VIII		Saturn	SD
18Ll30	Mozart		Jupiter	SR
19Ll33	Edison	Thomas	Vesta	SR
19Ll45	Princess Mary Donaldson		Juno	SR
19Ll51	Jobs	Steve	Hygiea	SR
20Ll08	Faraday	Michael	Mercury	SR
20Ll09	Rivers	Joan	Juno	SD
20Ll35	Simpson	Wallis	Chiron	SD
21Ll07	Lord Byron		Neptune	SR
21Ll29	Rampling	Charlotte	Chiron	SR
22Ll33	Lang	K.D.	Mercury	SD
23Ll02	Minogue	Kylie	Ceres	SD
23Ll14	Reagan	Ronald	Juno	SR
23Ll58	Bono	Sonny	Mars	SR
24Ll48	Fitzgerald	F. Scott	Mercury	SR
26Ll02	Garland	Judy	Ceres	SD
26Ll03	Winfrey	Oprah	Neptune	SR
26Ll27	Garfunkel	Art	Mercury	SD
27Ll18	Rampling	Charlotte	Jupiter	SR
27Ll38	Hanks	Tom	Neptune	SD
28Ll05	Borg	Bjorn	Vesta	SD
00SC04	Rampling	Charlotte	Juno	SR
00SC26	Silkwood	Karen	Juno	SR
00SC29	Prince William		Jupiter	SD
00SC41	Kahlo	Frida	Juno	SD
01SC36	Calment	Jeanne	Jupiter	SR
02SC11	Galileo		Vesta	SR
02SC31	Bieber	Justin	Juno	SR
02SC59	Manson	Charles	Mercury	SD
03SC20	Faraday	Michael	Venus	SR
05SC11	Pistorius	Oscar	Venus	SD
05SC24	King Edward VIII		Juno	SD
05SC50	Ono	Yoko	Juno	SR
05SC52	Simone	Nina	Juno	SR
07SC20	King Edward VIII		Hygiea	SD
07SC34	Ford	Harrison	Juno	SD

Appendix Two

07SC39	Wilson	Brian	Juno	SD
07SC42	Court	Margaret	Juno	SD
09SC20	Hearst	Patty	Saturn	SR
09SC21	Houston	Brian	Saturn	SR
09SC21	Travolta	John	Saturn	SR
09SC40	Darwin	Charles	Uranus	SR
09SC40	Lincoln	Abraham	Uranus	SR
09SC56	Menendez	Erik	Venus	SD
11SC47	Evans	Cadel	Uranus	SR
11SC52	Simon	Paul	Mercury	SR
12SC56	Prince William		Ceres	SD
13SC05	Pistorius	Oscar	Mercury	SD
13SC28	14th Dalai Lama		Jupiter	SD
14SC20	Corby	Schapelle	Juno	SD
14SC39	Bieber	Justin	Jupiter	SR
15SC51	Graves	Robert	Uranus	SD
17SC13	Whitlam	Gough	Juno	SD
17SC14	Rowling	J.K.	Neptune	SD
17SC35	De Havilland	Olivia	Juno	SD
17SC41	Parker-Bowles	Camilla	Jupiter	SD
17SC45	Simpson	O.J.	Jupiter	SD
17SC56	Kidman	Nicole	Vesta	SD
18SC07	Jobs	Steve	Juno	SR
18SC18	Weinstein	Harvey	Mars	SR
18SC24	Stevens	Cat	Chiron	SD
18SC25	Love	Courtney	Pallas Athena	SD
19SC05	Princess Diana		Hygiea	SD
19SC26	Love	Courtney	Juno	SD
21SC09	Jobs	Steve	Saturn	SR
21SC23	Clinton	Hillary	Mercury	SR
22SC54	Washington	George	Eris	SR
22SC57	Thomas	Dylan	Mercury	SR
23SC15	Swaggart	Jimmy	Jupiter	SR
23SC54	Williams	Robin	Juno	SD
24SC07	Earhart	Amelia	Saturn	SD
24SC14	Picasso	Pablo	Mercury	SR
26SC23	Pankhurst	Emmeline	Pallas Athena	SD
27SC31	Close	Glenn	Jupiter	SR
28SC04	Bieber	Justin	Pluto	SR
28SC05	Stosur	Samantha	Mars	SR
00SG32	Mandela	Nelson	Pallas Athena	SD

The Test of Time

03SG03	Edwards	Blake	Hygiea	SD
03SG07	Amundsen	Roald	Hygiea	SD
03SG58	Lewinsky	Monica	Ceres	SD
03SG59	Hitchcock	Alfred	Uranus	SD
03SG59	Travers	Pamela	Uranus	SD
04SG48	Campbell	Joseph	Pallas Athena	SR
05SG07	Nicholson	Jack	Mars	SR
05SG49	Coward	Noel	Mercury	SD
06SG01	Branson	Richard	Ceres	SD
06SG45	Lewinsky	Monica	Juno	SD
06SG49	Travers	Pamela	Chiron	SD
07SG52	Graves	Robert	Pallas Athena	SD
08SG02	Baudelaire	Charles	Ceres	SR
10SG06	Fleming	Alexander	Ceres	SD
10SG57	Branson	Richard	Hygiea	SD
11SG10	King Louis XVI		Pluto	SD
11SG44	Edwards	Blake	Mars	SD
14SG20	Travers	Pamela	Juno	SD
14SG22	Hitchcock	Alfred	Juno	SD
14SG40	Redford	Robert	Jupiter	SD
16SG28	Lady Gaga		Juno	SR
19SG05	Milligan	Spike	Pallas Athena	SR
19SG06	Battle	Kathleen	Jupiter	SD
19SG06	Henry	Lenny	Saturn	SD
19SG07	Jackson	Michael	Saturn	SD
19SG07	Plant	Robert	Jupiter	SD
19SG13	Ford	Betty	Pallas Athena	SR
19SG54	Brando	Marlon	Jupiter	SR
20SG14	Goodman	Linda	Juno	SR
21SG22	Jung	Carl G.	Mars	SD
22SG22	Lady Gaga		Uranus	SR
22SG28	Leno	Jay	Hygiea	SR
26SG23	Lange	Jessica	Vesta	SR
27SG57	Clinton	Bill	Pallas Athena	SD
00CP50	Grant	Ulysses S.	Vesta	SR
03CP07	Baudelaire	Charles	Uranus	SR
04CP27	Johnson	Lyndon B.	Juno	SD
04CP28	Kyrgios	Nick	Juno	SR
05CP04	Catherine the Great		Juno	SR
06CP03	Jones	James Earl	Mercury	SD
07CP56	MacLaine	Shirley	Juno	SR

Appendix Two

08CP14	Hitler	Adolf	Jupiter	SR
08CP26	Hanson	Pauline	Mars	SR
08CP54	Keating	Paul	Mercury	SD
10CP56	Bligh	William	Saturn	SD
11CP59	Bolt	Usain	Mars	SD
12CP28	Brennan	Eileen	Ceres	SD
12CP37	Cline	Patsy	Ceres	SD
12CP41	Sellers	Peter	Jupiter	SD
12CP56	Marx	Karl	Jupiter	SR
14CP23	Bryant	Martin	Hygiea	SR
15CP33	Fonda	Jane	Mercury	SR
15CP42	Browning	Robert	Juno	SR
17CP13	Dahmer	Jeffrey L.	Vesta	SR
18CP53	Russell	Rosalind	Mars	SR
20CP10	Leo	Alan	Mars	SD
21CP57	Applewhite	Marshall	Vesta	SR
22CP26	Wells	H.G.	Jupiter	SD
22CP56	Nadal	Rafael	Mars	SR
23CP14	Gillard	Julia	Saturn	SD
24CP23	Tomlin	Lily	Mars	SD
25CP04	Chapman	Mark David	Ceres	SR
25CP33	Kyrgios	Nick	Neptune	SR
26CP46	Beethoven		Venus	SR
27CP22	Gillard	Julia	Jupiter	SD
28CP26	Thunberg	Greta	Mercury	SR
28CP40	Brennan	Eileen	Chiron	SR
29CP04	Dahmer	Jeffrey L.	Pallas Athena	SR
29CP24	Robertson	Geoffrey	Ceres	SD
29CP50	Clooney	George	Saturn	SR
00AQ03	Borg	Bjorn	Hygiea	SR
00AQ06	Dali	Salvador	Chiron	SR
02AQ21	Marx	Groucho	Jupiter	SD
02AQ23	Nostradamus		Venus	SR
03AQ09	Shepherd	Cybill	Venus	SD
03AQ40	Simenon	Georges	Mercury	SD
04AQ01	Farmer	Frances	Vesta	SD
04AQ07	Gabriel	Peter	Venus	SD
04AQ23	Prince Harry		Hygiea	SD
05AQ30	Chapman	Mark David	Chiron	SR
05AQ31	Keeler	Christine	Venus	SD
05AQ41	Freud	Sigmund	Chiron	SR

The Test of Time

06AQ01	Milk	Harvey	Juno	SR
06AQ19	Eastwood	Clint	Juno	SR
06AQ26	Navratilova	Martina	Chiron	SD
06AQ57	King Edward VI		Pluto	SD
09AQ17	Reeve	Christopher	Juno	SD
09AQ29	Putin	Vladimir	Juno	SD
09AQ51	Kennedy	John F.	Hygiea	SR
09AQ58	Browning	Robert	Eris	SR
10AQ25	Wilkes Booth	John	Neptune	SR
10AQ58	Williams	Kenneth	Venus	SD
11AQ34	Wilson	Brian	Vesta	SR
11AQ36	Keeler	Christine	Mercury	SD
11AQ40	McCartney	Paul	Vesta	SR
11AQ46	Culpeper	Nicholas	Chiron	SD
12AQ19	Franklin	Benjamin	Mercury	SR
12AQ26	Armstrong	Lance	Mars	SD
13AQ06	Kennedy	John F.	Juno	SR
13AQ07	Fleiss	Heidi	Venus	SR
13AQ07	Trump	Donald	Ceres	SR
13AQ11	Sutcliffe	Peter	Ceres	SR
14AQ21	Jobs	Steve	Mercury	SD
15AQ33	Nightingale	Florence	Eris	SR
16AQ17	Keaton	Buster	Hygiea	SD
17AQ06	Navratilova	Martina	Pallas Athena	SD
17AQ10	Fisher	Carrie	Pallas Athena	SD
17AQ20	Berry	Chuck	Jupiter	SD
20AQ10	Belushi	John	Mercury	SR
20AQ40	Ali	Muhammad	Venus	SR
20AQ46	Hawking	Stephen	Venus	SR
20AQ56	Capote	Truman	Vesta	SD
20AQ56	Carter	Jimmy	Vesta	SD
20AQ56	Musk	Elon	Mars	SR
21AQ00	Weissmuller	Johnny	Saturn	SR
21AQ32	Assange	Julian	Mars	SR
21AQ33	Chamberlain	Lindy	Mercury	SD
21AQ39	Kennett	Jeff	Mercury	SR
22AQ23	Knievel	Evel	Jupiter	SD
23AQ43	Kennedy	John F.	Uranus	SR
24AQ29	Prince William		Vesta	SR
24AQ50	Roosevelt	Eleanor	Hygiea	SD
25AQ35	Bacall	Lauren	Mars	SD

Appendix Two

25AQ40	Keaton	Buster	Vesta	SD
25AQ48	Capote	Truman	Mars	SD
25AQ53	Carter	Jimmy	Mars	SD
25AQ56	Neal	Patricia	Venus	SR
26AQ02	Wilson	Brian	Pallas Athena	SR
26AQ05	Mann	Thomas	Saturn	SR
26AQ07	McCartney	Paul	Pallas Athena	SR
28AQ28	Clinton	Hillary	Pallas Athena	SD
29AQ10	Brockovich	Erin	Ceres	SR
01Pl38	Berry	Chuck	Juno	SD
03Pl58	Simpson	Wallis	Pallas Athena	SR
04Pl15	Stevenson	Robert Louis	Neptune	SD
05Pl01	Johnson	Boris	Saturn	SR
06Pl09	Foster	Jodie	Chiron	SD
06Pl25	Hutton	Barbara	Chiron	SD
06Pl41	Fox	Michael J.	Chiron	SR
06Pl57	Cruise	Tom	Hygiea	SR
07Pl17	Pavarotti	Luciano	Vesta	SD
07Pl22	Lang	K.D.	Pallas Athena	SD
07Pl57	Toulouse Lautrec	Henri	Eris	SD
09Pl31	Close	Glenn	Mercury	SD
09Pl38	Prince Philip		Uranus	SR
10Pl19	Toulouse Lautrec	Henri	Chiron	SD
12Pl13	Churchill	Winston	Eris	SD
12Pl41	Cruise	Tom	Jupiter	SR
13Pl35	Navratilova	Martina	Mars	SD
14Pl00	Fisher	Carrie	Mars	SD
15Pl02	Alzheimer	Alois	Chiron	SR
15Pl56	Travolta	John	Mercury	SR
16Pl04	Hearst	Patty	Mercury	SR
16Pl35	Williams	Robin	Ceres	SR
16Pl38	Calment	Jeanne	Mercury	SR
16Pl46	Love	Courtney	Vesta	SR
16Pl51	Simpson	O.J.	Pallas Athena	SR
17Pl24	Lang	K.D.	Juno	SD
17Pl58	Crane	Bob	Ceres	SR
18Pl04	Lady Gaga		Mercury	SD
18Pl47	Johnson	Boris	Chiron	SR
19Pl17	Blake	William	Uranus	SD
20Pl05	Biden	Joe	Ceres	SD
21Pl48	Douglas	Kirk	Chiron	SD

The Test of Time

24Pl10	Dillinger	John	Eris	SR
24Pl48	Stevenson	Robert Louis	Ceres	SD
25Pl37	Princess Diana		Pallas Athena	SR
26Pl09	Ledger	Heath	Mercury	SD
26Pl20	De Havilland	Olivia	Chiron	SR
26Pl30	Copernicus	Nicholas	Mercury	SR
26Pl38	Gandhi	Indira	Vesta	SD
27Pl23	Baudelaire	Charles	Mercury	SD
27Pl26	Kahlo	Frida	Saturn	SR
27Pl59	Irwin	Bindi-Sue	Jupiter	SR
28Pl52	Turner	Tina	Jupiter	SD

APPENDIX THREE

MULTIPLE STATIONS

From the many charts I have examined to date, there are a handful of well-known people and events with four, or more stationary planets. These are:

Donald Trump	(5)	Ceres, Jupiter, Juno, Chiron, Neptune.
MH370	(5)	Mars, Vesta, Ceres, Jupiter, Saturn.
Marshall Applewhite	(4)	Mercury, Vesta, Ceres, Neptune.
Bjorn Borg	(4)	Mercury, Venus, Vesta, Hygiea.
Julia Gillard	(4)	Ceres, Vesta, Jupiter, Saturn.
Granville Train Disaster	(4)	Mercury, Jupiter, Hygiea, Pluto.
Steve Jobs	(4)	Mercury, Juno, Hygiea, Saturn.
John F. Kennedy	(4)	Mercury, Juno, Hygiea, Uranus.
Jay Leno	(4)	Mars, Juno, Hygiea, Pluto.
Courtney Love	(4)	Venus, Juno, Pallas Athena, Vesta.
Spike Milligan	(4)	Mercury, Mars, Pallas Athena, Neptune.
Henri Toulouse Lautrec	(4)	Ceres, Hygiea, Chiron, Eris.
Whitlam Dismissal	(4)	Mars, Vesta, Pallas Athena, Saturn.
Prince William	(4)	Ceres, Vesta, Jupiter, Saturn.

REFERENCES AND NOTES

Note about chart data.

In some cases the birth time for the people and events listed is unknown, however since the orb for a stationary planet is a minimum of several days, people and events without an accurate recorded time have been included and can be examined. All data have been retrieved from various software and Internet sources, including Solar Fire databases and Astro-Databank (http://www.astro.com), and from my personal research of births and events in the public record. All charts are calculated using the Placidus House System with Solar Fire.

Where the time of birth in unknown, charts have been calculated using 12 noon, unless otherwise stated. All charts have been calculated using the 30 percent rule, so any planet moving at less than 30 percent of its average speed is flagged S.

The Rodden Rating System (below) for chart data has been used. In most cases the charts shown are AA, A or B.

AA	From Birth Record
A	From memory or News Report
B	From Biography
C	Source Unknown or rectified
DD	Conflicting or Unverified
X	Time Unknown
XX	Undetermined

ENDNOTES

1 Christophe Galfard, *The Universe in Your Hand*, Pan Macmillan, London, 2015. p.194.

2 http://www.bbc.com/earth/story/20160429-the-real-reasons-nothing-can-ever-go-faster-than-light accessed July 2021

3 Christophe Galfard, *The Universe in Your Hand*, Pan Macmillan, London, 2015. p.162

4 Dennis Elwell, *Cosmic Loom*, The Wessex Astrologer, Bournemouth UK, 2008 edition, p.6.

5 https://ivypanda.com/essays/the-psychology-of-serial-killers/ accessed July 2021.

6 https://www.worldometers.info/world-population/ April 2015.

7 http://sacred-texts.com/astro/ptb/ptb37.htm#page_54 June 2015.

8 Deborah Houlding, "An Introduction to Horary Astrology, Part 5: Accidental Strengths and Afflictions," *The Mountain Astrologer,* Oct/Nov. 2013, pp. 75–76.

9 Erin Sullivan, *Retrograde Planets: Traversing the Inner Landscape,* Samuel Weiser, Inc., 1992, 2000, p.125

10 *Ibid.*, p.126

11 For more details on the nature of these differences see https://tonylouis.wordpress.com/2018/08/26/average-daily-motion-of-planets-in-horary/#comment-8736

12 Data rounded to the nearest day. Asteroid data found at http://www.southastrodel.com/PageAsteroids000.htm July 2021

13 https://tonylouis.wordpress.com/2018/08/26/average-daily-motion-of-planets-in-horary/ July 2021.

14 The Moon plays a key role too, especially in infancy.

15 https://www.bbc.com/news/magazine-22122407 Accessed July 2021

16 *Still Me*, Christopher Reeve, Kindle Edition, Arrow Books, 1999, Chapter one.

17 There may be slight variations to the exact position of Mercury between 12 noon charts and the real time of birth, if it is unknown. This is only in the order of seconds of arc.

18 Jeanne Calment is so far the oldest person to have lived, dying at the age of 122.

19 Subject of the film *A Beautiful Mind*.

20 See Endnote 17.

21 6am chart.

22 David Koresh suicide 19 April 1993 Venus SD & Chiron SD.

23 Because Venus makes two conjunctions with the Sun, she is not always stationary when semi-sextile the Sun.

24 My first book, *Secrets of the Zodiac*, Allen and Unwin, 2009, examines this concept in detail.

25 My research into the Venus-Mars cycle as outlined in my book, *The Sacred Dance of Venus and Mars*, confirms that the Venus-Sun cycle commences at inferior conjunction and not at superior conjunction.

26 Mars rising and culminating was also often seen in the medical profession and in science. Michel Gauquelin, *Written in the Stars*, Aquarian Press, Northamptonshire, UK, 1988. pp.104-113.

27 Birth time note https://mountainastrologer.com/tma/birth-time-for-julian-assange/ Accessed July 2021.

28 https://www.independent.co.uk/arts-entertainment/books/features/julian-assange-we-just-kept-moving-2359423.html Accessed July 2021.

29 Mary L. Trump. *Too Much and Never Enough*, chapter one. Simon and Schuster, July 2020.

30 David Attenborough was born 8 May 1926 in Isleworth, UK. Time unknown.

31 It is most likely that Diego Rivera was born on 8 December 1886, although there is the possibility he was born on 13 December. Either way, Jupiter is in late Libra and within two degrees of Frida's Juno. https://www.astro.com/astro-databank/Rivera,_Diego

32 https://greekgodsandgoddesses.net/goddesses/juno/ September 2021.

33 Uncertain birth date https://www.astro.com/astro-databank/Borgia,_Lucrezia

34 https://www.astro.com/astro-databank/Borgia,_Lucrezia September 2021.

35 https://www.biography.com/political-figure/lucrezia-borgia September 2021.

36 https://www.sportscasting.com/o-j-simpsons-father-abandoned-him-and-it-had-a-devastating-impact-on-his-life/ Accessed June 2021.

37 https://www.biography.com/crime-figure/oj-simpson Accessed June 2021

38 Born in 1479 or 1480. https://www.astro.com/astro-databank/Borgia,_Lucrezia

39 A week before this disaster, Neptune, Venus & Juno all stationed retrograde. The disaster happened in heavy fog.

40 https://www.etymonline.com/search?q=focus September 2021.

41 https://www.smithsonianmag.com/history/madame-curies-passion-74183598/ August 2021.

42 https://en.wikipedia.org/wiki/Frances_Farmer August 2021.

43 https://allthatsinteresting.com/frances-farmer-lobotomy August 2021.

44 https://allthatsinteresting.com/frances-farmer-lobotomy August 2021.

45 https://en.wikipedia.org/wiki/J._Paul_Getty July 2021

46 https://www.smh.com.au/entertainment/celebrity/kidnapped-mutilated-and-unloved-by-miserly-tycoon-the-tragic-life-of-j-paul-getty-iii-is-over-20110208-1al6q.html August 2021.

47 https://www.theatlantic.com/technology/archive/2011/11/crazy-perfectionism-drove-steve-jobs/335842/ August 2021.

48 https://www.ncbi.nlm.nih.gov/pmc/articles/PMC4924574/ August 2021.

49 https://www.mensjournal.com/health-fitness/why-tom-cruise-making-stunt-history-mission-impossible-rogue-nation/ September 2021.

Endnotes

50 https://www.gutenberg.org/files/20203/20203-h/20203-h.htm September 2021.

51 Ibid. Chapters II & III.

52 https://www.rollingstone.com/movies/movie-news/philip-seymour-hoffmans-last-days-77972/ Accessed June 17 2021.

53 https://www.newcastleherald.com.au/story/6832338/timeline-in-the-whitlam-dismissal-lead-up/ Accessed June 20, 2021.

54 https://www.cnbc.com/2021/04/07/golf-star-tiger-woods-was-speeding-before-car-crash-cops-say.html July 2021.

55 https://www.astro.com/astro-databank/Culpeper,_Nicholas August 2021

56 Jack Nicholson played the role in film. His Chiron is not close to a station but it's worth noting its conjunct the South Node.

57 https://www.space.com/45-uranus-seventh-planet-in-earths-solar-system-was-first-discovered-planet.html August 2021.

58 Wikipedia references, Robert Beekes, *Etymological Dictionary of Greek*, Vol 2, Brill, 2009. 1128-1129. https://en.wikipedia.org/wiki/Uranus_(mythology) September 2021.

59 https://time.com/3574931/karen-silkwood/ September 2021.

60 https://www.pbs.org/wgbh/pages/frontline/shows/reaction/interact/silkwood.html September 2021.

61 https://skyandtelescope.org/astronomy-news/the-return-of-neptune/ September 2021.

62 His notes state that Venus was rising at the time. https://www.degruyter.com/document/doi/10.1515/astro-1997-0117/pdf

63 https://mathshistory.st-andrews.ac.uk/HistTopics/Neptune_and_Pluto/ August 2021

64 https://www.history.com/this-day-in-history/official-registration-of-hollywood August 2021.

65 Another theory states that the children were poisoned, but a number of researchers have concluded this was mere gossip.

66 The details of Mata Hari's life have been sourced from *Femme Fatale*, Pat Shipman, Orion Books, London, 2008.

67 https://www.etymonline.com/word/revolution#etymonline_v_12995 September 2021.

68 https://www.astro.com/astro-databank/Leo,_Alan July 2021.

69 Ibid.

70 https://solarsystem.nasa.gov/planets/dwarf-planets/eris/in-depth/ August 2021.

71 https://www.etymonline.com/search?q=disatser August 2021.

72 https://www.smh.com.au/world/mh370-experienced-significant-changes-in-altitude-20140315-34te1.html August 2021.

73 https://www.dailytelegraph.com.au/news/exclusive-extract-our-worst-train-disaster-remembered-in-a-new-book/news-story/418e540d2ce7aaa1eefafba2479d85e9 August 2021

74 https://www.theguardian.com/cities/2019/dec/08/bhopals-tragedy-has-not-stopped-the-urban-disaster-still-claiming-lives-35-years-on September 2021.

75 Data sourced from original article by Diana Rosenberg and Arlene Nimark, NCGR Journal, winter Edition 1985-6, pp11-16.

76 Mary Shelley, *Frankenstein*, Paragraph 6, Introduction to the 1831 edition. https://romantic-circles.org/editions/frankenstein/1831v1/intro September 2021

77 https://www.tor.com/2016/06/20/mary-shelley-waking-dream-frankenstein-astronomy/

78 https://en.wikipedia.org/wiki/Mark_Zuckerberg

79 https://people.com/royals/princess-diana-prince-charles-engagement-40-years-ago/ September 2021.

80 Helen Keller's time of birth given in Astro-Databank is 4.02pm, but listed as DD. Upon checking with archivist Philip Graves to verify the source this information, Philip kindly looked in his library for the original article mentioned in Astro-Databank. The magazine referenced and the author were found to be incorrect. In looking through his library, Philip located *Astrology, The Astrologers' Quarterly*, Volume 4, Number 4, December 1930-Feb 1931, which includes an article by M. Matthews, pp. 215-216. Mathews writes, 'Since my speculative map of Helen Keller appeared in *Astrology*, the time of her birth has been obtained from her secretary by an American gentleman. It is "about 4 p.m." This works out 2½ minutes past four by the epoch, which I give.' So 4.02pm is a rectified time by Matthews, but based on information provided by Keller's secretary in 1930. We can probably now classify 4.00pm as category A data.

81 https://digital.library.upenn.edu/women/keller/life/life.html July 2021

82 https://digital.library.upenn.edu/women/keller/life/life.html , Chapter 4, July 2021

83 Ibid Part III.

84 Ibid Chapter XIX.

85 Ibid Chapter XIV

86 Anne Sullivan was born on 12 April 1866, Feeding Hills, MA, though 14 April is cited in many sources. https://www.astro.com/astro-databank/Keller,_Helen August 2021.

87 https://en.wikipedia.org/wiki/Birthday_problem#cite_note-nonuniform_birthdays-5 see note section 1. September 2021.

www.ingramcontent.com/pod-product-compliance
Lightning Source LLC
Chambersburg PA
CBHW081346080526
44588CB00016B/2390